TOUGH CASES

TOUGH CASES

Judges Tell the Stories of
Some of the Hardest Decisions
They've Ever Made

Edited by

RUSSELL F. CANAN,
GREGORY E. MIZE, AND
FREDERICK H. WEISBERG

THE
NEW
PRESS

NEW YORK
LONDON

Requests for permission to reproduce selections from this book should be mailed to: Permissions Department, The New Press, 120 Wall Street, 31st floor, New York, NY 10005.

Photograph of Judge Allie Greenleaf Maldonado on page 175 by Yosh Photography
Photograph of Judge Jennifer D. Bailey on page 255 by Michael Cotter

Published in the United States by The New Press, New York, 2018
Distributed by Two Rivers Distribution

ISBN 978-1-62097-387-5 (ebook)

LIBRARY OF CONGRESS CATALOGING-IN-PUBLICATION DATA
Names: Canan, Russell Frank, 1950- editor. | Mize, Gregory E., editor. |
    Weisberg, Frederick Howard, 1944- editor.
Title: Tough cases : judges tell the stories of some of the hardest
    decisions they've ever made / edited by Russell F. Canan, Gregory E. Mize, and
    Frederick H. Weisberg.
Description: New York : New Press, 2018.
Identifiers: LCCN 2018020593 | ISBN 9781620973868 (hc : alk. paper)
Subjects: LCSH: Trials—United States. | Judicial process—United
    States—Case studies.
Classification: LCC KF220 .T66 2018 | DDC 347.73/7—dc23 LC record available at
https://lccn.loc.gov/2018020593

The New Press publishes books that promote and enrich public discussion and understanding of the issues vital to our democracy and to a more equitable world. These books are made possible by the enthusiasm of our readers; the support of a committed group of donors, large and small; the collaboration of our many partners in the independent media and the not-for-profit sector; booksellers, who often hand-sell New Press books; librarians; and above all by our authors.

www.thenewpress.com

Book design and composition by Bookbright Media
This book was set in Janson Text and Didot

Printed in the United States of America

10 9 8 7 6 5 4 3 2 1

Contents

Introduction

AS ANY JUDGE WHO HAS SERVED ON A BUSY TRIAL COURT CAN attest, there are many assignments where the cases come at you so hard and fast that there is barely time to step into the box and take your stance before the next one comes zooming in. And that is true of the "easy" cases. This book is not about those. It's about the rare times in a judicial career when a judge has to wrestle with a problem so complex, or so emotionally draining, as to test the fortitude and impartiality of even the most competent and experienced jurist.

In busy trial courts, these cases can appear in the garb of criminal, civil, probate, or family cases. Often the judge is unable to find any guiding legal precedent and is forced to navigate uncharted waters in search of the "just" result. Sometimes controlling legal precedent exists, but following it would lead to an unjust result. And then there are cases where the judge has very wide discretion to apply a vague legal standard, such as "the best interest of the child" in contested child custody proceedings, or to find the "right sentence" in a criminal case, where the statutory range might run from no prison time at all to life in prison.

Some cases are hard not only because of the subject matter, but also because they capture the attention of the entire community and become highly politicized. This can be especially challenging for elected judges, who know that whatever decision they make may become fodder for an opposition campaign when they next stand for election, and may ultimately cost them their judgeship. These political realities do not lessen a judge's duty to decide each case in accordance with the facts, the rule of law, and by reference to neutral principles. But politics can make the exercise of that duty more agonizing, as any decision is likely to be unpopular with at least one large segment of the population.

Judge Robert H. Alsdorf of Washington State writes of one such case in "Can an Elected Judge Overrule Nearly a Million Voters and Survive?" His high-stakes ruling could have cost him his judgeship but, when he explained his decision in a detailed opinion, the public accepted the ruling and came away with a better understanding of the rule of law. In "Elián," Judge Jennifer D. Bailey of Florida explains her handling of the highly publicized Elián González contested custody case, describing how she stood up to pressure from outside forces attempting to influence her decision, including Congress and the President of the United States. A third chapter in the same category is Federal Judge Reggie B. Walton's description in "United States v. I. Lewis 'Scooter' Libby" of the trial of Vice President Richard Cheney's Chief of Staff in an obstruction of justice case that was closely watched by the White House and much of the rest of the country. A final example in this category is the story of "Terri's Judge" told by Judge George W. Greer of Florida, who found himself randomly assigned as the judge called upon to decide, between competing interests and under the glare of national attention, whether Terri Schiavo—comatose and in a persistent vegetative state—should continue to live or be allowed to die.

Many of the other selections are less well-known but no less fascinating. They chronicle the struggles of conscientious trial court judges to find justice within the confines of the law when the path is either unmarked, or is clearly marked but pointing in the wrong direction. The authors, each with years of experience on the bench, tell the stories of how they dealt with the cases they found to be among their most challenging. Judge Gregory E. Mize of Washington, DC, describes in "Brave Jenny" his handling of a very emotional child neglect matter, where he was compelled to remove a young girl from her mother but was stymied in his effort to reunite them by the mother's lack of insight into her mental illness, which presented a continuing danger to the child. In another child custody case, Judge Gail Chang Bohr of Minnesota, in "A Judge's Hidden Struggle: Overcoming Judicial Culture," had to choose between accepting the stipulated agreement of both parents to share custody of their child, which in most cases would be virtually automatic, or rejecting the agreement and awarding custody to a third party based largely on her instinct, later borne out by events, that neither parent had the capacity to protect the child's best interests.

Judge Russell F. Canan of Washington, DC, writes in "Rough Justice" of a case in which he struggled with following the law when it appeared that a jury in a criminal case was about to return a verdict that would require him to impose a harsh mandatory sentence, a sentence that he considered manifestly unjust under the facts of the case. In "Crazy or Cruel: The Trial of an Unexplained Filicide," Judge Frederick H. Weisberg, also from Washington, DC, describes his experience presiding in the trial of a mother accused of murdering her four daughters and living alone with their decaying remains for many months until her landlord discovered them in the course of evicting her for nonpayment of rent. The trial put the judge squarely at the intersection of law and psychiatry, when in a highly unusual turn of events the defense attorneys challenged their client's mental competence to refuse to present a defense of not guilty by reason of insanity. In "Uneasy Lies the Head That Wears a Crown," Judge Mark Davidson of Texas describes his delicate handling of what started out as a relatively routine divorce case involving a prominent member of the Houston legal community, but then spun almost out of control after the wife accused her lawyer of raping her during the course of his representation.

Two chapters take the reader completely outside the traditions of American jurisprudence. In "Walking with my Ancestors: Tribal Justice for Salmon Running," Judge Allie Greenleaf Maldonado, a tribal judge for the Little Traverse Bay Bands of Odawa Indians in Michigan, describes how she took a risk with a seemingly incorrigible defendant in a felony drug distribution case and, against the odds, managed to shift the focus from what would normally be an almost certain conviction and prison sentence to a more healing approach, which enabled the defendant to see the path to sobriety and a productive future. Judge Edward S. Wilson takes us not to his home state of Minnesota, but to Kosovo, where he was assigned as an international judge for a United Nations mission to preside over the prosecution of several members of a notorious organized crime syndicate charged with a series of violent jewelry store robberies. His story, "Building Justice in Kosovo," presents a lesson in the application of the presumption of innocence and the reasonable doubt standard in the context of a society that has not fully embraced those principles or the rule of law.

In "A Quiet Grief," Judge Lizbeth González of New York tells the sad story of one that got away. While she was trying to help the parties work out their differences in a very contentious landlord and tenant dispute, tragedy struck. Finally, the one relatively inexperienced judge among the contributing authors, Judge Michelle M. Ahnn, in "Every Case Is a Tough Case for a New Judge," writes of her personal transition from an experienced public defender in California to a neophyte judge presiding over a criminal misdemeanor calendar. As she describes it, every case was a hard case requiring her to distance herself from her former client-based advocacy and to decide each case impartially based solely on neutral principles.

Overall, the aim of the collection is to demystify judicial decision making and to make the process accessible to ordinary people who would not otherwise get a ringside seat and who may assume, understandably, that judges can simply do whatever they want. For the many people who think the system is unfair and fails by a wide margin to "do equal justice to the poor and to the rich," as all judges must swear to do, these up close and personal stories should help such skeptics appreciate the complexity of the job and, at least in some cases, the agony in its execution. Whether it persuades or not, however, our goal is to offer a firsthand and nuanced account of hard cases, as told by the judges who actually had to decide them. We hope that all who read it will come away with a renewed faith that our justice system—sometimes maligned and not always perfect—is still the best in the world and, together with a free press, the bedrock of our democracy.

Russell F. Canan, Gregory E. Mize, and Frederick H. Weisberg
Washington, DC
May 2018

1

Terri's Judge

JUDGE GEORGE W. GREER

 *Judge George W. Greer was elected to the Sixth Circuit Court of Pasco and Pinellas counties in Florida in 1992 and served for eighteen years before retiring in 2011. While on the bench, he presided over trials in all divisions of the court and served as Chair of the Florida Conference of Circuit Judges in 1999–2000.*

IT'S PALM SUNDAY WEEKEND, MARCH 20, 2005. I'M IN AN UNDISclosed location under the protection of the sheriff of my county with my wife, our Yorkie, and our host. We have just settled in, when I turn on the television to see the Majority Leader of the U.S. House of Representatives, Tom DeLay, flanked by a bicameral and bipartisan group of congressmen, calling me a terrorist and a murderer. I'm a thousand miles from DC, but for a fleeting moment I think: what if they send the federal marshals for me? What if they come and take me down to Guantánamo? That one moment was the most scared I've ever been. But it was a brief moment, and it passed. My wife stayed up late with our host that night following the story and the bluster and flurry of two branches of government trying to undermine the third. But I carried my dishes in from the living room, put on my bulletproof vest, walked the dog down a back road of Florida's intercostal waterways, and went to bed. I had already said all I had to say on the subject. I slept soundly.

That weekend the political response to the Terri Schiavo case had reached a fever pitch. The case that had ended up on my desk in the Circuit Court for Pinellas County, Florida, more than five years earlier in July of 1999, was coming to an end. On the Friday before Palm Sunday, Terri Schiavo's feeding tube had been removed in accordance with my order, and she died twelve days later on March 31, 2005, at 9:05 in the morning, at the Hospice of the Florida Suncoast. In these last months of the case, the Governor of Florida, the President of the United States, Pope John Paul II, and my very own church had all weighed in. But even though this looked like a tough case from the outside, the legal questions put before me in the Terri Schiavo case were, perhaps surprisingly, not difficult decisions for a judge to make.

And, by the time my wife and I had packed our bags to return home a few days later, I understood that not only was my fleeting fear not irrational, it was, maybe, the only sane response for a man watching his country's leaders turn the bedrock principles of federalism and privacy upside down. Guantánamo might have been a stretch. But my split-second fear spoke to something bigger: how small a big, overreaching government can make a man feel. How a government without checks and balances and separation of powers starts to feel like anarchy. It says something to me that what got to me wasn't having plain-clothes deputies assigned to protect us at our house or accompany my wife to get her hair done, or even the checking under the car or scanning the courtroom that became part of my day-to-day routine. I trusted the men and women whose job it was to protect us. I had great faith in law enforcement. I knew they were taking care of us, and, outside of that one moment, I always felt safe.

What ended up getting to me was seeing my government left unchecked. Seeing Congressional leadership stand up on television with these guys I knew—one I had even exchanged Christmas cards with for years—just tossing aside any substantive part of the deliberative process of a democracy. The Congressional compromise playing out that weekend produced a bill to allow federal courts to intervene in a final state court decision. The bill's passage was unprecedented in both scope and procedure: there were no committee hearings, no testimony as such. The parts of the Constitution that did not serve them were just tossed aside. These same lawmakers, big on the amendments—most on the Second, some on the First—somewhere along the way forgot about the primary document. Forgot about Article III in the United States Constitution that establishes judicial independence; that precedes all the amendments that follow. While the judiciary doesn't have the purse or the sword, making it codependent with the other two branches in those respects, an independent judiciary as constitutive of a full and free democracy is designed to ensure the independence of decision making. But here, in the course of the Schiavo case, both the state and the federal governments intervened to overturn a final state judicial decision: Governor Jeb Bush intervened within the state upsetting the separation of powers, and President George W. Bush intervened at the federal executive level, upsetting both the separation of powers *and* attempting to undermine state rights.

Hearing the senior Congressional leadership call me a terrorist was unnerving first on a personal level. This was my party, after all. How much hot water was I in? Would they come to snatch me up? Later, I was able to see this on a broader political level: this is what can happen when one party has absolute power. Anything can happen. The hallmarks of democracy can get tossed aside. I was watching, front and center, what would become an epic test of our country's separation of powers.

The question that landed in my probate court in 1999 was simple and clear: Did Terri Schiavo make reliable oral declarations as to what she would want done given the present circumstances? I presided over the trial from January 24 to 28, 2000, found the evidence clear and convincing that Ms. Schiavo would have chosen to remove her feeding and hydration tube, and on February 11, 2000, I granted the petition from her guardian and husband, Michael Schiavo, authorizing him to discontinue life-support.

More than five years, fourteen appeals, five suits in federal district courts, an intervention by both a Governor and a President, and four denials of certiorari from the U.S. Supreme Court later, Theresa Marie Schiavo passed this life on March 31, 2005.

I want to note at the outset that this is just the story of the case from my perspective. In theory, and as a matter of law, a lawsuit has a beginning and an end: an initial petition is filed with the court, which proceeds through resolution to conclusion, either by way of a final judgment in the trial court or by way of a final judgment from an appellate court. In truth and in fact, though, a story about a lawsuit, as with any story about the world we live in, has no clearly defined beginning or end. Events begin long before the petition is filed, and so the perspective of any story is necessarily limited and incomplete. The case of Terri Schiavo is no exception. As the presiding trial judge in the case, I tell a story here that is about, more than anything, the unique and fundamental role that judicial decision making plays in our lives and sometimes in our deaths.

Terri Schiavo grew up in the suburbs with her Roman Catholic parents, Mr. and Mrs. Robert Schindler, and one brother and sister—first outside of Philadelphia and later in New Jersey. She was by all accounts a shy girl. She struggled with her weight. Her father would sharply criticize her appearance. Right before she left for college in 1981, she lost almost a hundred pounds using a commercial diet program. Then, in a psychology class in Bucks County Community College, she met Michael Schiavo and at twenty and twenty-one, respectively, after a year-long engagement, they got married, honeymooned at Disney World, and shortly thereafter followed her parents down to St. Petersburg, Florida. Terri worked at the Prudential Insurance Company, and Michael managed a McDonald's restaurant. Then, in the early morning hours of February 25, 1990, Michael Schiavo called 911. When the paramedics arrived, Terri was in full cardiac arrest. She never regained consciousness.

The medical evidence presented during the trial suggested to me that years of dieting caused a potassium imbalance that led to a cardiac arrest that cut off the oxygen supply to her brain, causing irreversible brain damage. Terri's weight loss—from 250 pounds down to 110 when she collapsed—came at an enormous price; she was diagnosed as being in a persistent vegetative state, a neurological status primarily defined by movements that are reflexive and predicated on brain stem activity alone, as opposed to conscious and responsive.

In May, three months after her collapse, Terri was discharged from the hospital to a skilled-care rehabilitation facility, and in June of 1990, Michael Schiavo was appointed guardian. No one in the family objected to this decision, and during the first few years the whole family worked amicably together to give Terri the best possible care. During this first year, Michael took Terri to California for experimental "brain stimulator" treatments. He also paid for a hairdresser to come every two weeks to style her hair. The family even tried at one point to bring her home and care for her there. After three weeks they realized that they were not able to meet her needs, and they all agreed it would be best for Terri to return to a facility that could provide twenty-four-hour professional care.

Michael spent nights next to Terri sleeping on a cot, often staying with her all day at the different facilities. He bought Terri the latest fashions: stirrup pants and matching tops from the Limited, Picasso perfume. During the trial, the then-guardian ad litem—a person appointed by the court to act on behalf of an incapacitated person—described Michael as "a nursing home administrator's nightmare" because of his attention to Terri. There were reports of nurses in tears. One of the nursing homes took out a restraining order on him because of his relentless advocacy on Terri's behalf. The guardian ad litem testified that Terri "gets the care and attention from the staff . . . as a result of Mr. Schiavo's advocacy and defending on her behalf." Later, one of the refrains of the nurses at the nursing home was reported to be something like, "He may be a bastard, but if that were me, I'd be glad he was my husband."

In 1992, Michael successfully litigated a malpractice suit against

Terri's doctor for not catching her low potassium levels when she came to him with fertility concerns. Michael did so in his capacity as plenary guardian—a role that authorized him to exercise all legal rights and proceedings on behalf of Terri and to make decisions on her behalf (distinguished from the guardian ad litem, whose role is simply to make recommendations) and was awarded a large settlement in February of 1993.

Up until the moment money entered the picture, Terri's husband and parents by all accounts were on the same page. Besides living together to cut down on expenses, they had agreed on medical care and various medical procedures in an effort to restore Terri's capacities. Terri's parents even encouraged Michael to date. But once the damage award funds were received, their relationship began to fracture.

On Valentine's Day 1993, a little less than three years after Terri's collapse, her parents and her husband almost came to blows beside her bed over the medical malpractice money, and they did not speak to each other from this point on. The testimony that I would hear during the trial in January of 2000 differed on what may or may not have been promised to whom and by whom. What was clear to me then, and continues to be clear to me now, is that the relationship between Terri's husband and her parents ended because of money, and, specifically, because Michael was unwilling to divide his malpractice award equally with Terri's parents, Mr. and Mrs. Schindler. Money overshadowed the whole case and created potential conflicts of interest on all sides.

In 1994, a year after the settlement award, based on medical advice he received, Michael Schiavo refused to authorize medical treatment for an infection that Terri had developed. Mr. and Mrs. Schindler filed a petition to remove him as guardian based on allegations of abuse, neglect, and adultery—Michael was now living with a girlfriend. Although the Schindlers ultimately withdrew the petition, Michael decided to follow Terri's parents' wishes and authorized treatment for the infection.

There was not much legal activity after that until May of 1998, when Michael Schiavo petitioned the court to allow for the removal of Terri's PEG tube (a percutaneous endoscopic gastronomy tube), that had been providing Terri's sole means of nutrition and hydration since she was first admitted to the hospital.

I was assigned this case in July of 1999, quite by accident. I had recently become Chair of the Florida Circuit Judges Conference and was moved from the criminal division to probate to give me the flexibility I needed to fulfill my chairmanship duties. In my circuit, the criminal judge's calendar is packed. In probate, the division of the court that mostly deals with wills and guardianship cases, the case load generally allows a judge to perform other duties outside the courtroom. But here came this case.

Before the case got to me, the official record contained pleadings, motions, and orders appointing and subsequently discharging the guardian ad litem. Before being discharged, the guardian ad litem filed a report concluding, first, that Terri Schiavo was in a persistent vegetative state with her "chance of any improvement to a functional level [being] essentially zero" and, second, that Michael Schiavo was a competent guardian, but because of his competing interest as sole heir, could not alone recommend withdrawing life-support. Since I didn't know anything about the case when I got it, I read the law, read the file, got up to speed, and set the trial date.

The two questions I had to answer were: Is she in a persistent vegetative state? And if so, what would she want done? This was the first case in my career where I was being asked to withdraw life-support, and to date I have only had two. It is a profound charge for any judge. But the evidence in this case was clear, and by the time the bailiff announced that court was adjourned after five days in the courtroom, I knew that it would be the responsibility of making this decision that would be hard, not the decision itself.

The instant I saw the CAT scan of Terri's brain, I knew the answer to the first question. The CAT scan evidence presented by Dr. Barnhill, a neurologist certified by the American Board of Psychiatry and

Neurology, made starkly clear that Terri Schiavo was in a persistent vegetative state. Throughout the trial there was zero medical evidence to refute this fact and zero medical evidence that she could possibly recover from this state. Dr. Barnhill presented two images: on the right, a CAT scan of a healthy brain and on the left, a CAT scan he took of Terri's brain in May of 1996. Looking at the two, side by side, showed the vast difference in the size of the ventricles of each brain. In a healthy brain, the four cavities of the brain—the ventricles—make up a small, black, butterfly shape that is surrounded by healthy greyish brain tissue. In Terri's brain, the butterfly-shaped ventricles were nine times the size of a healthy brain's ventricles, Dr. Barnhill explained, because they had filled with spinal fluid after atrophy occurred once the oxygen to the brain was cut off. Pointing to the image of the large, black, butterfly shape of Terri's CAT scan where "there used to be brain," the doctor concluded that not only was there no longer the capacity for cells to communicate with each other in Terri's brain—what medically counts as consciousness—but that this damage was "irreversible."

The extent of my medical training is one class in law school called "Law and Medicine," so I had to rely a lot on expert witnesses. Before this case, I'd never heard of a persistent vegetative state. Years before, I had had a good friend suffer a similar event to Terri Schiavo; we thought at the time he was in a coma. His wife ultimately had to take him off life-support, but before she did I went to see him a lot. One of the confusing things about people who are in a persistent vegetative state is that, despite the severity of the brain damage, they still go through sleep-wake cycles. During some of my friend's wake cycles, I would talk to him and think: I'm going to use the right words. I'm going to say all the key phrases we used to use, and I'll get him out of this thing. I had real hope that he would come through.

I don't know if I thought of him the day I saw Terri's CAT scan, but I do remember thinking from time to time of my own experiences with seeing someone you love who is unresponsive for so long, and also about how much hope I really did have for my friend. But the evidence in front of me was clear, and I now understood the medical context for what a persistent vegetative state meant to the neurological functioning of the brain. The two options in front of me were to leave her as she was, in a persistent vegetative state with no chance of recovery, or to withdraw life-support and allow her to pass away.

The second question I had to answer was, what would Terri want?

Probate laws, like most laws, change as the world around them does. Since the 1970s—because we keep getting older, because medicine and medical technologies keep evolving, because of shifts in cultural norms—states have been revising their probate laws. By now, laws have changed regarding the end of life: How do we make decisions? What counts as life-support and what counts as getting in the way of a peaceful death? Who decides all of this and when? The controlling legal authority in Florida is a case brought to the Florida Supreme Court in 1990 when the state opposed the withdrawal of feeding tubes from Estelle Browning, an elderly woman whose living will expressed her wishes not to be kept alive on artificial life-support. The ruling in *Guardianship of Browning* is that the right of personal autonomy is not taken away if someone is incompetent to make the decision him or herself.

The Florida Constitution enshrines the right to privacy. The Florida Supreme Court in *Browning* begins with the premise that everyone has a fundamental right to the sole control of his or her person. That includes the right to refuse medical treatment. If the person is incapacitated, the guardian upholds the fundamental principle of personal autonomy either by consulting an advance directive, making a substituted judgment if her wishes have been made known, or determining her wishes by looking at her values and lifestyle, or determining what is in her best interest when nothing is known about her preferences. According to *Browning*, an incompetent person "has the same right to refuse medical treatment as a competent person." The Florida Supreme Court in *Browning* adopts the concept of substituted judgment saying, "one does not exercise another's right of self-determination or fulfill that person's right of privacy by making a decision which the state, the family or public opinion would prefer." In other words, since Terri did not have an advance directive, the decision in front of me was to see what the evidence proved she would have wanted. The legal precedent in front of me was clear.

The substituted judgment doctrine says: go on a fact-finding mission, figure out what the incapacitated person would want to do under the present circumstances. If she were to sign a living will, what would the living will look like? What would it say? I looked on my role as a jurist as not terribly difficult. You need to figure out what the facts are, you need to figure out what the law is, and you put those two together and your judgment emerges. The law made it clear that my job was to see if I could determine what Terri would want to do. As a judge, the substituted judgment doctrine meant that while I would hear from her friends and her family and would need to assess the credibility of their testimony, the only person's desires that had weight were Terri's. I would be substituting my judgment for hers, and using the facts and evidence from her life to get me there.

One of the criticisms of using substituted judgment is that it gives some solace for the judge. I can't disagree with that. Substituted judgment is not a question of what anyone besides Terri would want. It is not my judgment, the judgment of her parents, or the judgment of her husband. Once there is clear evidence to determine what she would have wished, the decision is understood as her decision.

And there was really zero evidence that she would want to continue in that vegetative state.

I heard a lot of testimony, and most of it had little or nothing to do with the decision in front of me. I heard from witnesses who ran the gamut of credibility. For all of the witnesses, I was able to observe their demeanor, hear inflections, and note pregnant pauses. Determining the credibility of witnesses is a large part of the work of a trial judge, and you look for any little clue as you try to decide if what you are hearing makes sense. A lot of this you do with your gut. I think we all spend much of our lives assessing the credibility of people around us and we all have different ways of doing this. For me, I listen to figure out if what I am hearing adds up. And if it does not add up, I try and find out why.

The testimony that rang true about Terri's feelings about life-support and end-of-life decisions came from Michael Schiavo, his brother Scott, and his sister-in-law Joan Schiavo. Scott testified that at a funeral luncheon for his grandmother, Terri said, "If I ever go like that just let me go. Don't leave me there. I don't want to be kept alive on a machine." Following a movie that they watched together about a man in a coma, Joan Schiavo said Terri told her that if she goes that way, she wants the tubes and everything taken out. Michael Schiavo told the court that after seeing someone on television on life-support, Terri said she would not want to live like that. Their stories were consistent from the depositions to the trial, and they all held up against cross-examination.

Additional testimony about Terri's feelings on life-support and end-of-life decisions came from Terri's mother, Mrs. Schindler, and a childhood friend of Terri's. The testimony of these two witnesses largely had to do with Terri's reaction to the Karen Ann Quinlan case—another right-to-die case about a young woman, dieting, who collapsed and never regained consciousness. I did not find Terri's mother's testimony convincing; nor did I find her friend's credible. Mrs. Schindler testified that Terri, at eleven or twelve years old, told her that she thought everyone should just leave Karen alone. This was in the 1970s, when the case was getting a lot of media attention. I heard the mother's testimony, but I felt Terri was too young at the time for this testimony to counterbalance the opinions Terri expressed to the Schiavos later in her life.

Terri's friend's testimony just did not add up. She testified that while she and Terri were watching a rerun of the film about Karen Ann Quinlan, Terri expressed her wishes to not have life-support withdrawn. But the friend's story jumped back and forth in time and did not hold up to cross-examination or remain consistent between the pretrial depositions and when she testified during the trial. More than anything, it did not make sense to me that comments Terri may have made at twelve years old should be understood as true reflections of what Terri would want now in her current situation. I also felt that these two statements Terri was said to have made—one to her mother, and the second to her friend—in reference to Karen Ann Quinlan did not carry the same weight as statements Terri was said to have made later to her husband, her sister-in-law, and her brother-in-law regarding herself and what she would want done if she were ever to have to make a decision to withdraw life-support.

The testimony I heard that Terri would not have wanted to live in a persistent vegetative state with no hope of recovery was credible and rose to the level of clear and convincing evidence. On February 11, 2000, I granted the petition of Michael Schiavo to discontinue artificial life-support.

Some people have asked if this was hard to decide, either because the parties purporting to know her judgment might have ulterior motives, or because it was hard to assess who knew her wishes better—her husband or her parents, who had known her longer. But I listened to the witnesses. I heard the testimony. The parents' side, even though they testified, never gave me any evidence that was either convincing or credible. They argued she would want to live, but they didn't show me anything to support that.

The decision in this first trial was not difficult: zero medical evidence she is not in a persistent vegetative state; zero compelling evidence she would want to continue that way. There was going to be a lot of dirt kicked up about this case, but the facts in front of me were clear, the law was clear, and judges are trained to decide. As a judge, you weigh what is in front of you and you decide. On the merits. In a case to withdraw life-support, the fact that someone could die as a result of a judge's decision is already a given. It was my case. There were good lawyers on both sides. I had to decide, and I did. I ruled, and ruled with confidence.

One story that did trouble me after the case and after Terri passed away was a brief exchange I had with a professor at Boston University Law School. I had gone there to receive a very nice award, and while I was there visiting, I met a professor in a motorized wheelchair on a respirator. He looked to me like he was in his fifties, and I asked him, "Were you in this condition when the university hired you?" He said yes and I said, "Good for them." Then he told me something that gave me pause: "I never thought I would want to live on a respirator." That was powerful to me. It made me stop and think. What do we really know about what our lives would look like after cataclysmic events? Are living wills credible documents if we can't know what we will be like on the other end of things? Of course, the professor's brain was totally intact; this was an entirely different situation from the one Terri was in. But it did stay with me, and I thought, life *does* look different after certain events. Life can have even more meaning after we end up where we didn't think we were going to. But again, there has to be consciousness. Meeting this professor did not make me doubt my decision, but it did make me ask, what do we really know on this side of tragedy?

The thrust of the appeal of my first decision was that no guardian ad litem had been appointed for the first trial. That had troubled me too. When I asked where Mr. Pearse, the guardian ad litem appointed by another court, was, I was told that he had been discharged by the court. Well, OK. Nobody asked for him to be reappointed. I do not believe having a third person asking questions and cross-examining at the trial would have changed the outcome at all. There was, as I have said, good counsel on both sides, and Mr. Pearse did testify and his report was in evidence. All the same, I was in agreement that the question of guardian ad litem should be resolved for future cases.

I entered a stay of the first judgment until the appellate process was concluded. A stay simply suspends action in a case until all appeals are completed. The advantage is to make certain we get a correct ruling. The disadvantage is that the process can take a long time. That is the delicate balance.

On January 24, 2001, the appellate court unanimously affirmed my decision to permit the removal of the PEG tube. In this decision, Judge Altenbernd, writing for the Second District Court of Appeal, found that there was sufficient evidence for me to make my ruling. Other appeals during this time were taken to both Florida's state courts and the federal court system, and all declined to overturn my decision. Once the stays expired, I had ruled Michael could set a date to remove the PEG tube and allow Terri to begin the natural dying process.

On April 24, 2001, when the stay was lifted, by my order Terri Schiavo's PEG tube was removed for what was to be the first of three times.

At this point in the case, there was no hoopla. There was interest, there were the three cameras that had been set up the first day of the trial along the side of the courtroom. But nobody interfered; there were no marches, no threats, none of that. When I walked the dog, it was just me and the dog. What gave this case legs was a ruling in a separate civil lawsuit, by a "duty judge," a judge who sits in when the assigned judge is not available. In a last-minute effort to keep their daughter alive, the parents had filed a tort suit in civil court alleging physical violence against Terri, two days after Michael as guardian removed the PEG tube. The duty judge was in an unenviable position: he had no case law in front of him to turn to, it was late in the day, and he heard the story of a young woman's life, now in his hands. He granted an injunction and ordered the PEG reinserted so Terri could be medically examined. The tube, two days after it was removed, was put back in. From this point on, the case changed from being just a court case to being the center of a national—and at some points, international—spectacle.

A duty judge is really someone who is just stepping in. Maybe the assigned judge is on vacation, maybe she needed to step away, but, in any event, the parents' motion fell in this duty judge's lap and he ordered the tube reinserted. And then everything changed. The underlying tort suit alleging physical abuse was ultimately dismissed for lack of prosecution, which was telling because I think it showed the parents didn't have a valid claim. But the injunction was appealed and reversed, and the appeals court judge, a perfect gentleman, did not beat up the duty judge, just very kindly said, in essence, "You overstepped your bounds. You had no business doing this."

In July of 2001, the appellate court resolved the question raised earlier of the guardian ad litem, affirming my discretionary decision to proceed without one. The trial court would essentially serve as guardian ad litem to Terri Schiavo. This was brand-new law. I never thought to ask the appellate judges what their thinking was; I don't like to put people on the spot. What the ruling did, though, was put a greater burden on me by making me the party directly responsible for her dying. Essentially, it shifted the agony of "pulling the plug"—a terrible and coarse expression that started to be used around this time in the case and I think previewed the polarization that would come—from the husband to me, the judge. Again, I am not sure what the thinking behind this was, but I imagine this additional responsibility sunk in for me, and I worked hard to protect the privacy of the woman right in the middle of all the bitter division surrounding the case.

The same appellate decision sent the case back to me for a second trial to consider Terri's parents' claim that there was new medical evidence that would have changed Terri's mind about whether she would have wanted to live or die. This trial was to involve testimony from five doctors: two chosen by Michael Schiavo, two by the parents, and one chosen by me, if the parties could not agree on the fifth. The court concluded with an acknowledgment of the delicate balance of a timeline in this case saying, "The judicial process must be sufficient to assure the accuracy of the proxy's decision, but not so slow as to deprive the ward of a final decision—one way or the other."

I scheduled the trial on the claim that there were new medical treatments available, for October 2002. I was very aware of the delicate balance of time and also determined not to waste any time of the five doctors who were brought in to examine Terri and testify. On day one, her treating doctor would come in to set the stage. On days two through six, the five new doctors would each give testimony. Day seven would be closing arguments, and then I would rule.

The second trial again took place in the historic old courthouse that was right in the center of downtown Clearwater, Florida. From the time the bailiff announced the court was in session on October 12th until he announced we would adjourn on October 22, I knew by the number of people and cameras in the courtroom that what was going on outside was different than before. But my job was the same. Both trials required me to make a determination. The second one presumed the determinations in the first to be true: Terri Schiavo was in a persistent vegetative state and she would not want to remain on artificial life-support under these circumstances. The second asked, given that the court had found, under substituted judgment, that Terri would not want to live like this, was there any new treatment that would cause her to change that decision and elect to take the new treatment as opposed to discontinuing the nutrition and hydration tube? That was the entirety of the question in front of me during the second trial.

It was important to me that the doctors' examinations, taking place during the summer months before the second trial, were respectful and not needlessly invasive to Terri's body. I ruled that each of the five doctors would give her treating physician the tests they wanted to run, and the treating physician would run and coordinate those tests. I said, "We are not sticking a needle in her five times for five blood tests. We will do it once." Throughout the second trial I tried to protect Terri's privacy. The internet and social media had arrived in full force at this time, and I didn't want her hospital room to be full of cameras, I didn't want videos of her circulating around, and I wanted to make sure that these medical tests were as minimally invasive as possible.

The first thing I did was to issue an order defining the phrase "new medical procedure" as used by the appellate court to mean anything she had not undergone. I did not want to end up in the circular logic of what "new" means. I wanted to turn over every stone here and see: Is there *anything* out there that would work? The first trial had a two-part question, but this trial just had one.

The two doctors that the parents selected spoke about the potential of two treatments—hyperbaric therapy and vasodilation—to help Terri. Hyperbaric therapy is a therapy that submerges the patient in water in order to use that water pressure to get large amounts of oxygen into the bloodstream; it is similar to treatment for the bends. Vasodilation is a treatment that widens the blood vessels to decrease blood pressure. Ultimately, although the parents' two doctors introduced these as potential therapies, I found, based on the overwhelming evidence presented by the other medical experts, that neither would be effective treatments for the particular injury that Terri sustained.

The two doctors for the husband, one of whom was explicitly pro–assisted suicide, both testified there was no medical treatment that would substantively or positively change Terri's condition. The fifth doctor was selected by me, since the parents and husband were unable to agree on a doctor together. With help from friends in the medical community, I selected a neurologist at the Cleveland Clinic. He told me he had no preconceived ideas about the case and that he was willing to serve. I had no idea what he would say; I just wanted an honest opinion. And he ended up being the guy I hung my hat on. He was neutral, objective, thoroughly professional. In his testimony, he explained to the court the agony and soul-searching he did to arrive at his opinion that there were no treatments that would improve Terri Schiavo's quality of life in her persistent vegetative state. I would have loved to hear otherwise. The facts of this trial, though, were clear.

I reviewed all the testimony and evidence thoroughly. Although this trial presumed the question of Terri's neurological status had been answered, because there were new concepts such as idling neurons that were brought up, I felt compelled to consider them. I spent extensive time reviewing the two-hour footage that one of the parents' doctors had testified documented conscious response. The majority of the doctors testified that these were not conscious, but rather reactive responses. Were it a conscious response, the same stimuli would produce the same response time after time. The neurological medical question at stake in the video footage was whether Terri was *consciously* responding or *randomly* reacting to stimuli.

At first blush, she did seem to smile and look lovingly at her mother and to follow the Mickey Mouse balloon placed in front of her. These were the short snippets from longer video documentation that would find their way to the media. But after a thorough review, I counted 111 commands and 72 questions put to Terri, and only very few actions that the doctor said were considered responses. Based on the credible evidence, if she were cognitively functional there would be consistent and reproducible responses. I found this to be not the case at all and so found my first decision regarding her persistent vegetative state to stand. At the conclusion of my deliberations, it was clear to me that there was no new treatment that would change the substituted judgment made during the first trial. Neither hyperbaric therapy nor vasodilation would be effective since Terri was not capable of conscious response. On November 22, 2002, I denied the motion for relief from judgment and, per directions from the appellate court, ordered that the PEG tube be withdrawn at 3 p.m. on January 2, 2003. The following month, I stayed the ruling until an appellate court could hear the case.

I hoped the appellate court would uphold my second decision just as they had my first, and they did. What I did not expect was what would start to become the new normal outside the case. Much of the reaction against the withdrawal of life-support was based on religious beliefs about the sanctity of life, but it was not until the end of the second trial that these reactions became, ironically, violent. At the end of the second trial, I got the first threat against my life. It would not be the last. Each morning, putting on my bulletproof vest became a part of my daily routine. Bloggers started covering the case and raising outer orbit issues. Everything, they said, was a conspiracy: the Greek ancestry of one of the lawyers and one of the doctors in the case, the private campaign contributions my wife made to local politicians. One blogger even put our home address on her blog. Later, a driver from the flower shop delivered dead flowers to my wife with a note saying, "no food . . . no water." Over the course of the case, two arrests were made of people who made threats against me. One pled out and the other was convicted by a jury. Law enforcement was at our house from late 2004 until mid-2005 to protect us. While I felt safe as a result, the experience was especially unnerving for my wife, although I did not know it at the time.

When the duty judge made his decision, almost overnight the media doubled in size, and anti-abortion activists showed up en masse to the courthouse and to the hospice where Terri was. I couldn't figure out why anti-abortionists cared about the Schiavo case. There's no unborn person here. None of it added up, until a few years later, in 2004—right in the eye of the political storm of this case—I was presented with another petition to withdraw life-support. This time it was for a man. These cases are profound. No one takes them lightly. This second case, though, was particularly unnerving for me: The man was more or less my age, he was also a lawyer, had two kids, as I had, was a runner like me, and had been remarried, as I had. I heard the case and ultimately decided to withdraw life-support. One small article ran in the *St. Petersburg Times* on page nine. Right at the same time the whole world seemed to be focused on Terri Schiavo, no one made a peep. I asked someone—a very credible source connected to the Governor—do you think we'd have all this to-do if we were talking about a Terrence Schiavo? And he told me, this has nothing to do with Terri Schiavo. It has everything to do with *Roe v. Wade*.

I have thought about that comment a lot. And I have thought about the absence of reaction to my decision to withdraw life-support from the man in 2004. My guess in all of this is that the anti-abortion movement was concerned that if a woman could withdraw life-support and choose to die, it's not a far stretch to say she can have an abortion. Gender I think played a big role in the anti-abortion movement's rallying around this case.

But I pretty much shut out all of this at the time. As judges, we are not supposed to be persuaded or stampeded by what goes on outside a case. When Jerry Falwell or Pat Robertson made statements on television, I'd change the channel. The Schiavo case at the time struck me as a family tragedy that was taken up by anti-abortion and "right-to-life" groups like the National Right to Life, Operation Rescue, Focus on the Family, and Traditional Values Coalition. My friend told a reporter around this time, "Hey, Judge Greer *is* the religious right," and he was correct! I became a Southern Baptist as an adult and still consider myself to be one at heart. But things were changing in the church, and I didn't understand where they were politically sometimes. At the time, when protesters began to gather at the courthouse, I didn't know that I would later be exiled by my own pastor. I am still puzzled by it all.

I stayed my ruling until the appellate courts could decide. Once they had and after the Florida Supreme Court refused to review their decision in August of 2003, on September 17, 2003, I ordered that the PEG tube be removed on October 15th. And then things got even more puzzling. Shortly after I set the date for the removal of the tube, a two-page letter arrived from Governor Jeb Bush writing in support of the parents and telling me that, after receiving thousands of emails, he felt he "had to do something." I read it—even though I probably should not have—and filed it with the clerk.

On October 7, 2003, Governor Bush filed a federal court brief in support of the Schindlers' attempts to stop the removal of the PEG tube. Three days later, Federal Court Judge Richard Lazzara ruled that he had no jurisdiction to hear the case filed by the Governor, and on October 15, 2003, for the second time, Terri Schiavo's nutrition and hydration tube was removed by my order.

Six days later, however, on October 21st, Governor Bush signed an executive order—authorized by legislation that was written and passed by state lawmakers (although sought and signed by the Governor himself)—to reinsert Terri's PEG tube for the second time.

I watched all of this unfold in disbelief. If the first time the tube was reinserted was a stunning misfortune resulting from the ruling of an unlucky duty judge, this was an outright stunt. And it was a calculated stunt. Here were two branches of the government coming together to essentially undermine the third branch of government's final judicial decision. I still don't know what to make of a lot of it. I do remember thinking at the time that the Republican leadership, unable to push through the marriage amendment to federally establish marriage as the union between one man and one woman, saw its base rallying around what had at that point become a cause célèbre for the anti-abortion movement. And they jumped on board.

The legislation that was passed in the Florida House of Representatives on October 20th and, with a lot of arm-twisting by the Governor, on October 21st in the Florida Senate, was known as Terri's Law or HB 35-E. The new law allowed the Governor to issue a "one-time stay in certain cases." A little box was drawn around Terri Schiavo's case with such narrow parameters that the bill would essentially apply only to her. It was passed in an unusual evening session. There was no testimony, no debate, and the supporters of the bill read from handouts provided to them by the sponsors of the bill.

What was going through my head at the time was not how this affected judicial process in Florida, but how it affected Terri Schiavo. She had, at this point in 2003, been declared by every credible medical expert to be in a persistent vegetative state for almost fourteen years. The court had found there were no medical treatments that would change this condition. Why were the Florida legislature and Governor Jeb Bush intervening to void her wishes? What explained the urgency to keep her alive when the court had conclusively found—*twice*—that this was contrary to her wishes? I knew this was a violation of foundational legal principles.

Our highest appeals courts eventually agreed. Michael Schiavo challenged the law the week after it was passed, and his new case was assigned to Circuit Judge W. Douglas Baird. In May 2004 (about the time I was ruling in my second "right-to-life" case), Judge Baird ruled that it was unconstitutional for the legislative branch to get involved in the functioning of the judicial branch. Judge Baird wrote that Terri's Law was "an unconstitutional delegation of legislative power to the governor and because it unjustifiably authorizes the Governor to deprive Florida citizens of their constitutional right to privacy." In the ruling, he cited Justice Antonin Scalia, who established the principle that Congress cannot get involved in overturning a final judicial decision "for even the very best of reasons." That is pretty black-letter law. Judge Baird ruled Terri's Law violated Terri Schiavo's right to privacy, her due process, and the separation-of-powers doctrine. Underscoring the constitutional role of checking power, he drew on Daniel Webster's observation that these limits set forth are to guard against men with even the best of intentions who might "promise to be good masters, but they mean to be masters." In September of 2004, the Florida Supreme Court affirmed Judge Baird seven-zip.

The Governor during all of this made much of the fact that he and his wife had a living will. There were times when I just wanted to ask him: Does yours say to keep you alive until the Second Coming if you are in a permanent vegetative state? Or does it say exactly what mine says? That if there's no reasonable hope for recovery, pull the damn plug.

The Governor did play to his religious base. A couple of months before Judge Baird's ruling, Pope John Paul II made a proclamation on "Life-Sustaining Treatments and Vegetative State: Scientific Advances and Ethical Dilemmas," saying that man is always man, never "vegetable," never "animal." This became the centerpiece of a court filing seeking a ruling on whether the papal statement would have changed Terri's mind. I ruled that since St. Peter, we have probably had tens of thousands of papal proclamations, and we are not going to try and determine which of those tens of thousands Terri would have followed. No, I said. We are not going there.

This was not a religious question. This was a legal question. God's law, I do believe, is a higher law, but God gave us the power of self-determination. We determine as mankind and as a nation how we should conduct ourselves. We have created the institutional framework in the Constitution, and that is what I took an oath to uphold. We cannot pick and choose whether the laws of the land suit our own beliefs. Most people wouldn't pay taxes if that were the case. This was not a hard distinction for me to make.

Once the Florida Supreme Court overruled Terri's Law, almost six months of more legal maneuvering ensued. On February 25, 2005, after issuing a number of stays in order to hear arguments and to outline my decisions from those arguments, I ordered that, absent a stay from the appellate courts, after five years of proceedings, this case must come to a close. I ordered the tube removal for March 18, 2005, and motions were then filed fast and furious. When I got motions to disqualify me from continuing to preside in the Schiavo case—and there were seven in all—I thought each time, I am not leaving. I am stubborn, but I also felt I had to do the right thing. Toward that end, I consulted the attorney for Florida's Sixth Judicial Circuit, sometimes taking hours to determine whether any of the motions to disqualify were legally sufficient. Counsel came to the conclusion that these motions had no merit, and so I denied them. All seven.

The first one was easy. The parents' side filed a motion because they didn't think they had gotten a fair shake. That is not a basis for disqualifying a judge, just because they rule against you. Filing an appeal to a higher court is the established way to correct legal error by a lower court judge. The case law is crystal clear on that. The first four motions to disqualify were appealed and I was affirmed. I never lost a single vote and all of them were three-judge panels on the appellate court. I also never lost a single vote on the seven-member Florida Supreme Court. Two motions to disqualify went up to the Eleventh Circuit—the federal appeals court—but the motions were found to be insufficient.

I felt responsibility to the judicial branch to hang in there and stand up to the two other intervening branches. I also felt that if the motion to disqualify me were sufficient, I would have to step down, though I didn't want to. In the face of seven motions to disqualify me, I've said, part jokingly, that I made seven bad decisions in the Terri Schiavo case. Seven doors opened up that I could have walked out of. But if I had, it would have reopened the whole thing up to some other poor judge, who would have had to go back to square one, because once a judge is disqualified, every decision can then be revisited.

On a Sunday in early March of 2015, I had a telephone hearing in the case scheduled on a sheriff's cell phone so that my own cell phone number would not be disclosed for security reasons. I was in my kitchen, having this hearing; it was late morning, maybe 10 a.m. The attorney for the parents said, "Judge, before you get started, there's a matter we need to take up." I said, "Do you mean the motion to disqualify me that you faxed my office last night at 12:15 a.m.?" "Yes," he said. "I've reviewed that, Mr. Gibbs. I also prepared and signed an order denying that motion that you will get in due course. Let's proceed." At that point in the case, I had to keep a close eye on my fax machine, because when a motion to disqualify comes in, it brings everything to a screeching halt. You have to dispose of any motion to disqualify before proceeding. I was watching closely for anything that would interrupt the proceedings.

On March 18th, the date I had ordered the tube to be removed, the U.S. House of Representatives Subcommittee on Government Reform issued five subpoenas: one that Terri Schiavo appear before it, one that Michael Schiavo appear and bring the "hydration and nutrition equipment," and three for personnel and physicians at the hospice. I had a telephone hearing set for noon on the motion to stay and the motion to intervene that the U.S. Congressional Subcommittee had filed, and I was on the way to the undisclosed location that the Pinellas County Sheriff arranged in order to ensure our safety. A friend was driving, and I called the number to connect me to all the attorneys, including the attorney representing the House Subcommittee. He told me how critical it was for members of the subcommittee to view the life-support machines in working order and in operation on the following Friday. I said, "I understand this is important work for your subcommittee and I appreciate that. Can you share with me how many other site visits besides the hospice are currently on the subcommittee's schedule?" "None right now," he said. We were almost to the undisclosed location when I heard this, and I knew I was going to treat the federal government just the way I treated the state government when it tried to intervene. I said, "This is not your issue. Motion to stay denied. Motion to intervene denied. Thank you very much," and I hung up.

On that afternoon of Friday, March 18, 2005, Terri Schiavo's PEG tube was once again removed by my order.

Later that weekend the U.S. House and Senate passed S. 686. The federal bill, like the Florida bill before it, drew a very small box so that the bill would apply only to Terri Schiavo. But the federal bill included an extraordinary provision that would allow a federal court review of a state court's final decision. Generally speaking, if a case is heard in state court, it cannot then be heard in federal court. You don't get a second bite at the apple.

One of the remarkable things that happened in the Schiavo case was the attempt to allow just that by both the executive and legislative branches. But congressmen cannot be sued for voting for an unconstitutional law, which means they can act with impunity. President George W. Bush signed the bill into law early Monday morning on March 21st. And then? Every federal court that was asked to review the matter, all the way up to the United States Supreme Court, refused to hear the case on grounds of jurisdiction.

But what nobody ever talked about and that still stands out to me, is the question of whether or not S. 686 was unconstitutional. Federal District Court Judge James Whittemore heard a motion for temporary injunction and denied it. Judge Whittemore ruled there was no showing that the parents had a probability of success in the trial, so he refused to order reinsertion of the PEG tube. But the constitutionality of the new federal statute remains untested.

It is worth noting here that in the first "right-to-die" case heard in front of the U.S. Supreme Court in 1990, *Cruzan v. Director,* Justice Scalia concluded that the states are the only ones with jurisdiction in such matters and that the federal courts have no business in this field. He wrote that since "we know no more about 'life-and-death' as justices of the Supreme Court than do citizens of a state, that is where the decisions should be made." The nine justices, he noted, know no more about end-of-life questions than do nine people picked at random from a phonebook. Justice John Paul Stevens, writing with the majority, added, "This Court need not, and has no authority to, inject itself into every field of human activity where irrationality and oppression may theoretically occur, and if it tries to do so, it will destroy itself."

Meanwhile, the Majority Leader of the House of Representatives, Tom DeLay, appeared on C-SPAN labeling the Florida courts in general, and I suppose me, in particular, "barbaric."

When I returned to Pinellas County, I was met with a threat from Governor Bush's allies in Tallahassee that state authorities might "rescue" Terri from the hospice under a vague authority to protect citizens. I entered an order on Wednesday, March 23, 2005, forbidding the Florida Department of Law Enforcement from taking possession of or removing her from hospice, and directing each and every sheriff in Florida to enforce my order. Early the next morning the Florida Department of Children and Families appealed my order to the Second District Court of Appeal, which resulted in an automatic stay. The stay was lifted at 11 a.m. by the appellate court, and ten days after President Bush signed S. 686 into law, on March 31, 2005, Terri Schiavo mercifully passed this life. Her life was short and tragic. When she died, after fifteen years in a persistent vegetative state—the last five years the subject of a bitter family struggle and a sometimes ugly political spectacle—I felt relief. For her, for her husband, and I hope someday for her parents.

For me, this case was always essentially about the right to control your own destiny. The right to die. The legal precedents in the Terri Schiavo case required the court to make a decision that a person herself would have made if she were able. The case stood on the legal grounds of the constitutional right of privacy in Florida. From the outside, this case looked like a perfect storm: religious fury, partisan spectacle, media saturation. But a judge's job is to block all of that out. The truth of the matter is that, even with the storm outside, inside the case was clear. When Terri Schiavo died, I felt that I had made the right decision.

When I saw the autopsy report, I was certain. As much as you read, and as well as you listen, and as hard as you think about a case, for a good judge there is always doubt. But when I saw that the portion of the brain to which the optic nerve is attached was completely missing, I was certain she could not see; there was no possibility she could have been tracking the balloon in the videos. And in a case like this, with so much uncharted territory, it was important to me to see that and not have any doubt that I had made the right decision.

But all this did come at a personal cost to me. In mid-March of 2005, as the political storm around this case was full blown, I opened a particularly hurtful letter from my new pastor. This letter, like all my mail, had been opened before me by my security detail—they intercepted all my voicemails and emails, put the snail mail through a scanning machine at the courthouse, and brought it to me twice a week. I was used to that. But this letter turned out to be a letter from our pastor telling my wife and me to withdraw our membership to the church and "get on the side of the angels." That was tough. Afterwards, I probably got twenty invitations to attend other religious organizations including half a dozen Southern Baptist churches, and three synagogues. Two rabbis called me at home, and one told me, "Look, George, we won't shove Judaism down your throat." I laughed and told him, "Rabbi, your book is the first half of my book. That's not a problem."

I don't know if I will join another church. I'm still a Southern

Baptist at heart. That was my religious community for thirty-five years. We were married by that church. I taught Sunday school there, coached church league basketball and softball. My kids were baptized there. My wife and I both were baptized there.

It is true that the polarization around this case was stark. There was no middle ground in the Schiavo case. She either lived or she died. But this was not a religious question; it was a legal question. There was a dispute, and it was brought to the courts to decide based on the facts brought forth and the law. It was Terri's wishes that I had to discern. I was not ruling based on my faith, but on the laws set forth in the federal and state constitutions. This fact was never unclear to me. The cost of getting tossed from our church was high, but that was never something that weighed in on my thinking as a judge. The oath I took was to uphold the Constitution, and so all the religious backlash—from the Pope to Drs. Falwell and Robertson, and then culminating with my own pastor—just did not factor in. In the end, you have to stand by your principles, and I tried to.

Maybe too much, one of my friends told me during the Bush administration. He asked if I would ever want to be appointed a federal judge, I told him, "Look, I went from the promising young Mr. Republican in this part of Florida years ago, to now W. wouldn't appoint me dog catcher." So, maybe in some ways it did cost me politically. But in August 2004, right in the middle of this case, I ran for election to retain my judgeship and won by an overwhelming margin against an attorney who was known for his opposition to my rulings in the Schiavo case. People at home knew my record, and I feel proud to have kept their support throughout.

I have always said that this case did not present a difficult decision. It was not a difficult legal decision, and it was not a difficult professional decision to stand by it and to stand by the judiciary and the principles it stands for. There was no other place Michael Schiavo and Terri's parents could have taken their dispute. The courts are established to break ties. They are there so that we all don't throw down at high noon. But the job itself is tough. It is a lonely job in a lot of ways. Judges cannot give or receive information outside of the courtroom about a case. We are not supposed to comment publicly or privately. You can't go to your barber and talk it through. All you can do is go to other judges. For this case, there was only one sitting judge, the judge for *Browning*, who had been through the questions I was facing. There was nobody across the hall to wrestle any of this with.

It is difficult not to be able to defend yourself. If someone calls me unethical, I cannot respond as a judge. The ethics say you may not comment on a pending or an impending case, which means if it is already there or it is coming, you cannot say a word. Those are good rules. They keep judges above the fray. They keep us from turning into one more political hack. But that doesn't mean it's easy to hear your character impugned. Especially from inside your own party. Especially from people inside your own church.

But I believe there is no greater work than this. The job of the judge to me is the zenith of the legal profession. The judiciary and the independence of the judiciary is what stands between democracy and total anarchy. It is how the founding fathers envisioned making sure that it is not the loudest people who control how we govern ourselves.

There were high costs in this case. And I am sure I made my fair share of mistakes. But I have never regretted becoming a trial judge. Not too many people have to stand up to their president, their congress, their governor, their legislature, and their church. And I would have never known for sure if I had the strength to do that if not for this case. I walked out with my head held high.

2

Rough Justice

JUDGE RUSSELL F. CANAN

 *Judge Russell F. Canan was appointed to the Superior Court of the District of Columbia in 1993 by President Clinton where he chaired a committee studying wrongful convictions. Judge Canan is the former Presiding Judge of the Criminal Division. Prior to his appointment, Judge Canan practiced civil litigation and criminal defense in the District of Columbia. In 1983, Judge Canan helped establish the Southern Center for Human Rights in Atlanta, Georgia, where he represented prisoners on death row and directed class-action civil rights lawsuits.*

WHAT THE HELL, I THOUGHT. I REREAD THE NOTE FROM THE JURY in chambers. "If we find the defendant not guilty of Assault with Intent to Kill While Armed, can we still find him guilty of Assault with a Dangerous Weapon?" The note was signed by the Foreperson, Juror #10.

How could they be asking this question? I had already told them twice they could do just that in my final legal instructions, right before they began their deliberations. I had also given them this instruction in writing to take back to the jury room. It was also crystal clear on the verdict form.

The jury apparently needed to hear yet again that Assault with a Dangerous Weapon, or "ADW" in courthouse slang, is what's called a lesser-included offense of Assault with Intent to Kill While Armed (AWIK w/a). The jury could indeed find that although the defendant had not intended to kill the victim, as required for AWIK w/a, he assaulted the victim with a dangerous weapon without intending to kill. There could be no mistaking. The answer to the jury's question was clearly yes.

The jury's apparent confusion about a very straightforward matter provided a rare glimpse into their decision-making process. Once this point was settled, their inevitable decision would just be a matter of time. And I was in shock. How could the jury possibly convict the defendant of ADW? Had the case been tried before me without a jury, I would have found him not guilty of both charges. It looked like I was going to have to accept a verdict that I personally disagreed with. This happens occasionally, though most of the time I agree with the jury's verdict, or, if not, I understand how they came to their conclusion in a rational way.

I could not understand this one, though. It didn't make sense to me at all. To make matters worse, there was no principled way for me to prevent the jury from reaching what I considered to be the wrong verdict. But it wasn't the possibility of an ADW conviction I was really worried about. It was the other charge in the case.

The defendant was also charged with Possession of a Firearm during a Crime of Violence (PFCV). Both AWIK w/a and ADW are categorized as crimes of violence in the District of Columbia, and a conviction for either one of them meant a sure conviction for PFCV. That was the real problem because PFCV, unlike ADW, carries a mandatory five years in prison, and there was nothing I could do about that, either.

At least for the ADW charge I could place the defendant on probation, and he wouldn't have to go to jail. He was in his forties with no criminal record. He was a single parent to two teenage girls and held a steady job. Sending him to prison would be devastating to the girls.

But even more than that, I believed he was innocent. I could see a miscarriage of justice coming down soon.

During judicial trainings judges work through all sorts of hypothetical sentencings. A classic scenario is a brutal rape and torture, where the accused sets the victim on fire and leaves her in a deserted field to die. A conviction for such a depraved crime would call for a very harsh punishment, probably a life sentence. Hardly anyone would disagree. But what if you thought the jury got it wrong, and you believed the defendant was actually innocent? Not that the government's case was weak or that there was a reasonable doubt as to the accused's guilt, but that you firmly believed he did not commit this vicious crime. As the sentencing judge you have wide discretion and could lock him up for life. There is, however, no mandatory sentence for this crime, and you could also place him on probation with no jail time at all. Do you respect the jury's judgment and impose the harsh sentence? Or do you use your own judgment and effectively go around the verdict by not locking up the defendant at all?

I think most judges defer to the jury's verdict and impose the harsh sentence, no matter how much it offends them. To do otherwise would turn our jury system upside down. But I wasn't faced with this difficult philosophical question. I was in real time with no discretion and no legal authority to reject the jury's verdict. Because the crime of PFCV carries a mandatory sentence, I would have to impose a five-year prison term.

The problem is that under the law, the standard for a judge taking a case from a jury and issuing a not guilty verdict is very high. After the prosecution puts on all of its evidence and completes its case, defense counsel routinely moves the court to acquit the defendant and throw out the charges. The law requires the judge to review the evidence in the light most favorable to the prosecution and allow the jury to make all credibility decisions. Simply put, the jury is the judge of the facts. The trial judge determines the law; the jury finds the facts, and the court must defer to the jury's judgment on them.

There is a very narrow exception which allows the judge to throw out a case if the government's case is so incredible that no reasonable person could find the defendant guilty. This is an exceedingly rare occurrence and was not the case before me.

I thought back to a case when I was defense counsel and a judge took a case away from a jury in a child rape trial because he just didn't believe the young girl's version of events. I, of course, was delighted for my client, as I believed he was innocent, but was still shocked the judge had freed him. The prosecutor was beyond ticked off, and when the judge left the bench he told me, and anyone around who would listen, that the judge was lawless and violated his oath of office.

Should I do the same in this case? Should I take the case away from the jury? I had the power to do so, and the government did not even have the legal right to appeal my decision to our court of appeals. The case would be over. Defendant forever cleared of the charges.

The facts were pretty straightforward. A community party was being held in the local neighborhood hall in a middle-income neighborhood of DC, and many neighbors were in attendance. The defendant, whom I will call Sam Johnson, was usually the DJ at parties and provided the music with sophisticated amplifiers. His teenage daughters were there, as were a number of young men in their early twenties, including best friends Joe and William. As the party went on, Joe insisted on taking over from Sam the role as DJ. Sam refused as he was worried Joe would blow out the speakers. Joe persisted because he didn't like the music Sam was playing. Sam relented but warned Joe not to play the music too loud to save the speakers.

The party went on, but at some point Sam saw Joe flirting with his fifteen-year-old daughter. Sam and Joe had words, but nothing came of it. Later on, Joe cranked up the music and blew out the speakers, just as Sam had feared. A loud argument followed but no violence. Sam had had enough. He decided to leave the party and pick up his gear later.

Outside the hall, in the fresh air, Sam encountered William, Joe's friend, and they immediately had words. William later claimed at trial that Sam pulled a gun and threatened him. William said he turned to run when Sam fired and hit him in the front of his thigh. He couldn't really explain how he was shot in the front when he had turned his back to flee. Maybe he got shot first and then turned to run. Everything happened so fast it was hard to remember exactly. William testified that Sam got in his car with the gun, sped away, and did not return. In my view, William was not very believable and came off as both arrogant and aggressive.

The law allows the opposing party the right to impeach or discredit a witness by confronting him in front of the jury with prior convictions of certain crimes. William was impeached with several serious crimes.

No other eyewitnesses to the shooting testified for the prosecution. There was no scientific, physical, or electronic evidence presented to corroborate William's story. The gun was never recovered, and no evidence was presented that Sam had ever owned or had access to a gun. Sam made no incriminating statements to the police or anyone else.

At the close of the government's case, all the jury had was William's very shaky version of events, bad blood between Sam, William, and Joe, and Sam's flight from the scene with the gun. Had the case ended right there, with no defense evidence, I would have easily found reasonable doubt and declared Sam not guilty. But this was a trial by jury and the jury would have the last word.

As expected, the defense made a motion for judgment of acquittal claiming the government had not proved its case. I had to deny the motion; it was the jury's responsibility to believe or not believe William. They could also find as a motive that Sam was angry because of Joe's flirtation with his daughter and the destruction of his speakers. Finally, the jury could conclude Sam acted like a guilty man because he fled the scene with the gun rather than call an ambulance and the police.

It was now the defendant's turn to put on evidence. I'm sure the jury wanted to hear Sam's version of these events. That seemed, however, unlikely. The conventional wisdom from the defense viewpoint is the accused should not testify at trial. While there are, of course, exceptions, the theory is the defense is generally better served attacking the prosecution and poking holes in the government's case. Once the defendant takes the stand and is cross-examined, the jury's focus and decision-making shifts to analyzing whether or not he should be believed. Many an accused has stolen defeat from the jaws of victory by putting on evidence after the prosecution rested its case.

The decision to testify is the defendant's alone. Counsel is there to advise, but the accused can testify even if his lawyer recommends otherwise. Sam's lawyer was very experienced and savvy, and I'm sure she read the case the way I did and saw the dangers of Sam's testimony. Plus, she had an ace in the hole.

Her first witness was a working man in his thirties who parked right across the street from the hall waiting for his date to come out of her home. He had a clear view of the scene under well-lit conditions. He didn't know Sam or William and didn't even live in the neighborhood. He had a regular job and no criminal record. There was no evidence that he was using drugs or alcohol. The perfect witness.

He saw William and Sam arguing face to face. He couldn't quite hear what they were saying, but he clearly saw William bring out a gun from his jacket and point it at Sam. Sam grabbed the gun, and they tussled. A shot rang out, and William went down. No turning of the back and running. The witness saw Sam run away. He saw many people run out of the hall to aid William. He knew enough to know that he didn't want to be a witness in a shooting and get caught up in a police investigation, so he left with his date. Sometime later, Sam's investigator knocked on his door. Apparently, his date had mentioned to others in the neighborhood that he had seen the shooting. Although he really didn't want to be involved, he understood the importance of testifying.

I could see the prosecutor was surprised. Unfortunately, too much of a criminal case is trial by ambush. The government is required by law to turn over to the defense physical evidence, such as photographs and expert reports, but generally is not mandated to turn over the names of witnesses or their prior statements to the police or the grand jury until trial begins. The law does require evidence that is favorable to the defense be turned over by the prosecutor before trial in time for the defendant to adequately prepare his case. But, in general, the defense basically has to do its own investigation.

The defense obligation to disclose information to the prosecution is even less. While a defendant also has to turn over to the prosecution physical evidence and expert reports, he is under no obligation to identify any witness to the crime before the day of trial and may even keep under wraps altogether any witness who may hurt rather than help his case. I'm sure Sam's lawyer thought long and hard as to whether she would make this witness available to the prosecution before the trial in an effort to have the government dismiss the case well before trial. The prosecutor was well respected and very fair minded. Faced with such a good defense witness and no strong corroboration of William's side of the story, it's possible the judge could have been convinced to dismiss the case.

In any event, it seemed to me a weak government case had now gotten worse. Surely all the testimony was over. It would have been entirely prudent for the defense to rest its case at this point. But Sam wanted to testify. His lawyer kept a poker face, but my guess was Sam's testimony was against her advice. Sam did well, though. He was originally from rural North Carolina and had a country way of talking. He came off as a hard-working man who was raising his two daughters alone. His testimony pretty much tracked the eyewitness. He admitted he ran because he was scared William's friend Joe would be after him, and he also didn't want to face the police. He hoped William would not press charges or give up his name and it would all go away. He tossed the gun in a sewer.

With all the evidence in, it was now up to counsel to give their closing arguments to the jury, followed by my instructions of law. This was a slam-dunk case for the defense. I expected a quick "not guilty" verdict, probably within an hour. It was, however, almost 5 p.m., and I had to recess the trial before the jury could begin its deliberations. I could sense the jurors were disappointed and wanted to get right at it, but I sent them home for the evening and asked them to come back at 9:30 the next morning.

Shortly after 10:30 the next day, Mr. Van Hook, the deputy courtroom clerk, came into chambers and said the jury had sent a note.

"If we find the defendant not guilty of assault with intent to kill while armed, can we still find him guilty of assault with a dangerous weapon?" It was signed by the Foreperson, Juror #10.

I had already instructed them in open court and in writing. The answer was clearly yes. That was the easy part. But I had a pit in my stomach and was deeply concerned.

Mr. Van Hook, a quiet and reserved man, rarely gave opinions on cases. He saw my response and said, "This one's a real surprise, isn't it?" We both shook our heads. "I'll call the lawyers to come to court," he said. Thirty minutes later he called and said all parties were in the courtroom and ready.

As I walked into the courtroom, Mr. Van Hook stood and announced, "All rise. This honorable court is now in session. The Honorable Judge Canan, presiding. Please be seated and come to order." As he is performing this ritual, I always take a deep breath, reminding myself of the important work ahead.

The case was called the *United States v. Sam Johnson*. Counsel and the defendant stepped forward and identified themselves for the record. I announced that the jury had resumed their deliberations at 9:30 that morning and at 10:38 sent a note. I read the note out loud:

"If we find the defendant not guilty of assault with intent to kill while armed, can we still find him guilty of assault with a dangerous weapon?"

I could see the surprised look on the lawyers' faces. Sam dropped his head.

"Counsel, I think we all know the answer to the jury's note is a simple 'Yes'. It's in both the jury instructions and on the verdict form."

I looked to the lawyers. "Counsel, what's your position?"

"I agree," the prosecutor said.

"I agree, as well," said defense counsel.

I wrote the word "Yes," signed my name, noted the date and time, and asked Mr. Van Hook to send it back to the jury.

The note had been addressed, and there was no more business before the court. I hesitated. Ordinarily, I would leave the bench and wait for the inevitable verdict. But the reality of what was about to happen caused us all to pause. It was very quiet in the courtroom. No one was moving, but there was nothing to be said or done. Or was there anything else I should be doing? Perhaps I should suggest to the prosecutor and defense counsel that they should consider reaching a plea bargain to avoid the mandatory sentence. Was it even appropriate for me to make such a suggestion, especially at this stage in the trial? I was not sure what to do, so I decided to do nothing and left the bench.

Back in chambers I contemplated a judge's role in plea bargaining. The Superior Court Rules of Criminal Procedure generally follow the federal rules. Specifically, Rule 11 says that the prosecutor and defense counsel "may discuss and reach a plea agreement." As for the role of the judge in plea bargaining, the rule is quite specific: "The Court must not participate in these discussions." This rule is based on the principle that a judge's power and prestige would have undue influence in the bargaining process and could easily intrude on the prosecutor's prerogative to charge defendants and, at the same time, subtly coerce defendants to waive important constitutional rights and plead guilty.

In many state courts the judge plays a critical role in the horse trading that plea bargaining has become. When I was a defense counsel, I occasionally took cases in other states. The custom in many counties was for the judge, prosecutor, and defense counsel to meet in the judge's chambers and "try and work it out." The defendant was not present, and the discussion was off the record. Usually there would be some small talk—courthouse gossip and telling of tales from past cases—and then we would get down to business. The prosecutor would generally open with the offer. I would make a counteroffer, and then the judge would start twisting arms.

Many times the judge leaned on the State to soften its offer by either allowing the defendant to plead to a lesser crime or agreeing to a lesser sentence. Many times this would work to the defendant's advantage. The prosecutor generally appears before the judge every day, and, in order to keep good relations, the State would usually go along with the judge's recommendation. The State also knew that even if it turned down the judge, should the defendant be forced to go to trial and lose, the ultimate sentence would often look like the rejected deal in chambers. If that were the case, what was the point of going to trial?

Sometimes, of course, the judge leaned on the defendant to be "reasonable." Usually left unsaid was the leverage the judge had to ultimately punish the defendant should he reject the offer, insist on going to trial, and then lose. Some judges were known for "hammering" a defendant at sentencing for exercising his constitutional right to go to trial. The consequences for going against the judge's recommendation could be harsh.

More often than not, a bargain would be reached with the main charge reduced and a specific sentence agreed upon. We would then go into court and finalize the deal, but that was a formality. Although the deal would be cut behind closed doors and out of sight from public view, for the accused it offered a sure thing rather than risking the wrath of an angry judge. For the State and the victims, it offered finality and a sense of closure when weighed against the uncertainty of trial, where anything can happen.

My own view is that transparency is almost always the right way to go. Judges should not be placed in a situation where it would be all too easy to abuse power against either side. The Superior Court proceedings are always on the record in criminal cases. They are both audiotaped and transcribed by a court reporter in open court. We never bring the parties in chambers and negotiate pleas in private.

Scholars and government researchers generally agree that roughly 90 to 95 percent of all criminal cases, both federal and state, end in guilty pleas. That being so, keeping the judge out of the process preserves judicial neutrality and prevents the court from exercising undue influence over the government and the defendant.

As I considered these basic principles I reassured myself that the safest and easiest thing to do in this case was to do nothing. The jury was obviously coming to the end of their deliberations, and the forthcoming verdict would be their considered judgment, a judgment I was legally bound to accept. However, I was faced with presiding over what I considered a grave injustice.

Before a trial begins, I always ask the prosecutor and defense counsel if there is any plea offer on the table that could resolve the case short of trial. More than a few times in the past, there was movement from one or both sides on the morning of trial. If I felt the parties were close to a deal I would remind them the court has no role in plea bargaining but could encourage them to reconsider their positions and make decisions that would be in their best interests.

I had never even gone that far while we were in the midst of a trial, much less while the jury was deliberating. By bringing up a plea now, would I be going outside my role and skirting, if not violating, the rule against judges participating in plea bargaining? Was I seeking to achieve some type of rough justice? Do the ends justify the means if the ends are just? After further consideration, I saw no harm in raising the possibility of a plea with the parties, and in my view I would not be violating Rule 11. I concluded that simply reminding the prosecutor and defendant that they could consider reaching a plea bargain was not participating in the discussions of the plea itself.

I asked Mr. Van Hook to call the parties back to the courtroom. This would be new territory for all of us.

I believed I could bring up a plea without violating my oath of office. It probably wouldn't work anyway. The government was holding all the cards, and the defense had no leverage. The thought of sending Sam to prison for five years still bothered me deeply. I decided to go forward.

Mr. Van Hook came into chambers and said everyone was present. I returned to the courtroom.

"Counsel," I said, "I'm well aware of the court's limited role under Rule 11 for plea bargaining, and I cannot participate in any discussions. I think, though, we all know the import of the jury's question and what the verdict will be in this case. The defendant has no record, is raising his children, and works. I just can't see where a five-year mandatory sentence would constitute justice. I strongly urge both sides to consider a plea, even at this late stage."

The lawyers looked at me and nodded their heads.

The prosecutor said, "I'll see what I can do."

Defense counsel said, "I'll try."

An hour later I was called into the courtroom. Remarkably, they had reached a deal. Sam could plead guilty to Assault with Intent to Kill, and the government would drop the AWIK while Armed, as well as the Possession of a Firearm During the Commission of a Crime of Violence. The key to the deal was that while AWIK was a major felony and carried a maximum sentence of up to fifteen years in prison, there was no mandatory jail time. I could, theoretically, and probably would, sentence him to probation. He would not have to go to prison.

But now came the hard part. Sam had to get through the plea in open court.

Sam had just testified under oath that the gun was not his and he acted in self-defense in the struggle for it. He was now going to have to state, again under oath, that it was in fact his gun and that he intended to kill William with it. The lawyers were in the courtroom, but Sam was just outside, in the adjoining witness room. I could hear him crying and hear his daughters crying with him.

I looked at counsel. Defense counsel shrugged her shoulders and opened her hands as if to say, "What can I do?"

We all just sat there, waiting for Sam to pull himself together.

I wished the prosecutor would simply dismiss the case, though I knew that was unlikely.

Then I heard two loud knocks on the door leading to the jury room. We all froze. Mr. Van Hook got up, opened the door, and was handed a piece of paper by the jury foreperson. He closed the door and walked back to his desk next to the bench. He wrote down the date and time on the note and handed it to me. The jury would remain in the jury room until we had all the parties in the courtroom.

I read the note and then announced it to counsel. "Counsel, the note reads: 'The jury has reached a verdict.'" It was signed by the Foreperson, Juror #10.

I looked to defense counsel. "Counsel, I'm willing to wait a reasonable amount of time, but if it's not going to happen, we will have to take the verdict. Please consult with your client."

She walked back to the witness room. Several minutes later Sam walked in, followed by his daughters. They were all sobbing. Sam walked into the well of the court and stood next to his lawyer while the daughters sat in the first row of the audience.

The taking of a guilty plea is very routine and almost automatic. Mr. Van Hook placed Sam under oath.

Next, defense counsel announced the terms of the plea bargain. In exchange for Sam's plea to AWIK, the government would dismiss the AWIK w/a, ADW, and the PFCV. The prosecutor agreed the terms were accurate.

It is then the judge's role to go over the terms of the plea agreement personally with the defendant and make sure his pleading guilty was done knowingly, intelligently, and voluntarily.

Routinely, I asked him his age, level of education, and whether he was born in the United States. He said he went as far as the ninth grade and was born in North Carolina. I asked a few more preliminary questions:

"Are you taking any medication or used any drugs or alcohol in the last forty-eight hours that would make it difficult for you to understand or follow these court proceedings?"

"No, Your Honor."

"Have you had enough time to discuss this case with your lawyer and think about your decision to plead guilty here today?"

"Yes, Your Honor."

"Mr. Johnson, I'm taking this plea under oath and what that means is if you lie under oath you could be charged with the crime of perjury or making a false statement. Do you understand?"

"Yes, Your Honor."

"You do not have to plead guilty and if you do plead guilty you will be waiving or giving up certain constitutional rights. Do you understand?"

"Yes, Your Honor."

We went through each of his rights mechanically.

"You would be presumed innocent and would remain innocent unless and until the government proved the case against you beyond a reasonable doubt. If the government could not prove the case against you, you would be found not guilty and free to go. "Do you understand?"

"Yes, Your Honor," he said.

"Next, you have the right to be tried by a judge or jury. A jury is twelve members of the community who would hear the case and decide if you are guilty or not guilty. If a jury didn't hear the case, a judge would. If you plead guilty you would be waiving or giving up the right to a jury or judge trial. Do you understand?" I asked.

"Yes, Your Honor," he said.

We went through all of his rights individually: right to defend himself through counsel, right to testify, right not to testify, right to cross-examine the government's witnesses, right to present witnesses of his own, and right to appeal. He understood all his rights. He was willing to give them all up.

He was advised that the maximum sentence for AWIK was fifteen years and a fine or assessment of no less than $100 and no more than $5000 that went to a fund for the victims of violent crime. He said he understood.

"Are you satisfied with the services of your counsel?" I asked.

"Yes," he said.

"Has anyone forced, threatened, or coerced you to plead guilty?" I asked.

He looked straight at me, or perhaps through me.

"No," he said.

"Other than the plea agreement that was announced by your lawyer, has anyone promised you anything else?

"No," he said.

"Has anyone promised you what sentence you are going to receive?"

"No," he said.

I paused. While I hadn't promised him a light sentence, I certainly communicated to both his lawyer and the prosecutor that I thought five years in prison was not fair. Of course his counsel would have told him that the judge thought a sentence of five years was too long. So, in reality, he thought I had promised him, through the back door, a sentence of less than five years. And he was right. I had not made an explicit promise, but everyone in the courtroom, including me, knew that the promise was implied. If for some reason I changed my mind at sentencing and imposed a prison term of five years, or more, he could rightly think I misled him. In the pressure of the moment, I did not realize I had made a side deal with the defendant.

I thought about scuttling the plea. I had gone over the line. But we had come so far, and I thought the plea was the right thing to do.

We pushed on.

"Are you pleading guilty to the charge of Assault with Intent to Kill because you committed this crime?

He looked straight at me again. "Yes." He then looked down.

"Mr. Johnson," I said, "I'm now going to ask the prosecutor to state in open court what evidence the government would have presented if this case came to trial and then ask you if that's what happened."

This is always the hardest question when I take a plea. Since we had already had a trial, the absurdity of this situation was not lost on anyone.

The prosecutor summarized the facts of the trial we just had: that Mr. Johnson had been in a verbal argument in the parking lot and then pulled and shot a gun at William with the intent to kill him.

Sam looked down the whole time.

"Mr. Johnson, is what the prosecutor said accurate?"

He hesitated and mumbled, obviously reluctant. He muttered something, barely audible.

Normally, in a routine plea if it appears the defendant is reluctant, or unwilling, to admit he committed the crime, I say to him something like "It appears to me that you are reluctant to take this plea. Please understand that no one is forcing you to do this. If you want a jury trial, you have that right. Because if I take this voluntary plea, it is final, and you can't come back tomorrow, next week, or next year and try and take the plea back because you don't like my sentence or for any other reason."

I didn't, however, say anything.

I looked at his defense counsel as if to say you know I can't accept this plea unless he says yes. She completely understood.

She whispered to him for a few minutes. He wiped away some more tears.

He looked at me and said softly, very softly, "Yes."

Almost by rote I launched into what I say at the conclusion of every plea that I have ever taken.

"The court finds that the defendant was advised of all his rights and with competent counsel has knowingly, voluntarily, and intelligently waived and given them up and that there is a factual basis for the plea so, therefore, I accept it."

I think everyone in the courtroom, even the prosecutor, breathed a sigh of relief. It had been difficult, but we all got the right result. Sam would be guilty but would not be going to prison. The end justified the means. But was this really justice? Maybe rough justice.

I asked Mr. Van Hook to bring in the jury. They looked very solemn as they took their seats.

I said, "Ladies and gentlemen of the jury, I want to bring to your attention a development that just took place in the courtroom. Mr. Johnson and the government have entered into a plea agreement where Mr. Johnson pled guilty to a charge, and the government dismissed other charges. Usually this kind of thing happens before trial, but, in this case, it happened while you were deliberating, and I just accepted the plea a few minutes ago. As such, we will not be taking your verdict."

I continued, "I very much appreciate your service to the court and community, and please be assured that even though we took the time to go through this trial your time was not wasted, and we now have a final resolution of this case. On behalf of the court and the community, you have my deepest thanks and you are now excused."

The jury looked at me quizzically. They got out of their seats slowly, surely confused as to what had just happened. Perhaps I should explain to them in detail all the circumstances, but I rejected that idea since it would be hard to communicate all the dynamics without communicating to them that I thought they were about to make a tragic mistake.

I didn't do anything, and they left.

I turned to the parties and routinely, almost again by rote, set a date for sentencing two months in the future, before which I would receive a presentence report from the probation office. Not that I really needed any additional information to render a decision on Sam's sentence, but we were now playing it by the book.

I returned to chambers. I needed to take a break from this drama, and, besides, I had to prepare for my next trial, a burglary where the defendant was accused of breaking into a home at 1:00 a.m., tying up a seventy-year-old man, former director of a local choir, and pushing him into a closet while the burglar cleaned out the house of all valuables.

I thought about what one of my colleagues said when I was about to go on the bench and start presiding over criminal cases: "We get to see a human parade of misery and try and make some sense of it all. Try to do justice as best we can."

I looked up and saw Mr. Van Hook standing quietly at my door. I had been lost in my thoughts. He asked to come in, and I said, "Of course."

He said, "I found this in the jury room. Thought you should see it."

It was the jury verdict form. It read:

> We, the jury, find Samuel Johnson:
> Assault with Intent to Kill while Armed: Not Guilty
> Assault with a Dangerous Weapon: Not Guilty
> Possession of a Firearm During a Crime of Violence:
> Not Guilty

It was signed by the Foreperson, Juror #10.

We looked at each other, and I slowly shook my head. Although, technically, the lawyers didn't need to know about the verdict form because it was now an unofficial document, I asked Mr. Van Hook to call the lawyers and let them know.

He said, "I think they already do since I saw them talking to some jurors in the hallway."

"Please call anyway and send them copies of the verdict form."

I sat back in my chair and gazed out the window. I looked at a lush, green park across the street and saw people coming and going into the courthouse, all, no doubt, consumed by their important cases.

I guess this goes down in the "no good deed goes unpunished category," I thought to myself. I didn't have time, however, to think this through. I had to prepare for the burglary trial. Mr. Van Hook went out to make his calls.

Two days later I received a motion from Sam's lawyer seeking to withdraw his guilty plea. As grounds for the motion, she said I had put in motion, out of a sense of justice, of course, a process that was, in the end, coercive and threatening and that her client's plea was involuntary as a matter of law and should be vacated. She said that, as a result of the intense pressure brought to bear on Sam, he deserved a new trial.

The government filed an opposition and rightly pointed out that if the verdict had been what we all thought it was going to be, the last thing Mr. Johnson would be doing was seeking to withdraw his plea. The government also noted Mr. Johnson took his plea under oath, that this fact alone should be given great consideration, and that maybe, at the end of the day, his acceptance of the facts during the plea was the truth after all, notwithstanding the jury verdict that was never formally accepted.

A few days later they all come back to court to hear my ruling. This was an easy decision. Sam's lawyer was right of course. I had orchestrated a turn of events that scared Sam—at the threat of five years of hard time, and with the unsaid promise from me that he would not go to prison—into pleading guilty to something I felt he did not do. I had crossed a line to do the right thing under severe pressure in exceptional circumstances.

I granted the motion to withdraw the guilty plea. We were back to the beginning of the case. I looked to the prosecutor.

He said: "Your Honor, the government moves to dismiss this case."

"Motion granted," I said.

I looked at both counsel. "Counsel, I appreciate your high level of competence and professionalism in this difficult case."

I turned to Mr. Johnson. "Good luck, Mr. Johnson. Your case has been dismissed, and you are free to leave."

Faced with the same case today, would I do the same thing? Sitting back in the comfort of my home it is easy to philosophize and say of course not. But would I be writing a different story if the jury had found him guilty, as we all thought they were about to do? I would be thinking of him doing five years in prison for something I thought was unjust. I would be thinking of his daughters.

A judge takes an oath to follow the law, an oath I take very seriously and like to think I have always done to the best of my ability. I skirted the line in this case and rejected the jury's prerogative to determine guilt or innocence to avoid what I thought would be a miscarriage of justice. Was justice ultimately done? I think, in the end, it was, but at a cost to my fidelity to the law. I don't think I would do it again.

3

A Judge's Hidden Struggle: Overcoming Judicial Culture

JUDGE GAIL CHANG BOHR

Judge Gail Chang Bohr was elected as the first Asian American judge in Ramsey County, Second Judicial District of Minnesota, in 2008 and in 2014 became a senior judge for the State of Minnesota. Bohr became a lawyer after a career as a clinical social worker; prior to joining the bench she was the first executive director of the Children's Law Center of Minnesota.

BEFORE I BECAME A LAWYER, I WAS A CLINICAL SOCIAL WORKER FOR twenty years, working with children and families. I consider myself knowledgeable about human behavior, in particular child and adolescent development and family dynamics. In addition, before becoming a judge, I was the first executive director of a nonprofit organization that advocated for child welfare system reforms and recruited and trained pro bono lawyers to represent children in foster care. So, I had many opportunities to see firsthand what happened to children whose parents did not have their best interests at heart.

In my nonpartisan election campaign for my judgeship, I was struck by how many people—non-lawyers in particular—confirmed my belief that my social work background and work with children and families were important qualifications to be a judge. More than one person remarked that listening to people and truly understanding their life circumstances was the hallmark of a good judge. They knew that I would apply the law as established by our highest courts and the legislature, and that I would take into account the "whole" person who stood before me.

I find child custody trials to be some of the most stressful experiences I have encountered as a judge. In typical custody cases, the parents are each vying for legal and physical custody of their child. Emotions usually run high because the subject of the case "is my flesh-and-blood offspring!" Lawyers may or may not be helpful. While I am not involved on an emotional level, I am very conscious of the potential impact my decision may have on each family. Indeed, I find decisions regarding custody and the amount of time the child will spend with each parent the most challenging. The age of the child and the willingness of the parents to cooperate sometimes complicate matters. I find that the younger the child, the more difficult the decision. One of my most difficult decisions involved an eighteen-month-old child. By the time the case came before me, her parents had arrived at an agreement for custody and parenting time that bothered me deeply. Even though I tentatively approved their agreement, I did not believe it was in their child's best interests.

The overarching principle that we judges rely on in child custody cases—after applying the relevant statutes and case law—is "the best interests of the child." In an attempt to reduce judges' discretionary decision making, state legislatures generally define the factors that a court must consider in determining "best interests." However, even after a legislature has established these relevant factors, the decision in each case is left with the judge. After all, this is not a computerized exercise. Thankfully, a judge's humanity can intervene.

Courts encourage parents to resolve disputes and make their own decisions regarding custody and parenting time. The thought is that when parents agree, friction and conflict are decreased, thereby creating a better environment for their children. There is then an individualized—not a cookie-cutter—approach to custody and parenting. Nevertheless, the judge still must find it is in the best interests of the child before signing off on any agreement proposed by the parents.

It was not always this difficult. Historically, custody decisions have evolved from the days when children were viewed as the property of the father. Mothers did not have independent economic means to support their children. Then, it was simply a matter of placing children with their fathers. Later, the "tender-years doctrine" displaced the "economic doctrine." Mothers were presumed to be more appropriate custodians because they were the ones who cared for babies and children of a tender age. Consequently, mothers were more likely to be awarded custody, and fathers were ordered to pay child support with court-defined visitation rights with their child. Beginning in the second half of the twentieth century and the beginning of the twenty-first century, we have seen more focus on the psychological development of children and a wider acceptance that good parenting is not strictly the product of one gender over the other. In fact, nowadays shared parenting is encouraged.

In my experience, children who are attached to their parents stand a better chance of becoming self-assured adults. Knowing more about how children develop and grow into confident and productive adults helps judges determine legal and physical custody and parenting time plans. It has also made the custody decisions more complex, nuanced, and individualized.

Infants and toddlers are seen to be more at risk when early development is disrupted. Time is of critical importance to babies and toddlers, who are rapidly developing and whose healthy development depends on their sense of security. A stable home environment fosters a sense of security founded on consistency, stability, and predictability. The child's secure attachment forms the foundation for the development of healthy relationships in the future.

The legal standard "best interests of the child" evolved from the concept of "*parens patriae*," which literally means "father of the country." During the seventeenth and eighteenth centuries, this doctrine made the protection of children and care of incapacitated adults the obligation of the state. The doctrine, when applied to the treatment of children, makes the best interests of every child the first and foremost consideration of the courts.

Custody of children is defined in two parts: legal and physical. Legal custody gives parents the right to make important decisions about the raising of the child on matters such as health care, religious upbringing, and education, among other important life issues. Physical custody gives the parent the care and control over the child's upbringing and the ability to direct the child's day-to-day activities, such as after-school activities and sports.

For me, family law cases conjure up the seminal custody case decided in ancient times by King Solomon. This story was told to us children as an example of the love of a mother for her child, not solely as an example of Solomon's wisdom. Unlike modern-day judges, the biblical Solomon is supposed to have received the gift of wisdom directly from God (1 Kings 3:16-28). The story goes that two women came to the King with a baby boy, each claiming to be his true mother. They both lived in the same house, and each gave birth to a son within three days of each other. There were no witnesses to the births, as no one else was at the house. The first woman said the second woman's baby died during the night. She further claimed that the second woman had taken the live baby from her while she was sleeping and switched the babies so that the second woman was nursing the live baby. Meanwhile, the second woman placed the dead baby with the sleeping first woman.

When the first woman arose in the morning to nurse her child, she saw the child was dead. But as she looked more closely at the dead child, it did not look like her child. The second woman denied the dead child was hers and instead claimed the living child.

The two women came to King Solomon and asked him to award the living child to the true mother. What was the king to do? He had no way of determining the "true" mother. There were no DNA or other tests for him to order. There were no witnesses to summon. Instead, to everyone's horror, the king asked for his sword and commanded that the child be divided into two and each mother be given half. Then the first woman, whose son was living, said, "Oh, my lord, give her the living child, do not slay it." But the second woman said, "It shall be neither mine nor yours, divide it."

The king quickly recognized the first woman as the true mother who had the child's best interests at heart. He awarded her the child, saying, "She is its mother." What is not expressly stated, but implied, is that Solomon, in his wisdom, realized that only the "true" mother would give up her child rather than sacrifice his life. Luckily for him, Solomon, the absolute monarch, did not have to comply with our modern "best interests of the child" standard when deciding which mother would be the better parent.

While modern-day judges cannot claim wisdom as a God-given gift, their appointing authorities believe their knowledge of the law and life experience make them especially qualified to decide difficult cases. Society effectively gives them a leg up in the wisdom department. The people who elected me declared by their votes that my experience in the law and my knowledge about people and human nature were assets in making decisions. Judges also have laws and cases to provide guidance in custody and parenting determinations. And, since the laws do not dictate a specific outcome or direction in individual cases, judges must exercise discretion in their decisions. It is through the exercise of discretion that the judge's bias or preconceived notions can come into play. Everyone has preconceptions. It is by recognizing and taking time to discover underlying assumptions that judges can set them aside to arrive at a fair decision. In the story that follows, I recount how I struggled to overcome my own preconceptions to reach a just decision in a difficult case.

Cathy and John (not their real names) were the unmarried parents of an eighteen-month-old daughter, Mira. Cathy was forty years old and John was thirty-eight. Before I got involved in their family, they had a custody order issued by a court in another Minnesota county where they previously lived. Their case came to me on a motion to change the location of the court that supervised a previous custody order involving Mira. At that early stage, a judge in my position typically receives minimal background facts. I learned that Cathy and John had lived together for almost two years and Mira was born a year into their relationship. Based on the report I received, the parents' bond seemed to grow out of their mutual dependency on drugs and alcohol. They freely acknowledged that when they were together, drugs were the center of their relationship, and drugs often led to hostility and animosity, including physical fights. At different times, each had a judicial restraining order issued against the other. Only later, I learned that both Cathy and John had been involved with the criminal justice system and had had prior child custody cases involving other partners in three different Minnesota counties.

As part of the change in venue request in the case that came before me, Cathy was seeking to change custody of Mira from John to her. Both admitted they had been chemically dependent. However, John had been sober for some months and lived with his parents, and Cathy was in inpatient treatment, which she expected to complete in a few weeks. After she finished treatment, she planned to reside in "sober housing" for a period of time sufficient to complete the chemical dependency program. Then, she intended to find another place to live so she could have her parenting time with Mira.

Most importantly from my perspective in considering Cathy's request was the fact that Mira was currently living with John in John's parents' home, and John did not plan to move. Significantly, the grandparents would provide a degree of security and stability for Mira that might be lacking if she were left to either parent alone.

In the beginning I also learned that John had obtained an order of protection against Cathy six months earlier in the rural county that originally had jurisdiction over custody and parenting time. That court had also ordered the change of venue to the county where both parties now resided. The protection order awarded sole temporary legal and physical custody to John. Cathy had then filed a motion to change custody to sole physical and legal custody to her. The motion came to me for resolution.

In Minnesota, at the initial hearing of a child custody case, we encourage the parties to stipulate—come up with an agreement—and settle. At this hearing, the judge typically instructs the parties to work together to find a solution to issues of custody, child support, financial assets, and other matters. The parties have the opportunity to go to a neutral mediator to work out their differences. The message many judges and I give is that, rather than going to trial, the parties know their children and their financial situation better than anyone else. We presume they are best suited to decide custody and parenting time and fair division of assets and finances. My practice is to let them know that I will conduct a trial if custody is still contested, but I believe they are better informed to make such intimate decisions about their family than I, a stranger.

As most judges will attest, custody agreements are the hardest to negotiate, especially in disputed cases. Feelings run high. The love that once was present often morphs into hate and anger. Hence the parties are likely to battle it out to the bitter end. Given our very full court calendars, we judges encourage and appreciate agreements about custody.

Since John and Cathy each wanted sole legal and sole physical custody, I was prepared for a contested hearing with witnesses. Instead, when I entered the courtroom, John's attorney said they had an oral agreement to present to me. If I agreed, they would submit their agreement in writing. Cathy did not have an attorney, which is not unusual in custody cases. Cases with self-represented parties usually result in a judge spending more time with the case, explaining the process and a party's rights. However, because John and Cathy's case was no longer contested, I was not as concerned about giving long explanations.

They presented as a united front. They had recently patched up their relationship. Both claimed they were sober. Cathy had only to complete the last phase of her treatment and then live in sober housing. They asked that I accept their proposed agreement for joint legal and joint physical custody with equal parenting time. Their plan essentially had Mira changing homes three times a week. Even the holidays would be equally divided. Mira would spend Thanksgiving, Christmas Eve, and Christmas Day with Cathy in year one and with John in year two. In the meantime, pending submission of the written stipulation, Cathy would complete her inpatient chemical dependency treatment. During this period, she would be allowed parenting time at least once a week. They also asked me to dismiss the order of protection John had obtained against Cathy.

At that time, Minnesota law required a judge to make findings on thirteen factors relating to the child's best interests. Notably, the first best-interests factor was "the wishes of the child's parent or parents as to custody." Furthermore, in situations where the parties have an agreement, the best-interest analysis is shortened, and the parties' agreement is more likely to be accepted. In that situation, there is a presumption that the parents' agreement is in the best interests of the child.

If John and Cathy had not reached an agreement at the status hearing, I would have followed my practice in all contested cases and ordered a custody evaluation. A custody evaluator, usually a child psychologist, would interview the child and the parents separately, and then observe the child's interaction with each parent in the evaluator's office and the parent's home. The evaluator then would complete a written assessment and make recommendations to the court, taking into account the statutory best-interests factors. If a trial was needed, the evaluator would testify. At the end of the trial, after making findings on each of the best-interests factors, I would render my decision. Trials can take up to a week or more with testimony and arguments. The parties also make motions for various things such as temporary child support. The cost is enormous for the parents, both monetarily and emotionally. In these situations, I often feel neither parent truly has the child's interests at heart. The fight is really about which parent will "win" and which will "lose." Before going down that path, I usually remind the parties that the lawyer fees on both sides could pay for a college education for the child.

From the beginning, I was concerned that John and Cathy's stipulated parenting plan would require eighteen-month-old Mira to move homes three times a week, nearly every other day. My previous career as a clinical social worker convinced me that children, especially infants, need stability and consistency. Such predictability in their surroundings helps them to form attachments and develop healthy relationships. In learning to master their environment, infants and young children develop confidence in their abilities. They grow, develop, and thrive.

Cathy was still in treatment. She planned to find sober housing so Mira could stay with her for parenting time. In court, Cathy said, "I would like to come to an agreement so that we can both be in every aspect of Mira's life." She conveyed that she and Mira had "a mother and daughter bond that is so powerful. We love and adore each other very much. She is happiest when I am around." Cathy also said that she needed Mira to help her stay sober.

As she talked, I felt she had switched places with Mira, and Mira was now the parent in charge of Cathy's behavior. Cathy's comments made me question the lack of boundaries and the role reversal sometimes seen in cases of chemical dependency where the child takes care of the parent. I expressed concern that this was too much responsibility to place on any child, more so regarding an infant. I reminded Cathy that Mira was not the parent.

As for John, he was eager to have the order of protection lifted so he could have contact with Cathy again. He planned to continue to live with his parents, who were helping to take care of Mira. He appeared to be in compliance with his treatment plan. John seemed happy that Mira's care would be left with his parents and that Mira was the key to keeping Cathy in his life. He was excited to share custody with Cathy, even though, he said, as a couple they functioned better apart.

With some misgivings, I agreed they could write up an agreement and send it to me for review and potential signature. However, because I was concerned about the effect on Mira of moving three times a week, I ordered the case be reviewed in a month's time.

Our challenge as judges is to make the child's well-being the heart and center of the decision in cases where custody is disputed. Coupled with that goal is the high-volume caseload of family court judges. Thus, when it comes to determining physical custody, there can be a big sigh of relief when parents agree on the parenting plan, including holidays and special days.

Even when custody is not disputed, I am still not off the hook in the best-interests determination, because by signing the stipulation, I endorse the parents' agreement as being in the child's best interests. I was very torn about making eighteen-month-old Mira move households three times a week. On the one hand, I was relieved not to have to conduct a trial, but on the other, I was uncertain about how this plan would affect Mira. And I wondered if I should impose my views about child rearing.

Almost immediately following the day the parties announced their agreement, I began to second-guess my halfhearted decision to sign off on John and Cathy's stipulation. As I often do when I am uncertain about my decision, I asked colleagues what they would do in a similar circumstance. More than one of them responded that if this is the parents' agreement, all I had to do was sign it. But again, I was not convinced this was the best decision for Mira. I continued to discuss it with some of my colleagues in Family Court. One of my fellow judges laughed when I brought up the subject yet again, asking, "Are you still talking about that case?" The decision weighed on me. It was not a matter of whether it would be appealed or not. In fact, there would be no appeal, because there was no opposition.

I continued to be haunted by the prospect of Mira, an infant, moving around so much. She would likely not have a stable environment to meet her evolving developmental needs and promote her sense of stability and security. Would her parents put Mira's needs first? It reminded me of something my parents would say as I was growing up, the ninth of fifteen children. We older children were charged with taking care of the younger ones, and if our parents saw us without the younger ones in tow, they would ask, "Who is taking care of the children?" Instead of Mira being in constant care of a parent, it appeared to me she was being used to fulfill her parents' own needs. Mira was the tool that John needed to keep Cathy in his life, and Cathy needed Mira to motivate her.

Even though I had orally agreed to the arrangement, John's attorney still had to submit it in writing. Nothing would change without an order from me. After a month of anxiety about Mira, I realized I had to act on my intuition—something I did not want to admit because it felt that I was biased. To counter that feeling, I decided to order a review hearing and an evaluation by a child psychologist, at the parents' expense, to prove that a parenting plan requiring Mira to move three times a week was in her best interests.

Discretion is commonly understood as the power of judges to make decisions independent of narrow and unbending rules of positive law, to decide and act in accordance with what is fair. Discretion must be based upon the particular circumstances of the case, informed by the judge's personal wisdom and experience, and guided by the law. Even then, discretion can sometimes feel like one is acting on one's bias or intuition.

When I ordered a review of the case, I fully expected the parties would be giving me their signed agreement. But by the time of the review hearing, the scenario had changed dramatically. John's attorney revealed that neither John nor Cathy had signed the document, even though the attorney had sent it to them for signature many weeks before. And the attorney asked to withdraw from the case.

I also learned that John had been living at Cathy's residence in violation of the sober housing rules. Cathy also violated the terms and conditions of her probation when she started using alcohol again and allowed John to stay with her. John had completely relapsed. He was using methamphetamines and abusing prescription drugs and alcohol. In addition, felony criminal charges of drug possession were pending against him. Not surprisingly, all of this caused a complete alienation from his parents. Mira, at least, was safe. She remained with his parents while occasionally staying with Cathy at the treatment facility.

Cathy's failure to complete treatment triggered a probation violation for felony first-degree driving while impaired before another judge in a different county. Having given her a chance at treatment, that judge later revoked probation and ordered that she serve her sentence in prison with a release date some years into the future.

The couple's dysfunctional relationship, immaturity, and inability to provide a stable environment for Mira became clear. I felt enormous relief that their stipulated agreement to share physical and legal custody, with its onerous demands on Mira to bounce back and forth between parents, had not come to fruition.

John's parents moved to intervene and obtain temporary sole physical and legal custody of their granddaughter. They alleged that Cathy and John placed Mira in immediate risk of physical harm and endangerment by relapsing on drugs and alcohol. I believed it was in Mira's best interests that she be raised by her grandparents, who were best able to provide her the stable and secure environment to meet all her needs, and I gave them physical and legal custody of Mira.

As in the King Solomon story, Cathy and John initially came to me with the seemingly fair solution to split Mira's time equally between them. It appeared to be an equitable solution, especially since it avoided a trial—a preferred custom and practice in my court culture. But equal parenting time felt to me like splitting Mira down the middle because it did not take into account what was best for Mira's developmental needs.

The case of Mira, John, and Cathy provided great lessons to me. First, where there is an agreement for custody, quite a bit of information can remain hidden from the judge. At the beginning, except for what the couple shared with me about their drug and alcohol problems, the full extent of their involvement with the criminal justice system and the loss of custody of their other children was not available to me and was revealed only during the later custody review hearing.

The more important lesson I learned was that judges must rely on their life experiences as well as on the law in making their decisions. As I grappled with this case, I at first wanted to make sure that my decision was a "judicial" one, based solely on my application of the law, and not a "social work" decision stemming from my experience with and knowledge of children and families. After the first hearing, I realized I was trying to justify my inclination to sign off on the parties' parenting plan largely on a court custom and on the court's practice of trusting stipulations and avoiding time-consuming and costly litigation. Deep down, I did not believe the parents' proposed agreement was the best plan for the child. My distrust of the parents' custody agreement surely was influenced by my social work experience. Now I believe I must call upon my intuitions and sensitivities—honed over my twenty years as a clinician—and use them to test assertions surfacing in the courtroom. A judge's life experiences must enlighten the pathway toward arriving at her decision of what is in the child's best interests.

4

Uneasy Lies the Head That Wears a Crown

JUDGE MARK DAVIDSON

 *Judge Mark Davidson served as a District Court Judge in Texas for twenty years before his retirement in 2009. He is now serving as the multi-district litigation judge for all asbestos cases in the State of Texas. While serving as a District Judge, he tried hundreds of jury trials. From 2002 through 2007, he served as the Administrative Judge of Harris County. He is the author of twenty-seven published articles on legal and judicial history.*

THE CASE I WILL GO TO MY GRAVE—BOTH JUDICIAL AND subterranean—believing to be the most difficult has haunted me for a number of reasons. It got very little publicity at the time and has likely been all but forgotten by the attorneys who litigated it. For ethical reasons, I will decline to name the parties, even by correct initials, to protect their privacy.

The case started with the most ordinary of situations—a divorce. A woman, AB, went to a lawyer, YZ, thought to be one of the best of the Harris County, Texas, family bar. He had written numerous articles on legislative and appellate developments in family law. AB's husband was a well-compensated professional, and there were complex discussions over property division. The issues were eventually resolved, and the parties obtained a divorce.

In Harris County, because of its large population and its vibrant business community, the district courts have been statutorily specialized for many years. At the time of this case, there were twenty-five civil courts, twenty-two criminal courts, nine family courts and four juvenile courts. Because of the increasing specialization of the bar, most lawyers spent the bulk of their time before one or two of the divisions. This led to claims by lawyers that the judges of each division held the lawyers as political hostages, since close personal relationships between lawyers and judges were thought to be helpful to one's clients. This was considered to be especially true in the family division.

Harris County was going through a change in the composition of the bench in the early 1990s. Judges were (and are) elected on a partisan ballot. Before the 1980s, Texas politics was often described as "two-party politics in a one-party state." During all of the twentieth century to that point, the bench was dominated by white, conservative Democrats. No Republican had even run for judge until 1972, and none had been elected until 1978. Although the civil and criminal judiciary had become evenly divided between Democrats and Republicans, the Harris County Family Law Bench was uniformly Democrat—defiantly so, each of the judges would tell you. Jury trials in Texas family law cases are rare, giving judges great discretion. On the other side of the bench, family law lawyers therefore tended to be Democrats.

Because media in Houston is expensive, many judges raised money on a year-round basis from lawyers with cases pending before them. Tales of judges calling a lawyer before a hearing and asking for a contribution for an election that was three years away were not uncommon—and boasted about by some lawyers who were frequent donors. Two judges who sought and received campaign contributions on a year-round basis were Judge Richard Millard of the 189th District Court and Judge Norman Lee of the 257th District Court.

AB's divorce case was filed in the 257th District Court, Judge Lee's court. I had done some work in family law in the beginning days of my law practice and had met him several times on a brief and informal basis. I knew he had a good reputation. Because each judicial division in Harris County has its own building, contacts between judges of different divisions were infrequent and, for the most part, impersonal. AB's case had been the subject of several contested pretrial hearings and was eventually resolved in a settlement. But after the divorce was final, things got very interesting.

AB went to Joseph M. Nixon, an attorney, to make a horrific complaint: she claimed that her divorce attorney YZ had attempted to seduce her while he was representing her in the divorce proceedings. When his advances were rebuffed, she told Nixon, YZ had sexually assaulted her. She was not claiming consensual sex as an act of negligence by YZ, or that things got out of control one evening and they engaged in consensual sex. She was claiming rape and money damages for her resulting personal injuries. (To my knowledge, however, she never brought a criminal complaint to the attention of the district attorney.)

Sexual relations between an attorney and a client is an issue wrapped in secrecy and legend. Lawyers who collected "couch fees" were at one time thought to be as common as Hollywood directors who had "casting couches" in their offices. These trysts are reprehensible, particularly because there is a fiduciary duty between an attorney and a client. In the context of family law cases, it is even more troubling. If an attorney attempts to seduce a client who is emotionally vulnerable, it almost certainly subverts the purpose of the attorney-client relationship.

Yet only a few states have found attorneys who have violated this very basic tenet of human and professional conduct guilty of professional misconduct. As I write this in 2017, only one state has expressly prohibited sexual relations between an attorney and a client. Texas lawyers were given the opportunity to do so in 2011 but rejected changes to the ethical rules, with 72 percent voting against a change.

Nixon approached Houston attorney Larry Doherty to assist him, and they sent a demand letter to YZ putting him on notice of the rape allegation. They hoped YZ would forward the letter to his legal malpractice insurance carrier. That didn't happen.

YZ went to a very good civil lawyer named Robin Ziek. She was (and remains) an outstanding commercial litigator. In 1992, although she had been practicing law for only five years, she had a record of collecting difficult debts. Given the ups and downs of the Houston economy, this was not always easy. She had been lead counsel in several cases before me, and I had always been impressed by her skill, tenacity, and professionalism.

Ziek, at her client's urging, took an aggressive tactic. She did not wait for a lawsuit to initiate a defense. She sued AB seeking collection of past-due attorney's fees. At the time of the filing of the suit and without notice to the other side, she asked for a judicial writ requiring garnishment (meaning seizure) of AB's bank account before final judgment was determined. The writ, if granted, would seize money in the defendant's bank account up to the amount of the debt.

In most Texas courts, pre-judgment garnishments are very rarely granted. Most of the time, an applicant not only has to show the existence of an undisputed debt, but unsuccessful past efforts to collect it and imminent damage if the asset is not seized.

Exactly how YZ knew the identity of the bank and the significance of the timing of the application for the account seizure would later be disputed. It turned out that AB was due to get a payment from her ex-husband as part of the divorce settlement the day before the writ was filed. YZ denied he used any information received from representing his client in the timing of the application. He claimed he had only used information that would have been available to someone who had access to public records, the divorce decree and property settlement agreement that had been filed with the court.

The day before Ziek filed the lawsuit, YZ's law firm was shown as making a $1,000 contribution to Judge Lee's campaign. It could be that the timing of the contribution was totally coincidental. However, Lee would not be up for re-election for another three years.* Both Ziek and Richard Sheehy, YZ's later attorney, fervently and credibly state today that they had no knowledge of the contribution at the time and only found out about it at the trial. Texas law required semiannual disclosure of contributions, and no public report of the donation would be made for five months after it occurred.

The day after the contribution, Ziek filed the lawsuit. She did not file the suit in a civil district court, where virtually all such collection suits were traditionally filed. She filed in the 257th District Court—Judge Lee's court of domestic relations. It is likely that in the ten years Lee would serve as judge of the 257th, he had never before and would never again consider a pre-judgment garnishment. He would consider this one, and he did so the day after the campaign contribution was received. Lee ordered a constable to serve a writ ordering AB's bank to hold the money, even against pending checks from third parties. To secure any damages should the writ be wrongfully granted, he ordered that a bond be posted in the amount of $5,000.

AB's lawyers Nixon and Doherty did not wait long after being notified of the garnishment to initiate action—they filed a lawsuit in the civil division against YZ seeking $3.5 million for the personal injuries caused by the alleged rape. It was randomly assigned to a civil case docket presided over by Judge Richard Millard.

Millard was a longtime judge who had switched to the Republican Party a few years before. By 1992, most civil judges in Harris County were Republican. Millard clearly did not appreciate the intrusion of the family law bench on the traditional role of the civil bench. He decided to hold onto the case at all costs. Then things got comical.

Judge Lee and Judge Millard both signed orders consolidating the two cases to their respective courts. Each judge kept the

---

* In 2005, the Texas legislature would enact a prohibition on judges conducting any fundraising more than six months before filing deadline for a new term, or more than ninety days after an election in which they were on the ballot.

district clerk's file in his desk to prohibit the other from getting it. Threatened interlocutory appeals or applications for higher court intervention were bandied about. Finally, the Administrative Judge of Harris County, Judge Miron Love, brought the two judges together and worked out a compromise—the cases would be consolidated into one case and transferred to a civil docket over which I had presided for four years.

I never asked Judge Love how I got picked for the case. Perhaps it was because I had some experience hearing family cases as an appointed temporary judicial officer. Maybe it was because I had not yet acquired a reputation as a legal or political partisan. Possibly it was because none of the lawyers had ever made a campaign contribution to me. The most likely reason is that everyone thought I was too new to the bench to be smart enough to say "No!" I got a courtesy phone call from Judge Love, and I was shortly the beneficiary of an additional case.

I knew all of the parties' lawyers. I had met Doherty and Nixon at political gatherings (in both political parties) before I became a judge. Both Ziek and Richard Sheehy, who had been hired by YZ's insurance carrier, had had several cases in my court. I knew all of them to be consummate professionals.

I realized quickly after getting the case that this was one in which no mediation, no moderated settlement conference, and no other settlement technique known to God, man, or the judiciary could succeed. If the pleadings filed by AB had simply sought damages for an act of consensual sex in violation of the lawyer's professional duty to his client, a settlement might have been possible. However, a rape admission by YZ would constitute an intentional tort not covered by his insurance policy, and therefore would require payment of money damages from his personal savings. Under these circumstances, I deduced that any settlement would constitute an admission of facts that neither party could make.

The lawyers for both sides were highly skilled, so managing the case through the pretrial phase required very little of my time or attention. I set the case on a fast-track trial, and the parties assured me they would be ready. They were. As late as the Friday before the Monday trial, I did not foresee the difficulty of the trial nor the toll it would take on me.

Trials in Houston start, for the most part, on Monday. I had ordered a Monday afternoon jury. Monday morning started with the usual pretrial motions, which were fairly routine. Since there were two pending lawsuits with the plaintiff in each case being a defendant in the other, AB's lawyers asked for a realignment of the parties—that is, that they be allowed to present her as the plaintiff in the case being tried. There was some justice in their motion. The damages sought by the plaintiff dwarfed the $38,000 bill that YZ was suing for. On the other hand, YZ had won the "race to the courthouse" and been the first to file. I decided that the amount of the claim did not justify switching the positions of the parties on the morning of trial, and denied the motion. In any event, the conflicting claims would be tried together and the jury would decide how much of either claim to award or deny.

Jury selection was another matter. I did not think that allowing the attorneys to question jurors in open court about any experience they or a family member might have with sexual assault was reasonably calculated to get honest answers. I also thought that jury duty was not a proper place to strip someone of dignity by having to discuss searing moments in their lives. I therefore prepared and distributed a short questionnaire to prospective jurors as to whether he or she had ever been a victim of sexual assault and if they had ever had a problem with a lawyer. When more than one-third of the panel answered one of those two questions in the affirmative, I conducted individual jury questioning in chambers to determine whether any such experience would stand in the way of them being fair and impartial.

Eventually, a jury was selected, and the case began. After unmemorable opening arguments by both sides, YZ put on a short and simple case. There was a debt for unpaid attorney's fees of $38,000, and he wanted to be paid. Then came cross-examination. YZ denied that he had sexual relations, consensual or not, with AB. As an aside, and not pursuant to any question put to him by either attorney, he went on to say, "I have never had sex with a client in my life."

This testimony was unexpected—at least by me. It would not have been admissible for an opposing attorney to ask a question eliciting information about his relationship with other clients. But he made the statement on his own initiative in the context of a question about the propriety of sexual relations with a client, and he wanted to make a point.

That put me in an ethical dilemma. Many years before, well before I became a judge, a close friend told me that she had hired YZ to be her divorce attorney. She told me that, in the course of representing her, he had attempted to have sex with her, an offer she declined.

I had not disclosed this to the parties before the trial because I frankly did not remember it. Solicitation of sex was quite different from what was alleged in this case. The question was, should I now disclose it? I decided that the information I had from my friend did not directly contradict YZ's testimony—he had not had sex with my friend, he had only tried—and that disclosing it might help AB's case. I did not call my friend and tell her that a casual conversation we had ten years before had given me an ethical challenge. Indeed, I have never disclosed this until now, twenty-five years later.

AB's testimony led off her side of the case. It was understated and emotional all at once. She talked about her emotional state going into the divorce and how she had confided in YZ. She testified that she had gone to his office after hours at his request for a short discussion on the progress of settlement talks. She then briefly testified to an act of sexual assault.

AB's attorneys called expert witnesses who testified that any sexual contact, even consensual, between a lawyer and a client in the context of representation in a divorce was negligence.

My biggest intellectual challenge was the last witness called by

YZ in rebuttal. His attorney presented an expert witness who was a credentialed forensic psychiatrist from California, Park Dietz. Dietz had testified in his pretrial deposition that he had reviewed AB's psychiatric records and had concluded that she was not telling the truth. AB's attorneys objected, arguing that well-established case law prohibits the introduction of expert testimony as to the credibility of a witness. I quickly and firmly sustained the objection. YZ's defense team then said they would offer the witness to testify that AB's psychiatric records and conversations with her psychiatrist "were not consistent with that of a victim of sexual assault."

This was a closer question. Although the effect of the offered testimony, if believed, was that AB was not credible, that was not the question that was to be asked, nor was it the answer that would be given. AB's attorney argued that this was just a clever way around my previous ruling. With some misgivings, I concluded that the proffered testimony was not expressly a violation of the Rules of Evidence and I overruled the objection. I was aware that I was giving AB a shot at an appellate reversal, if the admission of the evidence, once heard by the jury, turned out to be erroneous. I had always thought, and still do, that probative evidence that is not clearly against the rules ought to be admitted.

Along the same lines, I declined to let AB offer evidence of the campaign contribution to Judge Lee. Even though she had pled a cause of action for wrongful garnishment, I felt that injecting Texas's legal culture of campaign contributions to judges was more prejudicial than relevant. Because no one called Judge Lee to the stand, I firmly ruled that the evidence would not come in. Calling it prejudicial was as close to a public statement as I could make on the propriety of that conduct.

The trial had received a fair amount of attention in legal circles. I would learn later that Judges Millard and Lee were calling my staff seeking updates on the case. A family law seminar was going on, and I later was told that it was the talk of the seminar. However, it was not covered by the newspapers. That was a relief to me given the salacious nature of the allegations and evidence.

Both sides were prepared and eloquent in making their closing arguments to the jury. YZ's attorneys emphasized the absence of a rape complaint to the district attorney and the testimony of Dr. Dietz. AB's lawyer argued that the jury did not have to find sexual assault to find YZ liable to AB for breach of his duty as her attorney. After watching the closing arguments, a very prominent family law lawyer who had no connection to the case told a number of friends that he had no doubt the jury would rule for AB.

The jury deliberated for a day, long by most standards, and returned a verdict that surprised me. I always thought I could "read" jurors by their body language, and I thought the jury was sympathetic to AB. They may have been sympathetic, but the first instruction in the Texas Pattern Jury Charge manual is that "Bias, prejudice, or sympathy is to play no part in your decision." The jury ruled that YZ did not sexually assault AB and that YZ was not liable to AB on any of her claims. They awarded YZ his attorney's fees of $38,500.

After the verdict was read, I discharged the jury. YZ attempted to shake the jurors' hands as they left the courtroom, but all of them declined the offer. I would later find out that the jury verdict was announced at the family law seminar, and that the attendees gave an enthusiastic ovation in honor of YZ.

I went home after the trial convinced that this was a problem verdict, and that I was responsible. I questioned my ruling on the expert testimony and whether I should have told the attorneys the story my friend told me. More than anything, I felt that the jury had just flat got it wrong. But that was not my job. I was brought up as a lawyer believing that juries got things right. In my twenty-eight years as a judge, from before this trial to today, I have thrown out only four jury verdicts. I kept these thoughts inside of me and have maintained my silence until this writing.

When it came time to do so, I accepted the verdict, entered a judgment for YZ for the unpaid attorney's fees, and entered a take-nothing judgment for AB on her claims.

A precondition for filing an appeal of a civil case in Texas at that time was that one had to file a motion for new trial, bringing to the trial judge's attention all of the legal errors the losing party believed had been made. A motion for new trial was filed shortly after the judgment was entered, but the attorneys did not set it for a hearing until three days before it would be overruled by operation of law. Thus, I had to act promptly after the hearing. The oral arguments on the motion were short, since the trial had taken place only two months before, and everyone knew I would remember the trial. I was convinced that my ruling on expert witness Dietz had been erroneous and had led to the verdict. Perhaps I should have granted a new trial and let the parties go at it again. Then I had an idea.

Texas law allows a trial judge to condition the denial of a new trial on a "remittitur," or voluntary reduction of damages by a successful party. If a remittitur is agreed to, and there is an appeal, the damages are added back on if the appeal is eventually successful. That gave me a way to conclude a case I felt needed to be over for the benefit of all concerned. I was reluctant to force AB through the trauma of a second trial and felt that I was helping her get closure to this chapter of her life in not ordering a new trial. At the same time, I did not think it fair that she should have to pay the judgment against someone who had wronged her, at least to the extent of the questionable garnishment.

I ruled that the motion for new trial would be denied if, and only if, YZ agreed to remit the entirety of his judgment against AB. Failure to agree would lead to the granting of a new trial. Two days later, I would learn that YZ had agreed to give up his judgment, and I denied the new trial. The plaintiff did not appeal, and proceedings were over—or so I thought.

Six months later, a bill of review would be filed. Under Texas law, a challenge can be brought to a final judgment if it can be proved that the judgment is fraudulent. After the judgment, AB's lawyer claimed to have obtained affidavits from fourteen of YZ's former clients in which they alleged that they had sex with YZ. None claimed the sex was assaultive or involuntary.

Pursuant to local court rules, the case was randomly assigned to another judge, namely Judge Elizabeth Ray. She was new to the bench, succeeding a judge who left the bench after encountering ethical issues involving campaign contributions. I was unaware of the filing of the case until, quite by chance, I was asked to sit for Judge Ray on a random Monday morning and hear her weekly motion docket. When I saw Doherty and Sheehy, the attorneys for both sides in the prior case before me, I knew something was up. I was stunned when I saw the name of the case. Doherty came to court claiming to have pictures of YZ's underwear that had been left at two of the women's homes. I never saw the pictures, however. A brief exchange in chambers led me to announce that I should not hear the case, and we reset the pending motion before Judge Ray a couple of weeks later. I later learned that the case settled without any additional hearings. Judges rarely learn the terms of private settlements. I now know that some amount of money was paid to AB. If so, I took some comfort that AB likely achieved some solace.

My rulings in the case have bothered me for years. Although I would try cases with greater amounts of damages claimed and would hear other cases involving very personal matters, in no other case have I ever looked back and believed one of my rulings led to an erroneous jury verdict. As recently as five years ago, I remember having a nightmare about this case being retried and making the same ruling.

I think caring about all parties in a case is the hallmark of a good judge. When the obligation of a judge to follow the law intersects with a ruling the judge thinks might not be fair, a judge must follow the law. Sometimes that extracts an emotional price.

William Shakespeare wrote in *Henry IV*, "Uneasy lies the head that wears a crown." The back that wears a robe must be strong, but sometimes rulings that must be made on the spot are a challenge to the spirit and soul. Today, twenty-five years after this trial, I suspect I think about it as much as any of the parties or attorneys. I remain uneasy, but hope that, in the end, justice was done. For all judges, that should be the bottom line.

5

Brave Jenny

JUDGE GREGORY E. MIZE

Gregory E. Mize was appointed to the Superior Court of the District of Columbia in 1990 by President George H. W. Bush and assumed senior status in 2002. Before joining the trial bench, Judge Mize was first a trial lawyer and then general counsel to the District of Columbia City Council. He currently serves as a judicial fellow at the National Center for State Courts.

JENNY RESIDED WITH HER PARENTS, A SMALL BUSINESS OWNER AND a homemaker, in a rural suburb of Washington, DC.* Shortly after her sixth birthday, Jenny became so ill her parents took her to a local hospital for examination. The hospital diagnosed she was suffering from diarrhea, dehydration, upper respiratory infection, and intermittent fevers. She remained hospitalized for more than two weeks. When her symptoms kept reoccurring, she was transferred to Children's National Medical Center in DC for specialized attention.

---

* Jenny's name and other identifiers in this story have been changed to respect privacy interests.

Upon admission there, Jenny was diagnosed with "failure to thrive," diarrhea, and infected urine.

Jenny was assigned a room and, consistent with hospital policy, her mother, Mary, slept on a cot in the room. While at Children's Hospital, Jenny kept suffering from multiple bloodstream infections attributable to yeast, mold, and other bacteria. Mary was permitted to help the nursing staff in feeding and cleaning Jenny as well as assisting in the collection of urine and stool specimens.

During her first two months in the hospital, Jenny underwent a series of diagnostic tests. Yet hospital staff remained perplexed as to the causes of her infections. To keep hydrated and nourished, Jenny suffered numerous catheter insertions for intravenous feeding and groin catheters. Throughout this time, Mary devotedly stayed at Jenny's bedside.

During Jenny's third month in the hospital, the treating doctors and nurses reached a consensus that mother and daughter had an unnaturally close relationship. They began to suspect Mary was the cause of Jenny's fevers by introducing foreign substances into Jenny's IV line, specifically fecal matter or water from a nearby aquarium. They started piecing together various possible contributing factors. Used and unused syringes were usually present in Jenny's room. Mary was recently separated from Jenny's father and may have been suffering from depression or other emotional reactions to the breakup.

The attending physician strongly suspected Mary was suffering from Munchausen's Syndrome by Proxy. This rare psychological disorder prompts a parent to inflict physical injuries on themselves or their child to gain great attention from medical personnel or to make the child abnormally dependent on the parent. The methods used by the parent can take many forms. Jenny's hospital doctor surmised Mary, as Jenny's constant roommate, was secretly taking continuous steps to maintain her daughter's serious infections.

During the fourth month of hospitalization, the medical staff referred Jenny's case to DC's Child Protective Services Agency. Soon thereafter the city attorney's office filed a civil petition in the DC courthouse alleging Jenny was the victim of child abuse by her mother. The case, captioned "In the matter of Jenny Q," was randomly assigned to my docket. The government accused Jenny's mother, Mary Q, of three offenses: physically abusing six-year-old Jenny, withholding proper parental care of Jenny, and being incapable of caring for Jenny due to Mary's mental illness. Under District of Columbia law, these kinds of cases are not criminal in nature nor tried before a jury. Instead, to protect family privacy, the proceedings take place in a closed courtroom where only the judge makes legal rulings and findings of fact. If a case presents conflicting testimony, gut-wrenching facts, or scientific issues requiring expert testimony, the task of the fact finder can be quite challenging. Jenny's case presented all of these features. Jenny's mother denied any wrongdoing, so a trial had to occur. Pending the scheduled trial date, I ordered Mary to be physically separated from Jenny. I designated her dad as her sole custodian but permitted Mary to visit Jenny for limited hours while supervised by a medical professional or a court social worker. Significantly, once Jenny was separated from her mom, her fevers subsided. After the IV line was removed, all of her symptoms disappeared and she was discharged to go home.

At trial, over the course of five days, the petitioning government and Mary presented conflicting evidence. Seven witnesses testified including Jenny's mother, her father, treating nurses and physicians, and several medical experts. A printed transcript of the entire trial would have consumed hundreds of pages.

In a child abuse case, the government must prove allegations in its petition "by a preponderance of the evidence." Although no witness actually saw Mary perform harmful actions on Jenny, the testimony of several healthcare professionals was most helpful to my reaching a verdict. Treating nurses testified about the unusual and persistent desire of Mary to engage in the care of Jenny. She was constantly in Jenny's room trying to be hands-on involved in urine collections and IV tube maintenance. She rarely left the room but did leave when Jenny's father came for evening visits after his workday. Hospital housekeepers repeatedly retrieved empty alcohol bottles late at night from waste bins in Jenny's room. Mary on occasion appeared inebriated. These observations continued even after Mary was instructed about the strict hospital prohibition of alcohol on the hospital campus.

Three medical experts testified about Munchausen's Syndrome by Proxy generally and about whether Mary suffered from it. The government presented two experts, and Mary's attorney brought an additional expert to the witness stand. From them I learned that in the handful of documented cases where a child victim requires hospitalization, typical characteristics are:

- The child's prolonged illness involves confusing symptoms that defy diagnosis.
- The child has recurring hospital stays.
- The child improves dramatically after removal from the parent.
- The parent has medical training or expertise.
- The parent has a high level of interest and attentiveness to the child's needs while in the hospital.
- The parent has a cooperative and supportive attitude toward the hospital staff.
- The parent has a symbiotic relationship with the child.

The government's experts testified that, after reviewing the medical records, it was their expert opinion Mary suffered from Munchausen's Syndrome by Proxy, but Mary's expert witness, Dr. E, disputed that. He believed Mary had emotional problems that raised questions about her ability to parent successfully. Dr. E thought that, with professional help, Mary could learn to be a good parent. He further believed the court should intervene in the mother-daughter relationship at this time because he was not confident Mary had not done something to Jenny during her long hospitalization.

Throughout the trial Mary adamantly denied she harmed Jenny in any way. She vigorously asserted she was a model parent to Jenny and her younger brother. Mary also disputed she suffered from any psychological condition.

On the last day of trial, the government's lawyer, Jenny's court-appointed guardian ad litem charged with representing her best interests, and Mary's lawyer made their closing arguments. I took several days to reflect over the evidence and reread my numerous handwritten notes. I did so in the quiet of my chambers and on long walks in my neighborhood. At the end of my deliberations, I concluded Mary Q abused Jenny and suffered from a grave and rare illness that incapacitated her and made her a danger to her daughter. Reaching that verdict would be the first of many times when I'd go "to the mountain top" to ponder the "right thing to do." Although the evidence presented at the trial was distressing, events occurring after the verdict made this the toughest case I ever had.

Taking Care of Jenny

DC law provides, after a court finds a child to be neglected or abused, the court retains jurisdiction over the child and her parents until the harmful conditions are likely cured. Throughout the course of the litigation, the court is guided by the principle "do what is in the best interest of the child." In effect the court becomes a virtual parent of the child and supervisor of the faulty parent. Court supervision continues until the judge determines normal parent-child interaction is safe for the child or until the child becomes an emancipated adult.

On the day I rendered my verdict, I ordered Jenny to be in the sole custody of her father (John Q) and required that Mary stay away from Jenny except during weekly visitation supervised by a court social worker. Mary appeared stunned and crushed by the pronouncement.

The law also required me to hold a "disposition hearing" and issue a "disposition order" soon after the trial ended. This order must specify the ways Jenny was to be cared for and the steps her mom had to take to address her own Munchausen's condition. Believing the term "disposition" order hides its true significance (it does not dispose of a problem), I prefer calling it the "initial healing order." Jenny's younger brother was not governed by my order because he was not the subject of the child abuse case. Moreover, the divorce decree issued by a court in Mary and John's home state declared the boy would be in the custody of his father.

Approximately six weeks after the trial, I conducted a court hearing to figure out what I should include in the initial healing order. Before the hearing, I studied a detailed report from the court social worker assigned to Jenny's case. The report described the social worker's visits with Jenny, her father John, Mary, and several medical professionals familiar with the parties. One statement by Mary to the social worker stood out. Mary was quoted as saying, "My life is my children."

In preparing the initial healing order, I became concerned about the fact I had never actually met the most important person, the subject of everything I read and heard—Jenny. All of the writings and testimony described a kid who went from being a fever-stricken pincushion to a happy, spunky, seemingly normal daughter, sister, and second grader. I felt compelled to see her and talk with her directly. As in other cases where I need to make a delicate judgment call about a child, I notified Jenny's dad, mom, the social worker, guardian ad litem, and the attorneys for all parties that I wanted to meet with Jenny in my office for a simple conversation about "how things are going." I informed them that my law clerk, a young female lawyer, would be present to take notes and help make Jenny appreciate we were having a "get to know you meeting." Jenny's dad and others had already talked to Jenny about there being a court case with a judge trying to determine what was best for Jenny after her horrible experience in the hospital. Indeed, based on her conversations with therapists, Jenny understood that she was not able to be with her mom as before because "mommy gave me some bad candy at the hospital."

There being no objections from anyone about my meeting with Jenny, I personally met with her (now seven years old) in my office in the company of my law clerk. Jenny presented herself as a self-confident and articulate kid. When asked whether she was "happy or sad," she said she was happy. She described her second-grade class, her daily routines, and a few things about her long hospital stay. She said she was happy to be with her dad and "scared to be with mom" because "mom fed me bad candy and Pepsi at the hospital." She said she now feels good. "No headaches, fevers, or stomachaches." By the end of this delightful meeting, I felt relief and joy that my next decision would not be made in a theoretical vacuum. Instead I would be trying to protect a vibrant child who needed to continue her recovery from extraordinary injuries.

During the hour-long disposition hearing, I received input from Jenny's parents, their lawyers, the guardian ad litem, the city attorney, and the court social worker assigned to this case. I discussed with the parties various medical and social history reports generated by court staff.

Although Jenny was excused to attend school, her court-appointed guardian spoke about what court action she felt was in Jenny's best interests. In the end I concluded Mary was a danger to Jenny and would remain a danger until she admitted her wrongdoing, acknowledged her Munchausen's Syndrome by Proxy condition, and entered into a therapy regimen prescribed in court reports from medical experts. My initial healing order:

- Placed Jenny in the sole care and custody of her father,
- Required Jenny to receive psychotherapy to address any post trauma from her long hospitalization,
- Required Mary to engage in weekly therapy focused on issues presented by her attachment to Jenny and her Munchausen's Syndrome by Proxy,
- Directed Mary to regularly attend parenting classes,
- Limited visitation between Mary and Jenny to a maximum of two times per week and only when supervised by a clinical professional, and
- Prohibited additional supervised visitation between mother and daughter unless recommended by mental health professionals.

I also scheduled a "review hearing" three months down the road to see whether the requirements in the initial healing order were having any positive effects with respect to both Jenny and her mom.

What to Do About Mary?

Review hearings in these types of cases are designed to assure the child is safe and to determine whether the conditions imposed by the initial healing order are helping to cure harms the child suffered. In the first of many review hearings in Jenny's case, I learned Jenny was receiving therapy from the same child psychologist who treated her during the pretrial phase of her case. Jenny was happy to be living with her father, enjoying her neighborhood school, and generally "thriving."

Jenny's dad and mom were in the throes of a contentious divorce case in their home jurisdiction. Communication between them was strained, sometimes hostile. John Q, by virtue of a court order in the divorce case, continued to have sole custody of Jenny. And he was complying with my previous order allowing Jenny to visit with Mary under the supervision of the DC court social worker or a child psychologist.

Jenny's mom was not regularly attending required parenting classes or receiving any treatment for her Munchausen's Syndrome by Proxy condition. She explained that for her to travel the long distance from her home to Washington, DC, for parenting classes and therapy would interfere with maintaining her job in a local toy store. She was attending supervised visits with Jenny at a fast food restaurant near John Q's place of work in the family's hometown.

At the conclusion of the first review hearing, I kept in place all of the conditions of the initial healing order. I also advised Mary that there would be no hope of her having increased contact with Jenny if she did not seriously engage in therapy for her disease and attend classes on parenting and sound child nutrition.

During the next six months, things were going well for Jenny, but not so for Mary. Jenny continued therapy with her child psychologist. She was enjoying school and her home life with her dad and younger brother.

Mary and John's divorce became final. Their local court awarded the family home, mortgage-free, to Mary. John was required to pay monthly alimony to Mary for the next few years. John received sole custody of Jenny and her brother. Due to the ongoing nature of the child abuse case, the divorce court specified all issues relating to Mary's visitation with Jenny be controlled by my court orders.

Supervisors of the visits between mom and daughter reported Jenny was often reverting to infantile tantrums both during and shortly after the visits. Significantly, Mary was telling Jenny she would be coming home soon. We also learned Mary was offering wrapped candy to Jenny.

Outside of the visits, Mary was not regularly attending parenting classes. Although she engaged a psychologist to help her address her depression, that therapist was not providing therapy for Munchausen's Syndrome by Proxy. Indeed, the therapist reported that Mary does not remember doing anything to hurt Jenny at Children's Hospital. With respect to admitting she harmed Jenny, Mary stated, "I cannot make an admission because I believe I did not do it."

Jenny's therapist was dismayed that after almost two years, Mary had done almost nothing to address her behavior toward Jenny. Believing separation from Mary might help Jenny, he said, "Hopefully Jenny after prolonged exposure to only normal relations may come to recognize danger signs and eventually protect herself against her mother."

At the next hearing, all parties except Mary urged me to discontinue visitations until Mary engaged in meaningful therapy, developed insights into her relationship with Jenny, demonstrated ability to care for her children, and ceased to subvert Jenny's current home life with promises of returning home. Looking directly into Mary's eyes, I closed the review hearing saying I must terminate visitation until she undertook serious observance of the court's prior orders.

An Expert Chimes In—Again

At the fourth review hearing (three months later), I learned Jenny was now in third grade, enjoying her friendships, teachers, and school subjects. She was not having any tantrums or outbursts. John now had a girlfriend whom the social worker thought was a "positive, kind, and friendly woman" and "an excellent role model for Jenny." Jenny's therapist, teachers, and the court social worker praised Jenny's spunk and cheerfulness.

Mary switched jobs. She was attending therapy but only for depression. The court social worker urged me to order Mary's therapist be a specialist in Munchausen's disease. I reviewed a recent letter from the same medical expert who testified at the trial. The doctor stated few clinicians have experience in treating Munchausen's Syndrome by Proxy because it is so rare. As someone who had studied the few reported cases, she firmly believed a person with the condition must accept responsibility for causing her child's injuries. Not as a cure but as a first step to addressing her own condition and healing the relationship with her victim. The prognosis for successful treatment of Mary or anyone is "poor" because perpetrators are customarily rigid in their denial of wrongdoing and suffer a variety of serious personality disorders. She likened the situation to that of incest perpetrators. The best that can be hoped for is a reduction of risk through close monitoring of family functioning and appropriate therapy when family members are amenable to treatment. The treatment has to be child-driven rather than based upon the adult's wishes. If the perpetrator does not take responsibility, or, worse yet, if the adult puts blame on the child, the victim can come to sense she is responsible for her own injuries and believe her perception of reality does not count.

After hearing from all the parties and giving much weight to the expert's opinions, I ordered the social worker to search diligently for a therapist familiar with Munchausen's or sex disorders such as incest with some of the same resistance-to-treatment characteristics. I continued to prohibit visitations. I implored Mary to diligently engage in therapy with the court-identified social worker. I told her she must demonstrate genuine empathy for the impact of her offense upon Jenny. Unless and until that were to happen, a healed relationship with Jenny would be unlikely. Perhaps impossible.

Three months later, the court was able to secure the sought-after therapist in Washington, DC, and Mary started traveling to DC to attend therapy appointments.

More Concerns Start Bubbling Up

Before the next review hearing, I wanted to sit down and chat with Jenny again. To ready myself for that, I was thinking of my own communications with young kids. Everything I learned about Jenny reminded me of Irene, the main character in the children's book *Brave Irene*, one of my favorite books to read to my children—four of five being daughters. In the book, Irene endures sickness (hers and her mother's) while trekking through a snowstorm to fulfill a family obligation. I was confident Brave Irene would be an ideal token to give Jenny during our meeting.

At the meeting, Jenny as before was a pixie. Cheerful. Talkative. Not timid. Loving baseball and skating but not dolls so much. Naming her several friends and teachers. AND liking to read books!

Among the things I asked Jenny: If she was happy. "Yes" with a smile on her face. If she sleeps well. "Yes." Whether she knows why a judge is involved with her family. "I don't know why." Whether she remembers being sick in the hospital. "I am happy now." What makes her sick? "Nothing." What makes her sad? "Nothing." Do you wish for anything? "No."

At the end of the meeting I gave her *Brave Irene*. She received it with a big smile and grace—like a princess. After she left my chambers, I said to myself, "What an amazing little person!"

Weeks later her penciled letter arrived saying:

Dear Judge Mize,

Thank you for the book Brave Irene. I liked it a lot. I especially liked how Irene struggled through the storm. And then she got to a warm place. Everyone was glad to see her.

I hope your family is well.

—from Jenny

After meetings with Jenny, her case took on a deeper meaning. Review hearings became chapters in a story about a beautiful little person, a girl resembling my daughters and the many grammar schoolers I have met over the years. But unlike those girls, this case was a saga about a small child victimized by her mother, a girl who, unlike most of her friends, could not go home *or anywhere* to see her mother. That fact became a growing burden in my heart at every future hearing.

Mary's Spiral Downward

During the next five months, Jenny completed third grade. Her teachers reported she was doing "exceptionally well." One teacher remarked, "Jenny is enthusiastic and cooperative. She has excellent work habits . . . is a very special little girl. I believe Jenny has grown dramatically this year in independence." Jenny's therapist was still seeing Jenny every four to six weeks. He described her as an "autonomous little person, a neat little kid" who understands limits set by her father. In interviews with the court social worker, Jenny would change the subject whenever the topic of her mom came up. The social worker thought Jenny was the picture of contentment. "If there is a void created by her mother's absence, this officer fails to see it." Moreover, the social worker thought John Q was an excellent caregiver.

Meanwhile, Mary became unemployed. Her new Munchausen's therapist reported their weekly, two-hour therapy sessions thus far had focused only on Mary's chronic depression and low self-esteem. She lost much weight and several teeth. She was very worried about her children's emotional reactions to the events of the past two years: Do they feel abandoned by their mother? Can they express their feelings about the changes in their lives?

Mary was also showing a greater awareness of the dysfunction in her family of origin—especially the absence of nurturing and encouragement by her parents. In recalling her parents, she began to examine her own parenting strengths and shortcomings. Mary's therapist also described a fine line she was walking: the dilemma of balancing the integrity of her reporting to the judge who would decide Mary's future role as a mother, and the confidences she, as a professional therapist, had to keep with her client.

Since I required all therapeutic assessments of the parties be circulated to every other therapist and the parties' attorneys before each review hearing, we all learned Jenny's therapist and the medical expert on Munchausen's were concerned that Mary was still not acknowledging she caused injuries to Jenny and was responsible for the halt of visitations. At the conclusion of the hearing where the parties and I questioned these therapists, Mary asked that I resume supervised visitation between her and Jenny. Mary appeared worn, sad, and physically diminished in comparison to all prior hearings. I said no to her again. Intellectually it was the right thing to do. Yet my heart was heavy. Jenny was making great progress. Mary was increasingly disintegrating in parallel with my continuing denial of any visitation. I was feeling like part of the problem here and asked myself: Am I doing the right thing? Shouldn't there be two healings occurring? I directed the parties to consult with the therapists, and to submit written reports to address "whether supervised visitation is in Jenny's best interest." I thought this requirement would make the next hearing a big one for the parties and for my self-confidence.

Another Visit with Jenny

I felt it was important to see and hear again from Jenny. After notifying the parties as before, I met Jenny in my office with my law clerk present. I learned that Jenny, now nine years old, still loved her school. Loved art and her storytelling class. Did her homework every day in the kitchen or in her room. Her dad was home when she returned from school. In response to my questions, what makes you happy? "I don't know." Her favorite part of the day? "Every day." How is everyone at home doing? "My brother is fine. My dad is fine."

Eventually turning to more delicate subjects, I asked what she thought is the reason she comes to see me. She mentioned she remembered being in the hospital and thought that is why. I explained that I am responsible for keeping Jenny separated from her mom. That it is important for me to spend time with Jenny in order to be sure I am doing the right thing. After that, Jenny expressed wonder whether her mother was OK. She said she might write a letter to her mom. I reminded her that it would be OK if she wanted to do so. Jenny said she had not had much time but she did write to old friends and her daddy's mother. Jenny said she spends time with Ruth, her dad's friend. She likes Ruth.

Jenny said she sometimes wishes she could see her mom when she feels lonely, but that is not often. She said it would be OK to see her mom "one day in the future." It is "sort of" something she would like to do. She added, "I like my dad."

We closed the meeting with Jenny saying she likes to try new things. She would love to go to Oregon. And that she recently read *Be Careful What You Wish For.*

"Ground Hog Day"

A week before the "big" hearing on the visitation issue, the therapists submitted their written reports.

Mary's therapist recounted how her client was continuing to address her depression. Significantly, she said Mary, without "any form of admission of willful and/or designed harm to her children," was starting to "accept responsibility for the effect of her own past behavior and personality on her children's present emotional situation and development." Mary's therapist also visited with Jenny, and reported the child "presents as a petite, lively, verbally articulate, intellectually bright and creative child. She clearly reflects the protective world of her present environment." She further advised that Jenny "positively, and without any hesitation" said she was "receptive to direct questions concerning the possibility of a visit with her mother and did not indicate any fear that her present life situation with her brother and father could (or would) possibly be interrupted by such a visit." Indeed, Jenny said she was willing to see her mom again "someday." Consequently, Mary's therapist recommended resumption of twice-monthly, supervised visitation between mother and daughter.

Jenny's therapist focused on the three-year history of his involvement with Jenny and her family. He reduced his views to an equation. A (Mary's insight into her behaviors) + B (substantiated/substantial changes in Mary's behavior) + C (Mary completes parenting training) + D (demonstrated competency in parenting) = E (supervised visitation). He pointed to Mary's recurring failure to achieve the kind of insights the Munchausen's expert recommended. And he emphasized a stark contrast between Mary and Jenny's father with respect to learning parenting skills. While John completed three years of counseling by certified professionals with respect to parenting and child development, Mary had done the minimal.

He concluded by saying, "If 'E' in the equation is ever reached and visitation is reinstated, it should be monitored by a neutral party and such visitation be videotaped with the intent of using the tapes for coaching parenting skills."

In the courtroom, I wanted to hear Mary say what her approach would be to several hypothetical parenting challenges. For example, how do you set boundaries for kids? What would you do if your child had a tantrum in a crowded supermarket? What would you do if your child fell off a playground swing set?

I asked Mary to comment on her therapist's statement that Mary is able to "accept responsibility for the effect of her own past actions" on her children. Mary said she got "too close" to Jenny, was "too protective" of her. Sadly, she also said, "I would not do anything differently."

My comfort level with restoring supervised visitation fell through the floor. While I felt Mary showed progress in articulating the qualities of good parenting and dealing with typical child-rearing challenges, I was jolted by her denial of any responsibility for Jenny's abuse and injuries. I decided against visitation. Announcing those words felt like rocks in my throat.

To make matters worse, the court social worker informed us that the court fund to pay for Mary's monthly therapy was about to dry up. The cost of Mary's specialized therapy had consumed an outsized share of the fiscal year budget for all child abuse and neglect cases. The legal funding was not large to begin with, and the government wanted to maintain a fund balance to meet other case needs.

As we adjourned, I am sure my body mirrored the same sorrow and distress I saw on the faces of everyone in the courtroom. We had been meeting like this for almost three years, ending with yet another denial of Mary's request to visit with Jenny. As I kept an anxious mother away from her preteen daughter, I thought of what that would mean to my wife in relation to our daughters. I asked myself, could someone else take this case? Let someone else play the Oracle of Delphi! I could not wait to leave the courthouse after the hearing. I sorely wanted to be at home with family. When I did arrive to huddle with my crew, I counted my blessings and thought of Mary. Unlike my warm place, her home was probably quite stark and empty.

Mary Testifies

At the close of the prior hearing, I had the presence of mind to require each party to submit written statements before the next hearing. The statements were to address "why or why not limited visitation should resume in the near future." I also ordered the social worker to coordinate a "comprehensive background state-ment" of Mary's lifestyle and capabilities. This would include counseling she received, job prospects, housing conditions, income sources, "and other attributes or detriments." The comprehensive statement was to be delivered to the parties no later than one week before the next hearing. I was making a concerted push to get a bet-ter grasp on the suitability of Mary having a face-to-face meeting with Jenny. The next court event was going to be another crucial juncture.

To better prepare for the "why or why not" hearing, I called everyone to court for the sole purpose of asking Mary and her thera-pist some questions regarding the outcomes of therapy. They both consented to participate. Over the course of almost two hours, Mary responded to questions such as, what have you learned about par-enting from your mother? What have you yourself learned about disciplining children? Did you set limits for Jenny? What do you think neglect of a child means? How does a parent maintain a child's good health? What should a parent do for a sick child? She answered these questions confidently. She exhibited more insights into what constitutes good parenting than I had ever heard from her. Indeed more so than most other parents whose cases were pending on my court docket. But all did not end there.

Eventually we got to the question, what do you think this court case is all about? Mary said, "We are here because the hospital accused me of hurting Jenny." She went further to say, "Jenny got fevers right after John and I separated." Children's Hospital said I "tampered with the IVs." I then asked, what have you learned from that? She said, "I have learned I should have spoken up in the beginning and been assertive and stood up for myself which I have never been able to do. They want me to say I hurt Jenny or harmed Jenny or tampered with the IVs and I can't say that." Why not? "Because I didn't." She repeated, "I did not touch the IVs, I did not do none of that. . . . No one believes me, but I did not." Mary then broke down crying and we recessed.

After the recess, Mary went on to say the doctors and nurses "let Jenny have needles and IVs to play with." She described how on one day she saw Jenny put a needle in her IV tube. She said Jenny had "fear in her face." She alleged Jenny asked her not to tell the nurses. Mary said she didn't know how many times Jenny used the needles. Nor did she know where Jenny got the needles. "Maybe from the head nurse." She claimed one time Jenny wanted to put a needle in Mary's arm. Mary also claimed the nurses let Jenny change her own dressings and remove her stitches.

And lastly, Mary testified that at one of her last supervised visits with Jenny (shortly after the trial ended), Jenny told Mary someone told her that her mom made her sick at the hospital. To which, Mary further testified, "I told Jenny, I didn't feed you no poison. They are trying to blame mommy." And Jenny said, 'I know you didn't. It's our little secret.'"

Toward the end of the two-hour hearing, Mary, her attorney, and her therapist recommended I order resumption of supervised visitation. All others were equally as convinced, based upon Mary's denial of wrongdoing and blaming Jenny for inducing her fevers, that visitation should not resume.

Mary's astonishing assignment of blame to Jenny reaffirmed the correctness of my decisions thus far. I kept the current prohibition of visitation in place until the next hearing when the parties would more fully address the question of "why or why not" visitation. I asked myself again, would the preteen Jenny ever see her mother again?

The "Why or Why Not" Hearing

The government attorney started by recounting, in painful detail, the suffering Jenny endured over the course of months at Children's Hospital. After pointing out the conflicting medical expert testimony by advocates and opponents of renewed visitation, the prosecutor concluded by saying any resumption of visitation should be done "cautiously and in measured steps."

Jenny's guardian ad litem and her dad argued against any resumption of visitation. The Munchausen's academic expert submitted a letter expressing "shock" at Mary's blaming Jenny for her fevers and prolonged hospitalization. He thought Mary was acting like a classical Munchausen's perpetrator, assigning blame to others in order to gain attention and an advantage over her accusers. The guardian saw Mary's claims of merely being overprotective and not the cause of Jenny's illnesses as another indicator Mary had not made significant progress in treatment.

Jenny's dad said visitation with Mary "would hurt Jenny." He appreciated Jenny told a therapist she was willing to see her mom "someday." He "never gave up hope that Mary could be a mother to Jenny until she alleged that Jenny caused her own illness." He felt the "ludicrous claim" Jenny poisoned herself made clear Mary would likely abuse Jenny with a guilt trip and perhaps more physical harm. What touched me most was John's statement, "I understand you may be having a hard time legally, and as a parent yourself, in continuing to not allow visitation. What people outside this situation find almost impossible to realize is that there never was a mother-daughter relationship between Mary and Jenny. They were same age playmates, symbiotically acting as one. So Jenny to me has been deprived of a friend, not a mother. It is certainly unfortunate that Mary and Jenny cannot visit. However, some mothers die, some abandon their children, and others are just unable to play a role in their children's lives. And life goes on. Jenny's certainly has. She is amazing on many levels—all after not having to deal with or be confused by Mary."

Mary's attorney urged me to authorize carefully timed and supervised visitation for two reasons. One, Jenny's future development would likely be impaired if she did not have visits with her mom. And, two, a diagnosis of Munchausen's Syndrome by Proxy without an acknowledgment of responsibility by the parent should not be a disqualifying factor. To support the first reason, she provided the testimony of a highly credentialed child psychiatrist who treats patients at Children's Hospital. This doctor testified "a child having had an adverse experience with a parent and thereafter having no contact with the parent, will carry forward into adolescence and adult life both conscious and unconscious residual conflict. Positive experience with the parent under controlled circumstances will likely contribute to resolving such conflict and ultimately strengthen the positive aspects of their relationship." While recognizing it is important for a Munchausen's perpetrator to accept responsibility, the psychiatrist thought a positive visitation experience could nevertheless occur for Jenny without Mary's acknowledgment of responsibility. For example, carefully conceived (and enforced) ground rules for visitation could require Mary not to address the causes of Jenny's hospitalization until Mary came around to her own admission of responsibility.

At the conclusion of yet another lengthy, emotional court hearing, I denied resumption of visitation. There was no doubt Jenny was happy under current circumstances. The risk of confusion and emotional trauma to Jenny arising from visitations outweighed the great hurt Mary would continue to feel. My mental process looked like this:

Risks to Jenny vs. benefits to Jenny

– Jenny is merely a tool for Mary's self-gratification.

– Visitation will ultimately be futile if they cannot talk about the hospitalization.

– What happens if visitation, once begun, must be terminated for good reasons?

– Jenny's current developmental progress will be stunted.

+ Jenny's personal development in her teen years will benefit from maternal input.

+ Jenny will be reassured her mom is OK.

The Spiral Downward

If the prior three years were like a long slow drama, the next year was a one-act tragedy. Shortly after the "why or why not" hearing, Jenny sent a handwritten letter to Mary expressing love for her mom. This was permissible under prior court orders so long as John Q saw the letter prior to its sending. Mary sought my permission to write back to Jenny. Through her attorney, Mary also asked for supervised visitation. I promptly scheduled another court hearing. I read Mary's proposed letter. It simply said:

Dear Jenny,

I got your letter, it was so pretty, and I was so happy you wrote to me. I love you and miss you so much.

Love, Mommy xoxoxoxo

The hearing resurrected many of the same arguments made a month earlier. I was concerned to learn Mary was no longer receiving Munchausen's therapy because the government had stopped paying for it and she could not afford it. As a disheveled and forlorn Mary looked up at me, I denied her request for visitation. I repeated my prior reasons for the denial.

Afterwards, Mary's attorney filed a motion to withdraw from the case. Counsel stated that, for several months, Mary had not been responding to her telephone or written inquiries. The motion stated Mary and her counsel have "profound and apparently irreconcilable disagreement as to further compliance with court directives." I did not rule on the motion in the hope it could be addressed at the next review hearing. At the next hearing, I learned Jenny was continuing to do well at school and at home. She had recently attended an overnight camp and enjoyed the experience immensely. The court social worker reported Mary was not communicating with her. However, she was showing up at Jenny's school.

Mary appeared in court looking emaciated and quite sad. She said she went to Jenny's school to get school records John was not sending her. She had a part-time job, but her home was the subject of a proposed tax sale because she could not pay her taxes. She said she needed the home because her children needed a home to return to. Yet again, I kept all prior conditions in place.

On the third anniversary of the trial verdict, the DC government requested the case be closed. The prosecutor asserted Jenny was thriving in the custody of her father in a stable home environment many miles from Washington, DC. Hence there was no need for services to be provided by the DC courts. In addition he argued that, since the divorce decree issued in John and Mary's home state adequately set terms for child custody, there was no further need for the DC court supervision.

Jenny's guardian ad litem and her father opposed the request. John asked that I retain jurisdiction over this case only until all of the terms and conditions that currently applied to Jenny and Mary in the DC case were adopted and incorporated into the divorce decree issued by John and Mary's local court. Mary did not file a written response to the government's request. Nor did she appear at the scheduled hearing to say anything.

I granted the government attorney's request so long as the divorce court adopted the conditions suggested by Jenny's dad. I was convinced Jenny was fine and in good hands with her father. Conversely it appeared Mary had given up the fight. If she started to get more involved and a visitation dispute cropped up again, I felt the state court would become sufficiently involved. Moreover, the many thousands of dollars spent by the DC court system on maternal supervision and specialized therapies had maxed out. Any additional assistance to Jenny's mom was not going to come about through the DC case.

The Ultimate Conclusion

After Jenny's case was legally closed, it remained open for me. In the court files, the case was labeled "In the matter of: JQ." For me, it is more fitting for the case to be titled: "In the matter of: A Motherless Child." Or: "In the matter of: Human Court Playing God." Now decades later, memories of the dozens of dramatic courtroom hearings occasionally come back to haunt me. Why so?

About six months after the case "ended," I was sitting in my kitchen reading the daily newspaper. There was a short story about a boating incident on the Chesapeake Bay. State police found the body of a woman washed ashore. She went missing days earlier after falling off a cigarette boat in the middle of the night. Two persons on the boat dove into the water to try and save her but could not find her. State helicopters and dog units became involved in the search but without success. The woman's name: Mary Q.

After reading the newspaper, several questions kept revisiting me. Did Mary drink herself into a stupor and jump overboard? Was she sober yet so despairing that she intentionally escaped to the black waters? Was she thinking of Jenny? Suffocating in her guilt? Battling with her failure to accept responsibility for Jenny's injuries? Angry with the judge who would not budge—who did not give her a chance to see and speak for at least a little while with Jenny?

Even as I write this chapter, my mind and heart rubber band backwards. Memories and questions relaunch: I presided over many days of trial testimony—viewed medical charts, listened to treating nurses, plodded through literature from medical schools, and riveted on testimony from Jenny's parents. After the trial I read hundreds of pages of therapy assessments and social worker reports, followed by dozens of hours of question-and-answer dialogue in review hearings. Weeks and months passed between the many hearings. The mother-daughter relationship was a perpetual dilemma that would not resolve. Every hearing had a certain here-we-go-again quality. I asked myself at the start of each courthouse event, will there be a breakthrough today? Will Mary come clean and admit responsibility for injuring Jenny? Can Jenny and Mary reunite in a healthy way? Will I finally receive an insight that enables repair of their relationship?

In the end, I know I tried my best to do the right thing for Jenny. In cases like Jenny's, a judge must focus on what is in the best interest of the child. I think I fulfilled that mission to the best of my ability. The letter and spirit of the law was followed. Yet I do not find complete comfort in that realization. Questions linger. Does a judge have any responsibilities with respect to an abused child's family members? To the wrongful parent? What is the proper amount of concern to be given to the Marys of our world? Must doing what is best for a child exclude taking a chance on what could be restorative for a parent?

I continue to hope Jenny's wounds are mended. That she continues to be a living example of Brave Irene. That she may be an amazing mother. My own healing depends on such hopes.

Epilogue

About two weeks after I completed a "final" draft of this chapter, I wanted to track down Jenny and her father to obtain their permission to publish this story. My case records were more than twenty years old, so I started my search by reaching out to John's lawyer in the case. The attorney, remembering the case quite well, was confident he could reach Jenny's father and ask him to call me.

Within a day, John called me back. He was very enthused to speak. First, he wanted to report how well Jenny is doing. He was amazed at the coincidences surrounding my outreach to him. In the prior month, Jenny (at the time thirty years old) asked her father if she could review his voluminous records from the child abuse case. She wanted to read every detail about the case and then speak with the chief treating doctor and "her" judge. John eagerly gave me Jenny's email address and mobile phone number. He suggested I send her a copy of the story as well as my contact information. He informed me Jenny became an accomplished gymnast at Temple University and then a dental hygienist practicing in New Mexico and later in Maryland. My heart leapt for joy as I envisioned a strong, confident, and outward-oriented Jenny.

In a few days I received an email from Jenny saying she was thrilled I called her dad, and I sent the chapter to her. She wanted to speak with me when she returned to the Washington, DC, area in a couple of weeks. I suggested we meet for lunch at the National Gallery of Art near the DC Courthouse. She loved the suggestion. Lunch was "in the book"!

As I walked up the Gallery steps to meet Jenny at the security desk, I was a concoction of bewilderment and elation. I was about to meet Jenny after the passage of more than two decades. Is this really happening? How will I recognize her? What will we talk about? Will I learn things I would rather not know? Was the little victim now healed? Will my "toughest case" have a happy ending?

There she was! A young lady. Truthful eyes. A beaming, warm smile.

We instantly embraced. Our eyes swelled with blissful tears. We were speechless for drawn-out seconds. At a tiny Gallery Café table, food was a distant backdrop to reports about her life and family. She lived in a nearby DC suburb and practiced as a dental hygienist. Her dental group served many low-income clients. Although she is not married, she has a close circle of friends who meet regularly for fun and exercise. She is devoted and close to her dad and brother.

We spoke about my haunting memories of her case. She confided that she does not miss her mother. With the passage of many years and, most recently, after reading many court files and medical records, she is convinced her mom could never have had a healthy influence on her. Jenny believes her mom was the victim of her birth family's dysfunction and someone who was afflicted with chronic and severe clinical depression. For her, the most difficult part was not knowing what it is like to have a mother. Yet, she realizes life is about choices. "One can dwell on the past or decide to be happy and push through all the hardships and events that don't make sense." And one of her favorite quotes is, "The bad times make the good times better."

We ended our monumental reunion with another warm embrace and mutual expressions of hopes to keep in touch. Jenny followed through on that hope in this email message a few days later.

> A big thank you for lunch! As I rode the Metro back, I felt a huge feeling of closure. I know that my past and my childhood are something that will always be with me and something I'll always have to deal with, but I truly felt a sense of closure and happiness with meeting with you and knowing that you and all the witnesses/doctors/nurses/medical professionals fought for me. My dad gave me the actual trial transcripts last weekend and

I have been reading them every night. My mother was indeed a very sick person, and also very manipulative and I want to reiterate to you that you 200% made the right decision when you did not allow visitation between her and me. Up until this point, I always considered myself a victim of child abuse, but now I see myself as a survivor and the majority of that came from you reaching out to me.

As I write this epilogue, the ghost of Mary Q. seems a lot further away. Her beautiful daughter Jenny has replaced hauntings with deep feelings of thanksgiving.

Trial judge work in a big city is like standing in a waterfall of conflicts. Once one dispute is caught and resolved, another one immediately drops and demands fresh focus and resolution. A daily docket of criminal, civil, or family law cases requires dozens of decisions each workday. Some judgment calls such as setting a trial date are simple. Others present weighty and complex issues that necessitate careful, time-consuming attention. Almost every lawsuit compels a judge to decide issues of law and, very frequently, make findings of fact.

In this environment, it can be quite difficult for a judge to devote more than a limited amount of time to listen to legal arguments, question witnesses, read documents, and ponder what is the right and just thing to do. And post mortems are not common in this line of work. Once a case is completed, a judge rarely finds out what happened to the people involved or if his or her decision had its intended affect. On to the next case!

Since my appointment to the bench in 1990, I have made hundreds of thousands of decisions in tens of thousands of cases. This immense volume and the passage of years naturally challenge one's ability to remember any one decision or case. Yet, as a member of a large family and active participant in several communities, I am regularly asked by neighbors, strangers on an airplane, and even former jurors, "What was your toughest case?" To all, I respond without hesitation. It's the case of Jenny Q.

I tell Jenny's story not because I enjoy telling it. Now, decades later, her case haunts me. I do so principally because it prompts large questions about our human condition and the limits of the judicial office.

6

Every Case Is a Tough Case for a New Judge

JUDGE MICHELLE M. AHNN

Judge Michelle M. Ahnn was appointed to the Los Angeles Superior Court by California Governor Brown in November 2015. Prior to her appointment, she was a Deputy Alternate Public Defender in Los Angeles for fourteen years.

"ALL RISE, FACE THE FLAG OF OUR NATION, EMBLEM OF THE CONSTItution, symbol of freedom and justice for all. Department 3 of the Superior Court, Southwest Judicial District, Inglewood, is now in session. The Honorable Michelle M. Ahnn, Judge Presiding." Every morning, before I handle the first case, the bailiff in my court makes this formal opening. I asked the bailiff to do this because it reminds me of the principles that must guide my every decision. As I listen to the words, I take a deep breath to steel myself. I silently set my goals for the day—today I am going to be a patient judge, a knowledgeable judge, a fair judge. But then I sit down, look at a crowded courtroom and the stack of files I need to get through, and all my good intentions threaten to crumble. I begin to worry that I will not be able to give each case the time it deserves. I wonder if perhaps I missed something in my preparation for the motions that are before me on that day. I worry about my ability to be a good judge.

For fourteen years, I was a trial attorney at the Los Angeles Alternate Public Defender's office. When I first began with this office, I represented defendants in misdemeanor cases, mainly involving low-level offenses such as shoplifting or prostitution. Then, I was promoted to handle felony cases, which range from drug sales to capital murder. For the ten years prior to becoming a judge, I was assigned as a felony attorney to the Compton Courthouse. Most of my cases were gang-related and were serious or violent crimes such as murder, rape, robbery, and assaults.

In November 2015, I received a phone call informing me that Governor Brown had appointed me to be a judge. After my initial elation, I became apprehensive about where I would be assigned to sit as a judge. It could have been in any practice area—criminal, civil, family law, or dependency. Fortunately for me, I was assigned to a criminal courtroom to handle misdemeanor cases. I was relieved when I was told about my assignment because criminal law is in my "wheelhouse." In retrospect, the relief was premature, as I had not fully contemplated what it meant to transition from being a defense attorney to a judge.

With my background in criminal law, I felt that I had a good grasp on criminal law and evidence. I also thought that because misdemeanor cases involve less complex issues and less harm to society than felony cases, the decisions I would have to make as a judge presiding over misdemeanor cases would be straightforward and uncomplicated compared to the work I did as a public defender handling serious and violent felonies.

I thought that nothing would be harder than my experience representing a fourteen-year-old charged as an adult for a gang rape. My teenage client was accused of bringing three adult men into a room to rape a fifteen-year-old girl. The stakes were high. My client faced a maximum sentence of more than eighty years in prison, a sentence that would devastate his entire family including his parents, who were both hard-working and dedicated to their son. In order to defend my client vigorously, I had to question the alleged victim to show that the sex was consensual and not forced. In doing so, my cross-examination had to walk a fine line, remaining combative but not alienating to the jury. I had to keep in mind that no matter how much I believed in my client's innocence, the alleged victim was a young girl who had spent the past few years being bounced around different foster homes. The emotional stress of representing a client that young who faced so much time made this one of the hardest cases of my career as an attorney. The gratitude from my client and his family after the jury rendered not guilty verdicts on all counts was one of the best moments I had as a lawyer.

I have defended clients in the face of seemingly insurmountable evidence of guilt, especially as technology has advanced. In some cases, my clients posted incriminating pictures and videos on YouTube, Facebook, and other social media, flashing gang signs, displaying gang colors, and even boasting about committing the crimes they were accused of. As video cameras and surveillance videos become ubiquitous, the chances increase that a crime is being videotaped as it occurs. At the time, I believed there would be no bigger challenge than standing in front of a jury and arguing passionately and convincingly for the innocence of my heavily tattooed client who was caught bragging about shooting someone in the forehead just because the man happened to be in the territory claimed by the client's gang.

Because of these experiences, I came into this new job thinking that it would be easy—or at least easier. But I was wrong. Very wrong. My first year on the bench humbled me, haunted me, and taxed my nerves and wits far beyond any year I had spent as a public defender. It was a year of tough cases and hard decisions.

Ethical rules prohibit me from discussing a pending case, which includes any case in which the time for filing an appeal has not expired. Having been on the bench for only two years, most of the cases I have handled are still pending. So rather than discussing one particular tough case I have presided over, I'll explore how the transition from attorney to judge and how my newness to the job makes every case feel like a tough case.

I typically handle thirty-five to sixty cases a day. Two-thirds of those cases are routine matters that do not involve a lot of hard decisions. These are cases in which the defendant is accepting a prosecutor's plea offer, coming to court with a progress report from the counseling program they are attending, or requesting to continue the trial so that further investigation or preparation can be done. In the remaining third of the cases, I must tackle difficult issues such as determining whether to order a criminal defendant into custody or release him or her from jail, deciding to grant or deny pretrial and trial motions, and serving as the sole fact finder in bench trials.

Release or Bail—How Should I Decide?

Deciding whether to release someone from jail or set bail is the most frequent decision I must make daily. For most misdemeanor cases, the law requires the defendant's release unless certain conditions exist. If I believe the defendant is a danger to the community or will not return to court, then I can order that the defendant be held in custody until he can post bail. However, in most cases, the defendants cannot afford the bail amount, which means that they will stay in custody until their trial.

As such, a judge's decision whether to release a defendant or set bail has an impact on the defendant's decision about whether to accept a plea offer. As an attorney, I had hundreds of conversations with defendants about the facts of their cases and what choices they had in terms of accepting a plea or fighting their case. I learned as a defense attorney that a client's view on the merits of his case typically depended on whether the judge would release him. If the prosecutor's offer was time served, this would mean that the defendant would be immediately released from jail. In those instances, my clients who adamantly declared their innocence would change their attitude and plead guilty in exchange for the guarantee of their immediate release. Too often as a public defender, I felt that a client with a meritorious defense would waive his right to a trial and accept the prosecutor's plea offer if it would result in a sentence shorter than the time he would otherwise spend in jail waiting for his "day in court."

A defendant should never be forced to plead guilty to a crime he did not commit. But as a judge, I am tasked with the obligation to set bail without taking into consideration the reality that my decision might mean that a defendant will accept a plea offer rather than take his case to trial. I am sure this decision is hard for any judge, regardless of what job they had prior to becoming a judge. But during my first year as a judge, when all those conversations with my prior clients were so recent in my mind, I struggled to put aside my public defender mind-set and apply the law as required. At the same time, I wanted to avoid the other extreme of refusing to release someone whose background and case warranted release just to avoid being perceived as a defense-oriented judge.

The cases that weigh on my mind are the ones where the defendant is charged with domestic violence, but the victim wants the defendant to return home. Unlike most misdemeanor cases, if the crime charged involves domestic violence, a defendant's release is not presumed, and a hearing must be held to determine if the defendant should be released or bail set. Many times, the alleged victim comes to this hearing and adamantly denies telling the police that the defendant assaulted her. Other times, the alleged victim will minimize the defendant's actions when they beg me for the defendant's release. However, a bail hearing is not a mini-trial for the judge to determine who is telling the truth. Legal precedent requires that a judge presume the facts contained in the police report to be true during a hearing on whether to release a defendant or set bail.

In these situations it is gut-wrenching for me to face the victim and tell her that I will not release the defendant. Often the victims start crying because the defendant is the only source of income for the family and they will lose their home if the defendant cannot work. I often wonder whether it is paternalistic of me to protect a victim who emphatically states that she does not want nor need such protection. In these cases, I am left wondering days afterward about the correctness of my decision. If I set bail, I wonder how the family is surviving. If I release the defendant, I worry about the victim's safety. Yet, I cannot spend too much emotional energy wondering about the outcome of my decisions because there are more cases that I must rule on that day, and more the next day and the next.

I tend to refer to defendants as male because most of the defendants who come before me, especially those charged with domestic violence, are men. But I have had instances where the defendant charged with domestic violence is female, and these cases pose additional considerations that force me to do a lot of soul-searching about myself and my decision-making process. Once, during a hearing to determine if a female defendant charged with domestic violence should be released, the prosecutor could tell that I was leaning toward releasing her. Clearly frustrated, the prosecutor accused me of being biased. He insisted that I had refused to release male defendants who had committed similar crimes and who had similar backgrounds, so he believed that I should also set bail on the female defendant instead of releasing her.

I was taken aback by this accusation, but it made me wonder whether I was unconsciously stereotyping a woman as less dangerous than a man. Given my background, my education, and my work as a public defender, I hoped this was not true. I wish that there was some empirical way to capture data on factors that led me to release someone or set bail. But these decisions must consider so many factors that are unique to each case, and the reasoning for my rulings cannot be reduced to a spreadsheet. It was very uncomfortable to be accused of bias, but I was grateful for the reminder that in making these decisions, I must mentally check myself to make sure that I am neutrally applying the law.

It always seems like the cases with the hardest decisions about whether to release a defendant or set bail are the last cases of the day, when I am most tired. I go to pick up the lone file on my bench with relief, thinking that my day of making hard decisions is almost over. But then the prosecutor and defense attorney heatedly argue about whether bail should be set or the defendant released. I look around the courtroom, hoping that the answer will miraculously appear.

However, all I see are people waiting for me to decide. The exhausted bailiff who began his shift at dawn has his hand on the doorknob. He taps his foot as he thinks about the work that needs to be done to get all the custody defendants from the courthouse back to the jail. The defendant fidgets in his seat and looks at me with pleading eyes. In the audience, there are family members who have been in the courtroom all day waiting for their loved one's case to be called. They sit at the edge of their seats to get a better look at the defendant and at me, hoping to hear the words "the defendant is released." The attorneys eye the courtroom doors, ready to leave as soon as I say, "court is in recess," so that they can go back to their offices and work on their upcoming trials. The court staff is waiting for everyone to leave so that they can continue to work in quiet to update the files for all the cases we handled that day.

All of these people are looking at me, waiting for me to speak. My internal reaction, which I try to hide, is to think, "I don't want to make this decision." I desperately want to look over my shoulder in the hopes that another judge will come in and make this tough call. But it is my decision to make, so I take a deep breath and rule.

"He Is Remanded"—The Three Words That Are Hardest for Me to Say

It is one thing to keep someone in jail by imposing bail when he is already in custody. But for me, it is even harder to order someone into custody when he or she comes to court on their own. This situation can happen both before and after trial. If I have released a defendant pending his trial and he fails to return to court on the date

I ordered him to return, then I issue a bench warrant for his arrest. Often, the defendant will then come to court a few days later on his own to clear up the warrant, maintaining that he got his dates mixed up or some family emergency prevented him from coming back to court. If a defendant repeatedly misses his court date, I should consider remanding him into custody and setting bail because I lack any assurance that the defendant will follow the court's orders. But is justice served if I remand an unreliable defendant facing a low-level charge such as shoplifting? Or is justice better served if I allow that defendant to remain out of custody so he can work to earn money to repay the damage done?

This situation can also arise post-conviction. Usually when someone is sentenced to probation, there are certain conditions that must be fulfilled during the probationary period such as counseling or community labor. If the defendant willfully fails to abide by these conditions during the probationary period, I can impose jail time as punishment for the violation.

When I was a defense attorney, I spent a lot of time each day trying to persuade judges not to incarcerate my clients even though they repeatedly failed do what the court had ordered. My clients, like all of us, had other obligations such as work, school, children, or caring for a sick relative. Many of them had unstable housing situations or were homeless. Most of my clients had suffered trauma in their lives or were addicted to drugs or alcohol. Transportation was also a huge issue. Many of my clients did not have cars or reliable transportation, making it difficult to get to court and to the weekly classes ordered as a part of their probation. Sometimes, clients simply lacked funds to pay for the classes. Even with a fee waiver, domestic violence classes tend to cost about $25 per session, which quickly adds up when a defendant must attend class once a week for fifty-two weeks.

As a defense attorney, I warned my clients that if they had missed court or had been terminated from a counseling program, they should immediately go to court. And when they did this, I would beg the court for a second (or third, or fourth, or fifth) chance for my client. I argued that his decision to come to court on his own, even knowing that he could be remanded, showed responsibility on his part and a willingness to comply with the court's order. Essentially, if he walked into the court on his own, he should be given the chance to walk out of court. Most of the time, the judges I appeared in front of agreed to let misdemeanor probationers stay out of custody when they came to court on their own to allow them to continue with their counseling programs or perform the community labor. I do the same now that I am a judge. My primary desire is to see that the misdemeanor probationers learn from their conviction and have an opportunity to benefit from treatment and counseling in the hopes that this will prevent future criminal conduct.

There were so many times as a public defender when I would sit in the lunchroom with my colleagues and lament that a judge who was a former defense attorney would be tougher on my clients than judges who had been prosecutors or who came from a civil background. So, when I became a judge, I did not want my experiences as a public defender to jade me or cause me to be short-tempered with a defendant because I had already heard the same excuses over fourteen years as an attorney. At the same time, if a defendant repeatedly misses court or makes no progress in his counseling programs, I should consider imposing jail time.

During my first year on the bench, I had to order several people to be remanded into custody. It still unsettles me to do it because of my background and because of my work as a defense attorney. I knew from a young age that I wanted to be an attorney. My parents came to the United States from South Korea in the early 1970s and I was born here in the United States. Like many children of immigrants, I grew up making phone calls and being the voice for my parents, who felt that their English was not good enough to speak to strangers about business matters. Starting at a young age, I had to be my parents' advocate, so becoming a lawyer seemed like a good fit for me. From my childhood viewpoint, I thought there could be no job better than one that paid me to argue.

By the time I was in college, I had narrowed my interest in law down to civil rights or criminal defense because I liked fighting for the underdog. I am not a sports fan, but when I watch sports events with friends, I ask who is expected to lose the game and I cheer for that team. Also, I felt obligated to work in underserved communities. My parents came to this country with nothing but dreams and ambitions. They have done very well, but because they did not come from wealthy backgrounds, they never had the luxury to choose to do something other than look for jobs that would be financially rewarding. I benefited from their hard work and could go to college and law school. I had the opportunity to choose to do something I felt passionate about even though working at a law firm would have been far more lucrative than being a public defender.

I chose to be a public defender rather than a civil rights attorney for several reasons. In college, I volunteered at nonprofit organizations focusing on civil rights. While I enjoyed the work, it felt very slow paced, and the attorneys rarely went to trial. As a public defender, I would always have a steady stream of work and trials. I was drawn to the high-stress, think-on-your-feet approach public defenders must undertake. I loved being able to stand in front of a jury and argue with passion and conviction that my clients were not guilty. And I liked working one-on-one with the clients as opposed to representing large groups of people in the class-action lawsuits that tend to dominate a civil rights practice.

I had spent my whole professional life fighting to keep clients OUT of jail. Now, as a new judge, I had to face the reality that I had become the person who orders that they go INTO custody. I felt as if all my core values, principles, and beliefs—the very essence of who I was as a person—were sucked out of me the first few times I said to the bailiff, "He is remanded" and I heard the "click, click, click" of the handcuffs being put on the defendant. I do not doubt the correctness of my decision to incarcerate those defendants, but I was unnerved when I had to order it.

The first time I ordered a defendant into custody, I had to take a recess immediately afterwards to collect myself. My strong reaction caused me to question my decision to be a judge. Although those words, "He is remanded" will never flow effortlessly from my mouth, it does not shake me up as much as it did the first time. I have learned to keep extensive notes about the warnings and opportunities I have given the defendant so that I can justify to myself, and to the defendant, my reasons for ordering someone into custody. In these instances, I remind myself of the reasons I wanted to become a judge, and I stay focused on the fact that my role is now to serve justice as a whole, not just one client.

Learning the Law Again

As a defense attorney, I was familiar with criminal law and routinely made motions on behalf of my clients, both pretrial and during trial. In making these motions as a public defender, I conducted my legal research and argued my motions with the goal of winning that motion. If a legal precedent did not support my position, I did not read it as carefully as I did the cases that helped bolster my argument. As a judge, however, I cannot be result-oriented. I must approach each legal motion with an open mind that was not required of me as a public defender. Even case law that I was very familiar with must be reread with new eyes and an open mind.

During my first year as a judge, this caused many sleepless nights prior to a hearing. I would lie in bed and try to anticipate what evidence might be brought out during the hearing and the possible arguments attorneys might make. I would walk through possible scenarios in my mind: "If the witness says this, then I will rule this way." Or, "if the attorney cites this case, I will ask her about this other case that has a different holding." I felt the way a chess player must feel before a tournament, trying to anticipate all the possible moves the opponent might make. After tossing and turning and trying to quiet my brain, I would fall asleep but still dream about different scenarios that could occur during the hearing.

As an attorney, this would happen to me when I was in trial and trying to anticipate what a prosecutor might argue. Yet the mental gymnastics I perform as a judge are more difficult, because I must do this in a vacuum. Judges are not provided with police reports or witness statements. Usually, the only information we have prior to a motion or a trial is a brief oral summary of the facts. This restriction is so that my decision is based on the evidence presented during the motion rather than on extraneous or inadmissable things contained in police reports.

In contrast, when I was an attorney, I was given the police reports and knew what the witnesses might say on the stand because legal and ethical rules require the prosecutor to turn over witness statements of anyone the prosecution believes will be called as its witness. Based on the discovery provided by the prosecution and my own investigation, I would rarely be surprised by witness testimony during a motion or trial as an attorney. However, as a judge, I do not know beforehand what facts might come out, so I cannot prepare in advance. Instead, I have to make rulings on the spot. This lack of control and inability to fully prepare before the motion forces me to have even more sleepless nights than when I was an attorney.

Serving as the One and Only Juror

As a judge, I am sometimes asked to act as sole juror in a bench trial and decide which side wins. I have done this in both civil and criminal cases. The courthouse I work in is small and very busy, so I sometimes have had to handle small-claims cases (civil disputes where the amount sought by the plaintiff is less than $10,000). Common causes of action in small-claims cases are contract disputes, property damage, and disputes between landlords and tenants about security deposits or repairs. Litigants in a small-claims case do not have the right to have a jury trial, so those cases are always decided by a bench officer. In criminal cases, a defendant has a right to have a jury decide guilt or innocence in all misdemeanor and felony cases.

But sometimes, although not very often, both the prosecutor and the defendant will agree that a judge, rather than a jury, can decide the defendant's guilt.

Prior to becoming a judge, I had served as a juror in a civil case, so I had believed that presiding over a bench trial would be similar to that experience. The trial on which I served as a juror lasted seven weeks. While the trial was pending, I could not discuss the testimony or the evidence with the other jurors. When we did begin to deliberate and go over hundreds of exhibits that were admitted during the seven weeks of testimony, it was quite a shock to me. The twelve of us had listened to the same testimony and looked at the same exhibits, but we all had different views on what the evidence proved or did not prove. We also diverged on our views about the right outcome. I felt that the process of discussing and debating with the other jurors was essential in weeding through all the evidence to come to the right verdict.

I have handled a handful of small-claims cases and criminal bench trials during my first year and found them to be tough cases because, unlike my experience as a juror on that civil case, I have no one to discuss the case with. Judging at the trial court level is not a collaborative decision-making process. When there is a jury trial, I instruct the jury, "You must decide what the facts are. It is up to all of you, and you alone." As the sole juror in a bench trial, I still must follow the same instructions the jury would, so I cannot go to my colleagues and ask them how they would rule and base my decision on their input.

In rendering a verdict in these situations, I sit alone in my chambers, look over my notes, and try to decide if the plaintiff in a small-claims case or the prosecution in a criminal case has met their burden of proof. What if I miss a piece of evidence? Knowing that people can see the same piece of evidence differently, I worry that my prior work as a public defender causes me to view a piece of evidence or witness testimony differently than someone else might.

I found the small-claims trials to be easier to decide than the criminal cases because civil cases have a lower burden of proof. The plaintiff in a civil case has the burden of proof to prove their case "by a preponderance of the evidence." If the plaintiff can provide slightly more evidence than the defendant, then the plaintiff wins.

By contrast, the criminal standard requires the prosecution to present "proof beyond a reasonable doubt," defined by the criminal jury instruction as "proof that leaves you with an abiding conviction that the charge is true." So even if I believe that maybe the defendant did the crime or probably he did it, I still cannot find him guilty because "maybe" or "probably" is not a firm conviction that the prosecution has proven its case.

The First Year of Tough Cases

Facing the daily decisions of judging and the internal conflicts they raise within me made for tough cases, hard days in court, and long nights of soul-searching, especially during my first year. I feel that I suffered "decisional fatigue" in my first year on this job. My brain throbbed at the end of the day. I went home and did not want to make another single decision. I avoided restaurants with large menus because I felt overwhelmed by the number of choices. I made my family and friends choose what we did on weekends because I refused to make any decisions outside of work.

Now in my second year on the bench, I look back on my first year and wonder why I agonized so much over some of the legal and factual rulings I made. It is like the first few times I made lunch for my daughter to take to school. She has a bento-style lunch box with five compartments, which is the bane of my existence. Five compartments. That is five decisions that I must make at night when I am already tapped out from a long day at work making decision after decision. The first few times I packed her lunch, it took hours (no kidding, hours) for me to decide what to put in each of the five compartments. Does it contain a variety of foods from each of the different food groups? Do I have a good balance of salty and sweet? What about a balance of protein and carbs? Is this going to be enough food?

Now, having done it over and over, I can usually pack her a lunch in about fifteen minutes. This is not because I care less about what she eats, but because the process is more instinctual. I have learned from my mistakes of what works and does not work, and it is the same with the decisions I face as a judge. I still have my moments when I wish I could punt the decision to another judge, but experience has given me confidence in the rulings I make.

7

United States v. I. Lewis "Scooter" Libby

JUDGE REGGIE B. WALTON

 *Judge Reggie B. Walton has been a U.S. District Judge for the District of Columbia since 2001. He previously served on the Superior Court of the District of Columbia for eighteen years. He also served as President George H. W. Bush's Associate Director of the Office of National Drug Control Policy and Senior White House Advisor for Crime, an Assistant U.S. Attorney for the District of Columbia, and a staff attorney in the Defender Association of Philadelphia.*

A VARIETY OF FACTORS CAN MAKE A CRIMINAL CASE HARD FROM A judge's perspective. A case can be challenging merely because of the nature of its underlying facts. For example, if the facts have political implications, the country's politically polarized citizenry will inevitably subject any decision made in the case to partisan disagreement and criticism. The notoriety of the accused can also make an otherwise routine case difficult. So too can the lawyers involved in the case. The nature and magnitude of the alleged criminal conduct are also relevant factors. A case can also be difficult due to the evidentiary rulings that must be rendered both prior to and during the trial.

And finally, in the event of a conviction, determining what sentence to impose can confound even the most experienced jurist. When all of these factors are present in a single case, characterizing a case as hard does not adequately describe how taxing the case can be. And this was the reality that confronted me in presiding over the case of *United States v. I. Lewis "Scooter" Libby.*

Libby simultaneously served as Assistant to President George W. Bush and Chief of Staff and Assistant for National Security Affairs to Vice President Dick Cheney. Although Libby was not charged with committing an offense directly related to the politically charged events that formed the factual backdrop of the case, those events would be ever present during the trial, presenting challenges far greater than I had ever experienced during my more than thirty-year tenure as a judge.

The underlying events began with a sixteen-word statement uttered by President Bush during his 2003 State of the Union address and the United States' subsequent invasion of Iraq. In that address, President Bush stated: "The British government has learned that Saddam Hussein [the President of Iraq at the time] recently sought significant quantities of uranium from Africa." Less than two months later, on March 19, 2003, the U.S. military launched an attack against Saddam Hussein and the Iraqi government based on the premise that Iraq possessed weapons of mass destruction.

Following the invasion, on May 6, 2003, Nicholas Kristof published an op-ed in the *New York Times* entitled "Missing in Action: Truth," which for the first time made public a February 2002 trip to the African country of Niger by an unnamed former American ambassador, initially rumored to be at the behest of the Office of the Vice President, to investigate allegations that Iraq had sought to purchase uranium from Niger. The op-ed asserted that in early 2002, after returning from Niger, the ambassador had reported to the Central Intelligence Agency and the State Department that the allegations were false and based on forged documents. The article therefore called into question the veracity of President Bush's State of the Union statement; former Secretary of State Colin Powell's subsequent claim in a presentation to the United Nations, citing classified intelligence, that Iraq possessed weapons of mass destruction; and the validity of the Bush administration's stated reason for the military invasion of Iraq.

The ambassador referenced in Kristof's op-ed was former Ambassador Joseph Charles "Joe" Wilson, whose wife was Valerie Plame Wilson. Valerie Wilson was an employee of the CIA, and her status as a CIA employee was classified. In the months following the Kristof column, Valerie Wilson's employment with the CIA appeared in articles and news reports. The criminal charges brought against Libby arose out of the investigation to find the person who leaked to several members of the press that Valerie Wilson was employed by the CIA.

During the trial, the government presented testimony that on July 8, 2003, Libby met with Judith Miller, a *New York Times* reporter at the time, and, according to Miller, after asking her to identify him as a "former Hill staffer," Libby told Miller about Valerie Wilson's CIA employment status. Then, on July 10 or 11, Karl Rove, Senior Advisor and Assistant to the President, told Libby that Rove had told columnist Robert Novak that Valerie Wilson was a CIA employee, and that Novak would be writing a story about her. Also on July 10 or 11, Libby spoke to NBC Bureau Chief Tim Russert, who was also the host of the network's *Meet the Press* Sunday morning program, to complain about coverage of the Office of the Vice President on *Hardball with Chris Matthews* on MSNBC. According to Russert, neither he nor Libby mentioned Valerie Wilson. On July 12, according to testimony from *Time* magazine reporter Matthew Cooper, Libby told Cooper that Libby "had heard" Valerie Wilson was involved in sending Ambassador Wilson to Niger and also mentioned that Valerie Wilson worked for the CIA. On July 14, Novak published a syndicated column disclosing that Valerie Wilson was a CIA employee and that he had been told by two senior Bush administration officials that Valerie Wilson had suggested sending her husband, Ambassador Wilson, to Niger.

Near the end of July of 2003, the CIA made a criminal referral to the U.S. Department of Justice regarding the disclosure of Valerie Wilson's CIA employment status, and in the fall of that year, the Federal Bureau of Investigation initiated an investigation. Because Rove was a subject of the investigation, Attorney General John Ashcroft recused himself from any further involvement with the investigation, and his deputy, James Comey, selected Patrick Fitzgerald, the U.S. Attorney for the Northern District of Illinois, to investigate the referral as a special prosecutor.

Libby had already been interviewed on two occasions by the FBI before Fitzgerald was appointed special prosecutor. During both interviews, Libby told FBI agents that he learned about Valerie Wilson's CIA employment status from Russert during their conversation on July 10 or 11, 2003. Libby also told the agents that he "did not recall" Vice President Cheney informing him that Ambassador Wilson's wife worked for the CIA prior to his conversation with Russert, and therefore he was surprised to hear from Russert about her status with the CIA.

In January of 2004, Special Prosecutor Fitzgerald convened a grand jury in my court, the U.S. District Court for the District of Columbia, which started hearing testimony and issuing subpoenas for documents. Libby presented testimony to the grand jury on March 5 and 24, 2004. Consistent with what he had earlier told the FBI agents, Libby told the grand jury that when he spoke to Russert on July 10 or 11, 2003, Russert told him that Ambassador Wilson's wife worked for the CIA. Libby also told the grand jury that, during this conversation with Russert, he had completely forgotten that about a month earlier, Vice President Cheney had told him that Valerie Wilson was a CIA employee, or that anyone else had told him about Ambassador Wilson's wife's employment status.

As a result of Libby's statements to the FBI agents and his testimony before the grand jury, on October 28, 2005, Libby was charged in a five-count indictment with one count of obstruction of justice, two counts of making false statements to the FBI, and two counts of perjury. It would be more than two years before the trial would commence, and considerable time and energy would be expended by my two law clerks, judicial interns, and me addressing complex discovery disputes, resolving difficult pretrial motions, coordinating with court staff and the media regarding access to the trial by the public and the press, and working with the U.S. Marshals Service regarding courthouse security.

Upon randomly being assigned the case, I immediately realized that a major challenge would be ensuring that Libby would ultimately be judged by twelve impartial jurors untainted by attitudes about President Bush, Vice President Cheney, our country's military invasion of Iraq, and the events that occurred in Iraq following the invasion. Those concerns were heightened when I learned that the special prosecutor had conducted a widely covered news conference to announce the return of the indictment, during which he extensively outlined the evidence presented to the grand jury in support of all five counts of the indictment. As a former federal prosecutor myself, who held that position at a time when making pretrial statements to the media was strictly prohibited, I have an aversion to prosecutors engaging in such conduct due to the risk of tainting the potential jury pool. And obviously, that potential is enhanced when the case is a high-profile matter that will generate a great amount of media coverage.

I did not immediately intervene, anticipating that Libby's attorneys would make their own statements to the media on the courthouse steps right after Libby's first appearance in court, which is precisely how events played out. Although I did not endorse the defense's tactics any more than those of the special prosecutor, I concluded that I had to afford the defense the opportunity to level the playing field. Once both sides had taken their shot at trying to shape public opinion, I immediately admonished the attorneys that I would not tolerate any further pretrial statements to the media, and to their credit, they complied.

My understanding of the approach Libby's attorneys intended to pursue in defending Libby against the charges was informed by two pretrial motions filed by the defense. One was a motion to present the testimony of a memory expert, and the second a motion to introduce classified documents to show the number and complexity of the matters over which Libby was responsible for providing advice to the President and Vice President. Taken together, the motions seemed designed to lay the foundation for a defense that any false statements Libby made to both the FBI and the grand jury were the mistaken result of mental overload and were not made with the intent to deceive.

The challenge presented by the motion to introduce the memory expert was, on the one hand, providing Libby with the ability to support his position that a faulty memory was the explanation for his clearly false statements and testimony, while on the other hand, avoiding improperly permitting a purported expert to opine on a subject that a layperson could presumably appreciate without an expert's assistance. It is a fundamental principle of the law of evidence that the introduction of expert testimony is proper only if the subject of the testimony is beyond the ability of a layperson to understand. As the government argued, the jurors could, based on their own life experiences, assess the accuracy and frailty of memory, and therefore expert testimony on the subject was unnecessary. Libby's lawyers countered that many people have a misunderstanding about the capacity of human memory, and that expert testimony on the subject would be essential for the jurors to appreciate that a person with Libby's job-related responsibilities could innocently misstate or not remember a fact that most people with fewer or less weighty responsibilities would not forget.

After agonizing over how I should rule, I sided with the government and disallowed the expert testimony. In hindsight and considering recent scientific insight on the subject, I am not sure I would now reach the same conclusion. However, I do not believe the admission of the expert testimony would have impacted the outcome of the case. In any event, the expert testimony would have been admitted only as support for Libby's faulty memory theory, and the jury would have heard the expert's testimony only if Libby had decided to testify. As it turned out, Libby exercised his constitutional right not to testify, and there is no reason to believe that Libby's decision not to testify would have been different if his memory expert's testimony had been permitted.

The second motion implicated a federal statute entitled the Classified Information Procedures Act (CIPA). This statute was enacted in 1980 to address situations where criminal defendants desired to present classified information as part of their defense, which, before the statute's enactment, created a dilemma for the government—either allow disclosure of the classified information or dismiss the case. The statute protects unnecessary disclosure of classified information by requiring trial judges to balance the government's legitimate interest in concealing classified information with defendants' right to present relevant evidence in support of their defense. Resolution of this motion required a tedious balancing of these competing interests, which entailed the evaluation of hundreds of classified documents. This necessary, but extremely time-consuming and thought-provoking process, consumed several months and resulted in the issuance of six opinions (in addition to six opinions on non-CIPA-related motions). The end result was that the government prevailed on some of its positions, while the defense prevailed on others, which I concluded would give Libby the ability to show the jury that he had a very demanding job, both in volume and complexity, from which he could try to convince the jury that his misstatements were the result of mental overload, not malicious intent.

Having concluded the pretrial process, the next challenge was empaneling a jury that could give Libby a fair trial, which, for the reasons stated earlier, I knew would not be an easy task. Although I believed seating a fair and impartial jury was achievable, I realized that it would be a considerably time-consuming endeavor. In conjunction with the process of selecting the jury, I also had to develop a strategy for addressing the more than one hundred media requests for access to the proceedings, which up to that point had not been a concern because most of the proceedings had been conducted in private due to the need to protect against disclosure of classified information.

For guidance in dealing with the media in a case with comparable public interest, I contacted the judge who had presided over the Oklahoma City bombing case. His insight was tremendously helpful. With the help of my Chief Judge's administrative assistant, we convened a meeting with representatives from the electronic (television and radio) and print (newspaper and magazine) media. We insisted that they designate one electronic and one print representative from among their ranks who would bring issues and concerns to our attention so that we would have to deal with only two individuals. This requirement proved invaluable, as it saved us a considerable amount of time.

Because we obviously could not accommodate the in-court presence of all media representatives who desired to attend the proceedings and also make space available for the general public, we decided to have a second courtroom wired for closed-circuit coverage of the proceedings. However, a more profound and successful aspect of this initiative was the permanent conversion of a small courtroom on the first floor of the courthouse into a media room that was wired with several closed-circuit feeds and could accommodate approximately seventy media representatives. The benefit of this arrangement was that it became the preferred location for media representatives and gave them the ability to have immediate telephone access to their newsrooms. The willingness of the media to agree to the presence of only one print and electronic media representative in the courtroom during the individual questioning of the potential jurors, so as not to intimidate the jurors being asked to reveal sensitive and possibly embarrassing information about themselves, was also facilitated by the ability to view the questioning from the media room.

Because the District of Columbia is a Democratic, liberal-leaning jurisdiction, as indicated earlier, I knew that selecting jurors who would give Libby a fair trial would be a considerable challenge. President Bush and Vice President Cheney were unpopular in this District, and the Iraq war was opposed by a large segment of the American citizenry, and by a large majority in the District of Columbia. Accordingly, I had to employ a process to expose potential biases that could undermine the jurors' ability to reach a verdict based solely on the quality and weight of the evidence. That would necessarily require a wide-ranging, and what some potential jurors might consider intrusive, probe of the potential jurors designed to expose any perspectives that could impair the jurors' impartial consideration of the evidence.

I am not a proponent of written juror questionnaires because I believe that their use disadvantages individuals with minimal formal education. Therefore, I used a questionnaire that consisted of only one question regarding availability and submitted it to the potential jurors before they were actually summoned to the courtroom, to eliminate those who would be unavailable to participate in a trial projected to take up to two months to complete. Otherwise, with input from the attorneys, I crafted a multiple-question questionnaire that was read out loud to the potential jurors. Thereafter, the lawyers on each side and I questioned each potential juror in the courtroom outside the presence of the other potential jurors. The process was time-consuming, taking four and a half days to empanel the jury, but the effort was well worth the time dedicated because I am confident that the jurors selected not only had the capacity to be objective, but in fact were objective throughout the trial and rendered a verdict consistent with the evidence presented to them.

Having selected the jury, the next objective was to ensure that it would render a fair verdict, not influenced by anything other than the evidence. Therefore, the jury had to be protected from the media coverage of the trial and the circus atmosphere that engulfed the courthouse and its perimeter. Once the jury selection process commenced, the courthouse and the surrounding area were inundated with reporters, camera crew members, bloggers, and interested members of the general public. The situation, as anticipated, required the mobilization of court staff and the U.S. Marshals Service, in light of my decision not to totally sequester the jury.

Sometimes jurors in high-profile trials are totally sequestered, meaning that they are kept together, guarded at all times, sleeping and eating in court-approved facilities away from friends, family, and the general public. Because of the obvious burden on sequestered jurors, I ordered what is considered partial sequestration, whereby the jurors were met by deputy U.S. marshals at a designated location and driven to the courthouse basement parking garage. Throughout the day, they remained in a jury deliberation room that was equipped with a microwave oven and refrigerator and were provided breakfast and lunch throughout the trial. The jurors were also provided with several different newspapers that were screened by judicial interns so that articles about the case or related matters, such as the Iraq war, were removed before they were delivered to the jurors. At the end of the day, the Marshals Service transported the jurors to a common location for their return to their homes.

The challenge of presiding over the actual trial in this case was enhanced by the extraordinary quality of the lawyers representing both the government and Libby. The trial in this case was as well conducted by the lawyers as any trial I have witnessed during my more than forty-year legal career, and now more than thirty-four years as a trial judge. All of the lawyers' performances were outstanding, but the skills of special prosecutors Patrick Fitzgerald and Peter Zeidenberg, and defense counsel Ted Wells and Bill Jeffress, were nothing short of exemplary. While such high-level advocacy is always appreciated by a trial judge, it also enhances the stress level of the judge, knowing that every contested ruling will be scrutinized and challenged by whichever party feels disadvantaged, and sometimes by both parties. Moreover, if there were to be a conviction, Libby could be expected to appeal based on rulings that went against him at trial, and the last thing a trial judge wants is to try a two-month case to verdict only to be told by the appellate court that because of an erroneous ruling, the case has to be tried all over again.

The dispute between the parties centered on whether Libby's statements to the FBI and the grand jury regarding his conversations with two reporters, Tim Russert and Matthew Cooper, were false. The government called Matthew Cooper and Judith Miller as witnesses to establish that Libby had in fact told them about Valerie Wilson's employment status with the CIA. Miller had been held in contempt of court for refusing to comply with a grand jury subpoena when she declined to reveal who had told her that Valerie Wilson was a CIA employee. After being jailed for eighty-five days, Miller relented and agreed to testify before the grand jury and eventually to the trial jury that Libby was her source of the information about Valerie Wilson. The government also called Tim Russert, who, as noted earlier, was at that time the host of NBC's *Meet the Press*, as a witness. He testified that, contrary to what Libby had told the FBI and the grand jury, he did not tell Libby that "all reporters knew" that Valerie Wilson worked for the CIA.

I thought Russert's testimony about his conversation with Libby, during which he testified that neither party mentioned Valerie Wilson, was the most damaging evidence against Libby. I reach this conclusion because I believe it was difficult to convince the jury that Libby's memory was good enough for him to clearly remember that, contrary to Russert's testimony, it was Russert who told him that Ambassador Wilson's wife worked for the CIA, yet Libby was purportedly unable to recall that several members of the Bush administration had told him that Valerie Wilson was a CIA employee whose status was classified. Moreover, Russert came across as extremely credible, and his credibility was not diminished through cross-examination.

The government also presented the testimony of White House staff, State Department personnel, and CIA employees to establish that Libby had asked them if they knew (1) about Ambassador Wilson's trip to Niger, (2) who was responsible for sending him on the trip, and (3) if Valerie Wilson played any role in the decision to send Ambassador Wilson to Niger.

The government's theory was that Libby disclosed Valerie Wilson's CIA employment status to retaliate against Ambassador Wilson for calling into question President Bush's statement in his 2003 State of the Union address that Saddam Hussein may have acquired uranium from Niger, which was the ostensible predicate for going to war against Iraq. The government also submitted evidence suggesting that Vice President Cheney and Libby were troubled by the possibility that Valerie Wilson was responsible for her husband's trip to Niger, and by the suggestion that the trip had been taken at the request of the Office of the Vice President.

The defense attorneys aggressively cross-examined the government witnesses in their attempt to raise questions about their credibility. Primarily, the cross-examinations sought to show that several months had elapsed between their conversations with Libby and when they were asked to recount their recollections of those conversations, with the objective of raising questions about the accuracy of their memories about who said what. The defense also sought to show that White House officials were trying to make Libby the fall guy in order to protect Karl Rove, who was considered a more valuable asset to President Bush and his political operations. Rove, in addition to several other Bush administration officials, had admitted to telling reporters about Valerie Wilson's affiliation with the CIA, so the defense sought to show that Libby was being falsely sacrificed to protect Rove. The defense also called as witnesses several prominent reporters (Walter Pincus, Bob Woodward, David Sanger, Robert Novak, and Glenn Kessler) with whom Libby also had discussions concerning Ambassador Wilson's trip to Niger, and who testified that during those discussions, Libby never said anything about the Ambassador's wife, with the obvious objective of suggesting to the jury that the reporters who testified that Libby had told them about Valerie Wilson's status with the CIA should not be believed because Libby never mentioned her when he discussed the Ambassador's Niger trip with a number of other reporters.

At bottom, the defense's position was that the government had failed to satisfy its burden of proving beyond a reasonable doubt that Libby intended to or did obstruct justice, intentionally made false statements to the FBI, or intentionally provided false testimony to the grand jury. Rather, the defense's position was that Libby told the FBI and the grand jury his honest recollections at the time, and that to the extent any of those recollections were incorrect, his mistakes were innocent. Libby's attorneys sought to bolster their position about his mental state when he made the relevant statements by establishing that he had no notes of the conversations about which he was questioned, and therefore, he was unable to refresh his recollection or review the notes of other people or discuss with them their recollection of the events. Further, Libby's defense team suggested that the amount and scope of vital national security issues and information confronting Libby on a daily basis during the times he had the conversations he was asked to remember affected his memory of any brief conversations about the employment of Valerie Wilson when he talked to the FBI and when he testified before the grand jury. As noted earlier, the defense completed its case with Libby exercising his right not to testify. Although the jury never heard from Libby's "memory expert," I am confident that there was enough evidence for the jury to assess the credibility of the defense's claim that Libby had simply forgotten having leaked Valerie Wilson's CIA affiliation to reporters when he told the FBI and the grand jury that he had done no such thing.

Following the parties' closing arguments and my legal instructions, the jury commenced its deliberations on February 21, 2007. Unfortunately, the jury's deliberations were disrupted by an all-too-often occurrence in today's world of the internet and social media. Knowing the level of media coverage the case would generate, throughout the trial I constantly told the jurors that they could not let themselves come into contact with media coverage about the case, and specifically instructed them not to conduct their own independent research about the case, including computer research. Despite those repeated admonitions, one of the jurors disclosed to another juror that, because she felt she was not as informed about the facts of the case as compared to the other jurors, she had conducted a computer search about the case to better inform herself. Fortunately, the juror to whom the transgression was relayed reported the transgression and told the offending juror not to tell any of the other jurors what she had done. Upon the jurors' arrival at the courthouse, I was told what the offending juror had done. After I confirmed that the transgression had occurred and that the offending juror had to be excused, the parties agreed that the jury could continue their deliberations with only eleven jurors, which the law permits.

The jury ultimately rejected Libby's faulty memory defense and returned its verdict on March 6, 2007, finding Libby guilty of one count of obstruction of justice, two counts of perjury, and one count of making a false statement to the FBI regarding his conversation with Tim Russert. The jury found Libby not guilty on the remaining count of making a false statement to the FBI regarding his conversation with Matthew Cooper, which was understandable because defense counsel's cross-examination of Cooper raised serious questions about what Libby actually said to Cooper.

Based upon the legal standard for determining whether a person convicted of a crime who is subject to a sentence of incarceration should be released on his personal recognizance prior to sentencing, I concluded that Libby had demonstrated that he did not pose a danger to the community or a risk of flight, and I released him pending his sentencing. Prior to the sentencing date, I received more than 190 letters either in support of Libby being accorded leniency and not being given any prison time, or asking that a lengthy prison sentence be imposed. Most were in support of leniency and came from individuals whose names were unfamiliar, but others were from dignitaries like former Secretary of State Henry Kissinger, former Secretary of Defense Donald Rumsfeld, former Ambassador to the United Nations John Bolton, and former Deputy Secretary of Defense Paul Wolfowitz. The defense petitioned me not to release the letters to the public, which the media opposed, citing the First Amendment. The defense argued that releasing the letters favorable to Libby would subject the authors to criticism and discourage individuals from submitting sentencing letters to judges. While the position raised legitimate concerns, I concluded that the need for the court to be transparent compelled disclosure so that the public would know the information I considered when imposing Libby's sentence.

Sentencing is one of the most difficult obligations that comes with being a judge. The enormity of the task is enhanced in a high-profile case involving a convicted person with connections to the highest political offices in the nation—the President and Vice President of the United States. At sentencing, the courtroom and the other locations in the courthouse with closed-circuit feeds were packed with family and friends of Libby, interested citizens, and members of the media. As expected, the atmosphere in the courtroom was intense, as the government and the defendant passionately argued for or against the imposition of a prison sentence. It was only at the completion of those presentations when I came to the conclusion regarding what sentence to impose.

Considering the evidence I heard during the trial, the information in the presentence investigation report, the letters submitted in support of and in opposition to leniency, the U.S. Sentencing Guidelines (which had been declared merely advisory and not mandatory by the Supreme Court), and the factors the U.S. Code required be considered when imposing federal sentences, I concluded that a prison sentence at the bottom of the thirty- to thirty-seven month Guidelines range was the appropriate sentence. While Libby had lived a crime-free life prior to the events that brought him before the court, and by all accounts had otherwise provided valuable and outstanding service to the country as a member of the Bush administration, the conduct the trial evidence established that he had engaged in was reprehensible and cried out for punishment. Not only was he convicted for lying to the FBI and lying under oath before a grand jury and therefore obstructing justice; the trial evidence also clearly showed that Libby had disclosed the identity of a CIA employee with indifference to the harm that such a revelation could cause, because he did not know whether Valerie Wilson occupied a covert position as a CIA employee. Also of significance was the fact that the disclosure was seemingly made for the purpose of retaliating against Ambassador Wilson for challenging the Bush administration's stated reasons for invading Iraq. Moreover, Libby was a licensed attorney and, as a member of the legal profession, should have appreciated the corrosive impact that making false statements to law enforcement officials and lying under oath has on the nation's system of justice. Balancing all of these competing factors, I sentenced Libby to serve thirty months in federal prison. I then denied Libby's plea that he be allowed to remain free during the appeal he planned to file challenging his convictions. Threats against me and my family followed the imposition of Libby's sentence.

Shortly after the U.S. Court of Appeals for the District of Columbia Circuit upheld my decision to deny Libby's release pending the appeal of his convictions, but before Libby was scheduled to report to prison to begin serving his sentence, President Bush totally eliminated Libby's prison sentence by commuting it, and he justified his decision by characterizing the prison sentence as too harsh. The irony of the criticism was that the Bush administration had disagreed with the Supreme Court's ruling that the mandatory sentencing guidelines were unconstitutional, and, one month prior to commuting Libby's sentence, President Bush, through Attorney General Alberto Gonzalez, had requested that the bottom prison sentences of the sentencing guidelines, which the Supreme Court had made advisory, be legislatively adopted by Congress as mandatory minimum sentences. Following President Bush's commutation, Libby opted not to pursue an appeal, paid the $250,000 fine I had imposed, and successfully completed the imposed period of community supervision.

Upon being assigned the Libby case, I was told by one of my senior colleagues that I should fulfill the constitutional and statutory obligations imposed on federal judges to the best of my ability, but that I should also appreciate that regardless of how well I performed, there was the distinct possibility that Libby, if convicted, would be pardoned by the President. That advice sustained me throughout the challenging experience of this case. In the end, I believe the judicial system operated as envisioned by the country's founding fathers. The government pursued a matter of legitimate national concern—the leaking of classified information—and vigorously and fairly prosecuted crimes that undermine our law enforcement and judicial processes—lying to law enforcement officials and before judicial tribunals while under oath during the course of a legitimate investigation. Libby was also provided the quality of legal representation demanded by the Constitution. Citizens of the community assumed the awesome burden of serving as jurors and diligently performed that civic obligation as envisioned when the unique system of trial by jury was memorialized in the Constitution. Until recently, I concluded that my senior colleague had been only partially correct about the ultimate outcome of the Libby case, and that a former high-ranking public official supported by some of the most powerful public officials in the nation had been held accountable, at least to some degree, for crimes the evidence clearly showed he had committed. I was wrong.

On April 13, 2018, President Donald Trump fulfilled my colleague's prediction by pardoning Scooter Libby. As a basis for his pardon, President Trump stated that for years he had "heard that [Libby] has been treated unfairly." And the White House followed that statement with the suggestion that reporter Judith Miller's recantation of her trial testimony was proof of Libby's innocence. But in my opinion, both perspectives are simply false.

I believe that investigating who leaked the identity of the classified status of a CIA employee was a legitimate endeavor, and Libby's statements to the FBI and his grand jury testimony properly resulted in charges being lodged against him. He was represented by some of the best criminal defense lawyers in the country, and prosecuted by a team of lawyers who were absolutely fair. Even if Judith Miller's retraction of her sworn testimony is credited, a considerable amount of testimony from other witnesses was presented during the trial that clearly supported the jury's guilty verdicts. Finally, the assault on the jurors by some Libby supporters as a group of liberal partisans who convicted Libby not based on the evidence, but because of his association with the George W. Bush administration, is a spurious affront to the integrity of the citizens of the District of Columbia.

As the events that occurred subsequent to the trial demonstrate, when politics are at play in a case, sometimes the facts and the law ultimately do not matter. That reality and other factors made the trial of *United States v. I. Lewis "Scooter" Libby* a hard case, which is inevitable when high-level political figures are the subject of criminal prosecutions. Nonetheless, I am convinced Libby received a fair trial and his convictions were supported by the evidence.

8

A Quiet Grief

JUDGE LIZBETH GONZÁLEZ

Judge Lizbeth González was appointed to New York City Housing Court, elected to New York City Civil Court, appointed to New York City Family Court, elected to New York State Supreme Court, where she currently serves as a trial judge, and appointed to the Appellate Term, where she concurrently serves as an Associate Justice. She is also a past president of the Latino Judges Association.

I BEGAN MY JUDICIAL CAREER WHEN I WAS APPOINTED TO THE NEW York City Housing Court, where I sat for several years. During one rotation in the trial part, I was greatly troubled to see a tall, powerful-looking tenant walk into my courtroom followed by his son. Mr. Johnson was wild-eyed, and his son Aaron was severely autistic.* Mr. Johnson and the landlords with whom he had a dispute initially appeared before a judge in the resolution part to determine whether a settlement was possible or whether the matter should be dismissed on technical grounds. The case was ultimately sent to me for trial. Out of concern that this special-needs child faced eviction

---

* The names of father and son are fictitious.

if his father lost at trial, I asked for a summary of the facts to see if a settlement was still possible.

It took a lot of effort to deal with the parties. The self-represented father bellowed that he would not pay rent because repairs were outstanding. The managing agent, the building representative, and their lawyer were clearly rattled. The petitioner-landlord was a community housing association trying to do the right thing by its tenant. Although its representatives wanted to settle, Mr. Johnson wanted to vent. As he spoke, Aaron freely roamed the courtroom—not a problem (so long as he was safe) since only the litigants, court staff, and I were in the courtroom. I soon realized that the louder Mr. Johnson talked, the faster the boy moved. When Mr. Johnson became agitated, Aaron became agitated. I urged—then directed—the father to lower his voice since the attachment between them was clear.

Mr. Johnson was belligerent. The petitioner's representatives recounted the numerous times that repairs were attempted but access was denied; they nonetheless requested assistance in devising an access schedule and promised that repairs would be effected. I kept watching Aaron; he was tall and husky and maybe eleven years old.

Although my small trial courtroom was otherwise empty, the atmosphere became extremely tense. Like my court officer and court clerk, I found myself scrutinizing the father's body language and his hands, most especially, watching for any sudden movements.

I had no problem with Aaron until he climbed onto the courtroom benches and began to walk where people customarily sit. I sternly addressed Mr. Johnson and told him to control his son. At his father's command, Aaron stepped onto the floor, pacing back and forth as he randomly vocalized. That's when it clicked. By using his voice, the father could calm Aaron or use him as a distraction; that Mr. Johnson could manipulate his son to cause a commotion in court was also a concern. I called for a brief recess so I could contact the New York City Adult Protective Services (APS) supervisor located in our building, since APS is the Housing Court's best resource when adult litigants have physical or mental limitations that place them at risk. I asked the APS supervisor to arrange an emergency evaluation and a home inspection in conjunction with a caseworker from the Administration for Children's Services (ACS)—the New York City equivalent of Child Protective Services—to ensure that the boy was safe.

My jurisdiction ends at the door of my courtroom. When I reconvened the case perhaps thirty minutes later, the faces of the managing agent and his witness were ghastly—Mr. Johnson had apparently threatened to kill them while they were outside the courtroom. I asked them in the presence of their lawyer if they wished to press charges, but no, the building representatives wanted to make repairs and avoid a trial. I scheduled access dates for repairs and adjourned the case.

On the return date, I received a report that APS and ACS caseworkers had conducted my requested emergency home visit and evaluation—in the company of police—and determined that there was no need to remove Aaron or provide special assistance to his father. Once the parties were back in court, however, the behaviors repeated themselves. I was informed that apartment repairs were incomplete due to the father's interference; judging from his previous outbursts and some of his statements, it seemed clear that Mr. Johnson was the problem. I bluntly told Mr. Johnson that, but for his son, the nonpayment trial would have commenced. Since getting rid of a troublesome tenant is usually the goal of a landlord, I was surprised that eviction wasn't the priority of the community housing association: The building management asked for yet another opportunity to make repairs. I scheduled new access dates. But judges are routinely rotated. I was assigned to a different part and my jurisdiction over Mr. Johnson's nonpayment proceeding ended.

After serving my rotation in the trial part for several months, I was assigned to the housing part to adjudicate housing repair proceedings initiated by tenants. Unlike the trial part, which adjudicates one case at a time, the housing part, which hears matters about building repairs, is a bustling part filled not only with numerous tenants and landlords but also with city lawyers from the New York City Department of Housing Preservation and Development charged with the enforcement of the city's housing code. Imagine my surprise when Mr. Johnson and his son entered my courtroom. Aaron had grown and his dad looked wilder; I saw widespread concern spread in the audience in my busy courtroom as the boy began to vocalize and roam. I spoke with my court officer and told everyone that I would allow Aaron to walk about so long as he retained a semblance of calm.

I now had jurisdiction over the housing part proceeding commenced by Mr. Johnson against the community housing association. Mr. Johnson complained about repairs in his combative and angry way; the building representatives asked for new access dates.

These words are hard for me to write. I still sensed that something was deeply wrong. Judges aren't social workers or law enforcement officers, so I sent for the Adult Protective Services supervisor. I asked him to assemble another emergency inspection team and re-visit Aaron's home. I communicated my concern for Aaron's safety and knew that a thorough investigation would result—the APS supervisor was no slouch. Would my appointment of a guardian ad litem to represent Mr. Johnson have made a difference? Probably not. In New York City, Housing Court judges can appoint guardians at litem for tenants unable to advocate for themselves because of mental illness, infirmity, or age; the appointment of the lay advocate lasts for the duration of the case. But this wasn't Family Court: I had no power to appoint a guardian or an attorney for Aaron. Moreover, this was a housing part case where apartment repairs were at the fore. Here, the petitioner-landlord was cooperative, and Mr. Johnson agreed to be home so work could get started. I ordered the repairs, scheduled access dates and a short adjournment, and waited.

On the return date, I was informed that some of the outstanding repairs were completed. I also received the emergency evaluation report. The two protective services groups had visited the home, accompanied by the police. Mr. Johnson's conduct raised no red flags at home during his emergency evaluation. The agencies concluded that Mr. Johnson did not need assistance, and there were no grounds to remove Aaron from his father's home. I had no reason or authority to overrule the agency professionals: I didn't know the child protective services workers, but I certainly knew the adult protective services supervisor, who described the meticulous care with which he and the investigators conducted their evaluations. Mindful that the stress of the courtroom can bring out the worst in people and not reflect their child-caring ability, I accepted that everyone had done their job.

I conferenced the housing part matter before me, scheduled access for the balance of the apartment repairs, hawkeyed Mr. Johnson, watched Aaron, and waited to see how the case would unfold. I never saw them again.

Several years later, I was elected to the New York City Civil Court. I'm an avid newspaper reader and perused the New York sections early one morning. Then I saw it. I cursed and screamed. Inwardly I fall apart now as I did then. That Thanksgiving Day, I learned that Mr. Johnson had slashed Aaron's throat and left him in the bathtub to die. The paper said that ACS had received a recent allegation of neglect against Mr. Johnson, who had been arrested several times, once for assault. The agency initially sought custody of Aaron in Family Court, but consented to allow Aaron to remain at home and provide supervision instead.

Contrary to public perception, judges don't have limitless power. Would another investigation have changed the course of events? I don't know. Investigators and social workers are bound not only by protocols and legal constraints but also by the circumstances presented at the moment of their evaluations. Could I have done anything more? My heart bleeds. At the end of the day, my jurisdiction was defined by the nonpayment and housing repair proceedings that respectively came before me. Sometimes the consequence of a case transcends the litigation. During the time that I retained jurisdiction over the parties, neither matter was ready for settlement or trial—and my two court-ordered emergency investigations produced no results. I regret that I couldn't save Aaron. Online records show that Mr. Johnson went to jail and was subsequently released—I don't know why—but that won't bring Aaron back.

We judges do our best to ensure that justice is done. We bring opposing parties together and try to settle cases. When that doesn't work, we decide motions, make rulings and adjudicate trials to ensure that everyone has their fair day in court. Rest assured that like litigants and lawyers, we too suffer when things go wrong. I still grieve for Aaron.

9

Can an Elected Judge Overrule Nearly a Million Voters and Survive?

JUDGE ROBERT H. ALSDORF

 *Judge Robert H. Alsdorf is a retired Washington State Superior Court judge and currently a member of the State of Washington's Commission on Judicial Conduct. He served as a publicly elected general jurisdiction trial judge from 1990 to 2005. He has also served six years on the board of the ABA's international Rule of Law Initiative.*

IN 1999, CITIZENS OF THE STATE OF WASHINGTON WERE RUNNING out of patience. Year after year, for more than a decade, they had demanded reduction of a burdensome annual motor vehicle tax. For just as many years, the legislature had turned a deaf ear; the legislature classified the substantial revenues raised by the tax as general state funds available to support numerous popular state programs, not just transportation-related uses. Citizens were angered by the continued lack of constructive legislative response. I didn't much like the tax either. Only a year earlier, I had purchased a used car and found that the law required my tax to be calculated on a base value twice what I had paid for the car.

Washington's citizens weren't powerless to address such a situation. Because of the state's populist heritage, voters have the right to bypass the legislature and propose and adopt laws via a public initiative process. These initiatives can do anything the legislature can do except amend the state Constitution.

Taking matters into their own hands, a group of Washington voters proposed an initiative with two goals. The initiative, known as I-695, first took direct aim at the tax and decreed that all vehicles would henceforth be subject only to a flat annual $30 licensing fee. Second, it forbade any future increase in any tax, fee, or other charge by any governmental entity in the absence of an advance affirmative public vote.

While proponents of the initiative desperately wanted to reduce what for most drivers had long amounted not just to hundreds but even thousands of dollars in taxes over the life of their vehicles, theirs were not the only voices being raised. Opponents were equally firm in their conviction that passing the initiative would lead to a disaster. They argued that reducing the tax to a flat annual $30 fee would have a significant detrimental impact on the funding of state government, and that in the long term the act of subjecting every possible future tax and fee increase to a public vote would further aggravate that damage and be contrary to good public policy.

Feelings ran extremely high on both sides. Nonetheless, when the initiative to limit the motor vehicle tax came before the voters in November 1999, it won by a solid 56/43 margin, with more than 992,000 voting for and 775,000 voting against.

A Constitutional Challenge

Predictably, because of the initiative's anticipated impact, public and private entities and citizens immediately filed a series of lawsuits in late 1999 challenging the initiative's constitutionality. The cases were consolidated and assigned to my court in early 2000.

While complex constitutional litigation, pursued and defended by first-rate counsel, is virtually any judge's vision of a dream case, I immediately had reason to worry. No matter how I ruled, I could easily unleash angry interest groups who could put my judicial career at risk. The voters who hated the motor vehicle tax would be extremely upset if I overruled the initiative, just as the public and private entities and individuals that relied on the programs funded by this tax would be if I upheld the initiative.

The risk was not academic. It was serious. It was acute. I was an elected judge, and Washington's judicial elections are not merely retention elections. They are open elections, held every four years. The year 2000 was an election year. The filing period for my position was mere months after I would be ruling on the initiative. And, under Washington law, any number of lawyers who chose to do so could register to run against me simply by paying a small filing fee.

While both sides in the litigation could cause problems with my re-election efforts, it was obvious that the greatest danger came from the overwhelming number of voters who had really wanted and voted for tax relief. The risk posed by a ruling against them focused my attention admirably.

A senior member of the court suggested privately that if I were to conclude that the initiative violated the Constitution, I could simply have the case transferred to a retiring judge so that none of us would have to run the risk of being punished by the voters for making an unpopular decision. But dodging the case assignment was no more attractive to me than pandering to the wishes of likely vociferous critics. As I mulled how I would maintain personal and legal balance over the coming months, I decided just to put one foot in front of the other, taking each step as needed.

The first step was simple. I set a case management conference with all counsel in early January. I asked counsel to identify the variety of motions they intended to file in the seven consolidated cases, and we reached consensus on a filing deadline of late February. Oral argument would take place shortly thereafter, with my decision on all motions to be issued mid-March. It was understood by all that whatever my ruling turned out to be, it would be appealed directly to the state Supreme Court.

Preserving Objectivity and Neutrality

The briefs and supporting materials immediately began pouring in. They soon covered every available surface in chambers. I spent every spare moment digging into nearly a century of state constitutional litigation, beginning to digest the many issues and concerns that I would soon have to address. I enjoyed this mental exercise, but I could not ignore the darkness looming on the horizon. The longer I researched the topics, the more apparent it became that the initiative's constitutionality was in serious doubt, and if that were to be my final conclusion, I would have to strike it down, thereby putting my career at risk.

Being subject to Washington's quadrennial judicial elections was an occupational hazard we judges all accepted when we took a spot on the bench. But being subject to election can tempt any judge to pander to the public in a high-profile case, particularly in an election year. Fortunately, our general jurisdiction trial court counted among its members some very brilliant and courageous judges. Starting from my first days in court a decade earlier, I had sought out these experienced and occasionally battle-scarred judges to find out how they managed to keep their balance in difficult and highly publicized cases.

Drawing on their wisdom, I learned to transform dread of the next election into a heightened motivation to engage in thoughtful and transparent adjudication. Their approach can be distilled into several principles. The first relates to the essence of the judicial mind-set:

They don't pay me to be right. They pay me to be fair.

When I first heard this statement, not only did it not sound right, it sounded flat-out wrong. Of course, we judges want to be right. And if we aren't right, we should be and will be subject to reversal by a higher court. What I failed to understand when I first heard those words is that they refer not to the *what* of a judicial decision, but the *how*.

A few years before the motor vehicle tax cases were assigned to me, I had stumbled across the perfect illustration of this principle, that justice can more easily be achieved if we focus not on what most people consider to be the right result but instead on resolving underlying issues fairly and letting the end results take care of themselves.

My discovery was most unexpected. The topic of law had not even been on my mind. Taking a lunch break on a rare sunny Seattle day, I wandered into an old Seattle bookstore that had found its start during the Yukon Gold Rush and was closing after nearly a century in business. I happened to look into a small back room, now emptied of all books except one leather-bound volume lying on its side. The number 1 was prominently incised on its spine; the flaking title page identified it:

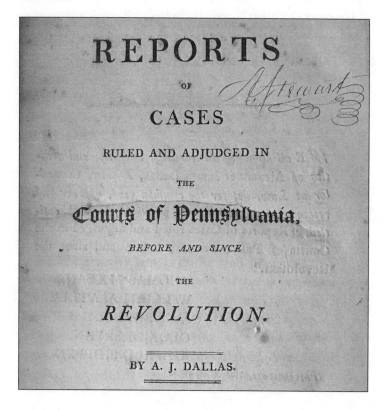

REPORTS
OF
CASES
RULED AND ADJUDGED IN
THE
Courts of Pennsylvania,
BEFORE AND SINCE
THE
REVOLUTION.

BY A. J. DALLAS.

The earliest case was from 1754, the latest was 1789. One decision almost immediately caught my eye, a case entitled *Respublica v. Malin*. It dealt with a charge of High Treason that had been appealed to the Supreme Court of Pennsylvania.

The facts were straightforward. The defendant had mistaken a group of American soldiers for British. He had approached them and explained he wanted to join their fight against the Revolution. He also had been seen a few days earlier mustering and parading with the British in a different county.

For most people in most countries, the "right" result would be to consider such a person a traitor and to kill him on the spot, or at the very least to execute him after a trial. But the Pennsylvania Supreme Court Justices decided otherwise.

The court ruled that because the defendant's simple statement of intent made to American troops had been accompanied by no affirmative action, and could not have succeeded in any event because the troops were American, it could not amount to an overt act of treason. The court also concluded that it could not consider the proffered evidence of the defendant having assembled and marched with British troops in a different county, because potentially treasonous acts taken outside the county of prosecution could not be admitted into evidence without proof first being offered of an affirmative act of treason in the county in which he was being tried. For those reasons, the Pennsylvania Supreme Court decided in September 1778, deep in the American Revolution, to reverse the conviction and acquit the defendant.

The court's fealty in *Respublica v. Malin* to neutral rules rather than to the "right" result, and the justices' adherence instead to process, to a careful consideration of all arguments, represent a fundamental step toward achieving the rule of law. I felt I was in the presence of a small but meaningful bit of American history. I bought the book.

Nobody disputes that the rule of law requires judges to be fair and to be seen to be fair to all, no matter a given party's merit or lack of merit. But as I prepared to shoulder the burden of ruling on this initiative, I had to figure out what this facile statement meant for me in real life. How to do it? How to achieve fairness? How to demonstrate it? Or is fairness simply in the eye of the beholder?

These questions brought to mind the second principle distilled from the judges in my court, one that is a corollary of the first but a bit more practical:

The most important person in the courtroom is the loser.

This principle too seems all wrong on first blush. It is natural to focus on and even give plaudits to prevailing parties. After all, they have won. As judges, we have determined that they were "right." And in a very real sense, speaking from the perspective of the law, we have also decided that the loser deserved to lose.

We have long been taught, first as lawyers and then as judges, that the key to rendering a proper decision is to exclude the irrelevant, the emotional, the human, to come to a conclusion driven solely by legal principle. We naturally proceed to discard whatever is irrelevant, despite the fact that remaining aware of emotion and other ostensibly irrelevant dynamics can actually promote justice. Turning to this second statement of guiding principle served to remind me that accurately identifying the winner is not, by itself, sufficient to constitute justice. The strength of a legal system is better gauged by the attention we pay to the losing party and by the respect for judicial process that such attention may engender.

Following that principle, whenever I have found myself beginning to reach a conclusion in a case, I step back and try to focus on what the party who then seems likely to lose considers to be the heart of its case. While on more than one occasion this process has revealed to me that I had actually overlooked a key issue and prematurely leapt to judgment, what is more important for these purposes is that actually and openly dealing with what a losing party believes to be its strongest points can help us make our rulings less unpalatable.

When I have reached my final ruling, I try to explicitly note for the losing party how laudable or understandable its motivation or key legal argument is, and then give a straightforward explanation of why that factor nonetheless cannot be used by the court to justify a ruling in its favor. Moreover, I attempt to do that early in my oral or written decisions so that before a party and its counsel learn that they have lost and, as often as not, immediately close their minds to any further details in the opinion, they would know that I had indeed heard and seriously considered what they had to say.

Of course, I do not always praise the losing side. There are times when a party is dishonest or unreasonably litigious or for other reasons deserves to be hammered rather than praised. But more often than not both sides are operating with at least a modicum of good faith. We can acknowledge this reality without losing any judicial power.

An Additional Hurdle

Given the importance of these complex cases to the entire state, our court leadership lightened my calendar and allowed me additional time to engage in what was a truly pleasurable duty of research and analysis. With that gift, and keeping in mind the first two principles I have described, I happily began to absorb details of the many different doctrines and challenges raised by the parties in their consolidated constitutional challenges.

I was then engaged in doing what I loved about being a judge, hearing directly from the parties and their advocates, and learning something new every day. But one day, in the midst of some abstract reverie on an obscure point of law I no longer recall, I realized with a start that I had a potential problem. I had overlooked another law rooted in our state's populist heritage: not only do our citizens have the right to propose laws by initiative, to reject laws by referendum, and to vote judges in or out of office; they can also remove a judge from a given case even after it has been assigned. This right is what our bench and bar have, through a long-standing but unfortunate choice of words, called an "affidavit of prejudice."

Despite that fraught name, no supporting evidence of actual prejudice or even conflict of interest is required. All that is required is a declaration asserting that a particular party does not believe it would receive a fair trial before the assigned judge. The mere filing of that document serves to remove the judge from the litigation, no questions asked. Each party can file this declaration only once, but every party, even those on the same side, can file one, which allows for multiple challenges in a multiparty case. What made this possibility even more problematic for me was that under Washington law, such a declaration can be filed even *after* oral argument so long as no substantive order has yet been issued. I had not yet issued such an order. This meant that I had to be very careful about how I conducted oral argument. It meant that an inadvertent choice of words in the framing of a question could be taken rightly or wrongly as tipping my hand one way or another. That risk of being summarily bounced after months of preparation made it even more important that in the conduct of the upcoming oral argument I assiduously attend to the third principle:

Make the parties part of the process of identifying and framing the central legal questions.

We had at our first scheduling and case management conference identified most of the substantive issues that would be raised by the legal briefs. The task for court and counsel at oral argument is to articulate the legal norms, standards, and inquiries that would ultimately provide the answers to each of the identified issues. Asking the parties to participate in the selection of the central legal query helps demonstrate to them that the final decision is indeed driven by underlying legal principles, not by the judge's personal policy preferences.

For this reason, my regular practice in oral argument was to invite counsel and the parties to work on the selection of these questions by saying, "It appears that [X] may indeed be the central question here. What I want from you is either a direct answer to that question or an explanation by you of what alternative question you believe is or ought to be key to the court's deliberations." Encouraging the parties and their counsel to propose counter-questions makes them part of a more neutral analytical process and helps any parties who are present for oral argument understand that court rulings are to be derived from principled decision making rather than from jumping directly to a preferred result.

In addition to identifying the central questions, it often is just as important to directly address who may answer whatever question is key. Who gets to, or who has to, decide what? Is a particular issue left to the executive branch to resolve based on political choices or principles? Is a decision constrained in some fashion by a legislative finding? Or by a statutory delegation of authority to an administrative agency that may exercise its own discretion? Or by a constitutional provision? Would a proposed ruling from a court constitute a forbidden judicial redrafting of a statute, that is, a judge trying to act like a legislative body? Identifying and distinguishing among multiple possible decision makers can be as instructive to the parties and their counsel as identifying the central questions.

Paying particular attention to the twin problems of how to frame the central questions and how to identify who might be entitled to answer them, I dug in deeper and completed my preparations for oral argument.

Oral Argument

The seven consolidated actions' complex briefing raised many factual and legal problems both broad and narrow. We had scheduled oral argument for a full day, and, as expected, it took nearly that long to allow all parties to be heard. Upon conclusion of counsel's formal presentations, I was immensely relieved that no side seemed to have taken umbrage as underlying legal questions were being identified and either framed or discarded, nor had any affidavit of prejudice been filed for any other reason. I committed to the parties that I would do my best to complete my analysis and draft my opinion within two weeks, as we originally had planned.

Making the Decision

It was not long after oral argument that I became firmly convinced that the initiative did indeed violate the Washington State Constitution. Despite the myriad issues that had been raised by the multiple cases, claims, defenses, and parties, it was really quite simple. There were two reasons.

First, the initiative's proposed requirement that all future fee increases be subjected to a public vote fit squarely within the Constitution's definition of a referendum. The Constitution established strict restraints on the topics a referendum could address and on the minimum number of signatures to be garnered in order to submit a referendum petition to public vote. Both constitutional limits were directly violated by the wording of the initiative. These two limits could not be changed without first amending the Constitution, which is something an initiative cannot do.

Second, as to the proposal to replace the existing hefty tax with a flat annual $30 fee per vehicle, I concluded that that provision standing alone would have been constitutional. The problem was that it had been joined with the referendum clause in a single initiative, and our Constitution forbade the joinder of two independent subjects in a single law. This constitutional restriction had been enacted in order to prohibit legislative "log-rolling", that is, the practice of joining an unpopular bill to a popular bill simply for the purpose of passing a law that might otherwise fail to obtain a majority.

Having reached those two conclusions, I realized that it would not be necessary to rule on the many other constitutional and legal challenges that had been raised in the seven consolidated cases. The two key fatal defects in the initiative had rendered the remaining issues moot.

Drafting the Decision

I was reasonably confident I had come to a ruling that was both right and fair. But drafting it would not be easy. Given the broad and even overwhelming interest, I felt I had to make it accessible not just to counsel but to the general public. A law review style of writing can be genuinely useful and appropriate in an academic setting, and in making the record clear for appeal, but it is often too opaque to be useful to laypeople. It can lead to stilted writing, with case and statutory citations creating stumbling blocks to smooth reading.

Rather than compose a decision in which I immediately followed each sentence or two with a formal legal citation or a quote, as is traditional, I tried to craft sentences that would be understandable to an average citizen with a high school education, saving for the end only those cites and quotes that are genuinely necessary for the reader or for the record on appeal.

Still, drafting this particular decision would be especially difficult. It was already painfully obvious that nearly a million highly motivated voters were about to become the "losing party." Convincing them that a single judge could strike down the results of an overwhelmingly popular vote was a high mountain to climb. How could I possibly demonstrate that I had paid sufficient attention to the arguments and wishes of the voters for them in the end not to feel overlooked or, even more seriously, abused?

So I started my draft of the ruling not by ignoring public will, but by showing respect for the vote in favor of the initiative and acknowledging it clearly in my very first sentence:

> Initiative 695 was affirmed in 1999 by a significant margin of the direct popular vote in virtually all areas of the State of Washington.

It was then important not only to reference immediately the fact that constitutional challenges to the initiative had been filed but also to describe what sort of analysis would enable a court to address such challenges to the public's expression of its will:

> Its constitutional validity and its reach are now being vigorously questioned. These legal challenges, which raise questions fundamental to a democracy, were filed in several counties by citizens and by public and private entities alike. They have been consolidated in this Court for resolution.

> The United States and its individual states have long been guided by the adage that we citizens have a government of laws and not of men. In accordance with this cherished principle, court rulings must be made by reference to law and not upon personal whim. A judicial ruling on the validity and reach of a legislative act passed by an elected legislature, or of an initiative or referendum passed directly by the citizenry, is controlled by constitutional law.

It was certainly worth emphasizing that constitutional challenges are not to be decided by reference to personal policy preferences, so I tried to gently nudge members of the public to remember that whether on the left or the right each citizen in her own turn must circle back to the Constitution to protect certain deeply cherished rights from the votes, laws, or actions of others:

> Wherever we citizens fall on the political spectrum and whatever our views on any given issue, we all agree that the touchstone is the Constitution. For example, one citizen may challenge a particular act or law on the grounds that it violates his or her right to bear arms under the Second Amendment. Another citizen may contest yet another act or law on the grounds that it violates his or

her free speech rights under the First Amendment. As citizens, we may and frequently do disagree on specific policies. Nonetheless, our agreement as citizens on a single point of reference, the Constitution, keeps American democracy healthy and viable.

Having described the nature of the case and the narrow grounds that would be used to come to a decision, I did my best to treat the soon-to-be-losing parties with genuine respect, to acknowledge the bona fides of those who had voted for the initiative:

> The Constitution of the State of Washington was drafted in keeping with the legal traditions of the United States, which find many of their origins in the American Revolution. One of the central cries leading to the American Revolution was "No taxation without representation!" Echoes of that revolutionary spirit are found in the passage of Initiative 695.

A flag-waving recitation that we are all bound by the Constitution could easily be perceived as self-serving and not at all persuasive to voters who not unreasonably found themselves fixated on the fact that a single judge had effectively overruled the votes of nearly a million voters. Therefore, throughout the opinion I sought both to reference voters' policy preferences with respect and to distinguish their bona fide policy preferences from formal constitutional restraints. This was not too difficult to do when dealing with the initiative's attempt to require referenda on all future proposed increases of taxes or fees:

> Arguments may be made that we have a runaway tax-and-spend government and that we need radical systemic change in taxation or in other areas in order to make our governmental entities responsive to the needs and the will of the citizens. Some citizens will agree. Some

will not. Whatever the wisdom of a particular proposed fiscal policy, the fundamental structure or system of our government can be changed only by constitutional amendment.

However, when dealing with the proposed flat $30 license fee I had the difficult task of informing the voters that, while that dollar limitation would have been constitutional standing alone, joining it with the de facto referendum requirement was fatal to its viability. I would have had to rewrite the initiative to eliminate that violation of the two-subject rule, and because judges are not legislators, that was something I could not do:

> When reviewing any law's constitutionality, a court is to interpret a law in such a way as to preserve its constitutionality, so long as that can be done without reaching absurd results. The only way Initiative 695 could be constitutional would be for the Court to arbitrarily eliminate one or more sections and redraft others. As the Court has already noted, courts are not to engage in the legislative activity of rewriting an initiative in an attempt to make an otherwise unconstitutional law constitutional.

A Final Check

I had completed my first full draft. I was reasonably confident that I had addressed what the parties and the appellate record needed. But I needed to take one more step. This last step is found in the fourth and final principled admonition concerning controversial litigation:

Before announcing what you intend to be your final ruling in any hotly contested case, double and triple check for emotion, bias, pressure, or other extraneous factors.

The first three principles inherently help counter the everyday confirmation bias that can cause any of us to jump to judgment and cherry-pick supporting facts and arguments. The fourth is intended to deal with the reality that despite our best efforts we judges also remain vulnerable to the same sorts of deep and hidden biases or pressures that can affect all humans. It actually can be easy to uncover such inclinations, even those that are buried. Simply identify and then flip whatever might have been a hot button in the litigation. This mental exercise is most easily applied in cases such as those involving gender, race, or religion. For example, in a dispute over child custody, ask yourself if the facts applied to the mother were applied to the father and vice versa, would you change your ruling and shift primary responsibility? If so, you are probably on solid ground. If not, you should figure out why not and be prepared either to understand and more clearly articulate your approach to gender or parenting or to revise your ruling.

Likewise, in a case involving a claim of police brutality and race, if you were to switch the race of the officer and the alleged victim, would any of your conclusions change? Or, in a case concerning a claim of infringement on religious freedom, would a non-mainstream religious group or practice receive the same ruling from you?

As to this tax initiative, there was nothing related to gender, race, or religion that I could easily flip. Nonetheless, ruling in any such high-profile case inherently gives rise to one obvious emotional factor: my firmly rooted fear of the electorate's likely rage at a judge with the chutzpah to rule against their perceived interests, in this case to deprive them of significant tax breaks. So I mentally flipped my ruling. That exercise made it clear to me that if I had upheld the initiative rather than striking it down, my emotional attachment to staying on the bench might have been a determining factor. It would have required me to seriously consider in chambers whether the decision I was about to announce was truly being driven solely by neutral principles.

At this point in the process I felt confident that while my rulings might be determined by the Supreme Court to have been in error, my decisions had been made fairly, and not from fear but in spite of it.

Issuing the Decision

I had completed my analysis. I had tried to draft a decision that would not be forever reviled as repugnant by those whose interests I had overruled. But my decision had to be presented to the public in a meaningful way.

The opinion itself was far too long to read in its entirety in open court. However, simply handing it out and immediately departing from the courtroom could be seen as arrogant or dismissive of the voters' interests. In the end, I decided to prepare a summary ruling consisting of the ten introductory paragraphs of my formal ruling, to which I added the key paragraph from each subsection of the ruling. And at the bottom of each page of the summary, I printed the Supreme Court web address where any reader who wished to do so could access the full formal ruling. This summary was slightly less than five pages.

Decision day arrived. The courtroom was packed. When I began reading, the room was absolutely silent. Once I completed the reading, which took roughly ten minutes, I directed my staff to hand out to the parties and to every person present both a copy of the summary I had just read and the full ruling itself, and adjourned the court.

The word immediately went out live on radio and TV from the courtroom that the initiative had been struck down. The firestorm was ignited. Verbal pyrotechnics were immediate. Minutes after I left the courtroom, court staff came to me and described a particularly chaotic scene. Reporters had barely finished breathlessly broadcasting the headline "The judge has ruled, 'The Initiative as a whole is unconstitutional'" when the prime sponsor of the initiative stood up in the middle of the courtroom and loudly began proclaiming his dissatisfaction. He heatedly accused me of wanting to be a king and dramatically tore an I-695 campaign placard into tiny pieces for the cameras, proclaiming:

> Does anybody else find this absolutely despicable, that 56 percent of the people, being outspent ten to one. . . . We don't give a damn what you want, if you want any control whatsoever over taxation in this state. No, you have no say whatsoever. I think today's ruling was despicable. I think it was abhorrent. I think it should give everyone shivers.

One television station compared his verbal outburst to the explosion that occurred that same month when our much disliked Kingdome was blown up in order to make way for a new stadium facility. Personally, I felt his response was well within his First Amendment rights. He had not disrupted court, he had waited until I had departed from this large courtroom, a public space, and only then did he command the attention of the press.

Talk radio and numerous web sites were inundated with statements of outrage. Man-on-the-street interviews were mixed, with more than half disapproving of my ruling. For days, my office was swamped with letters and emails. They ran the full gamut from "Love you Judge" to "In revolutions we hang people like you from the nearest lamppost." And for the first few weeks one man called my chambers about 2 a.m. almost every night, leaving lengthy and wordy messages on my answering machine grumbling about my ruling and expressing his frustration that any judge in a democracy would have the temerity to rule as I had. I called him the Midnight Rambler.

The day after I had issued my decision, the *Seattle Post-Intelligencer* printed a headline above the fold that I was not at all happy to see. Echoing the initiative's sponsor's repeated prediction that I would soon be voted out of office, the headline read, simply, "Ruling certain to have judicial and political fallout." Nevertheless, while my own personal future with the electorate continued to look uncertain for all the obvious reasons, I found no reason to complain about the great bulk of media coverage. Most newspapers actually saw fit in the first few days not only to publish the summary I had read in open court, but also to include the Supreme Court's web address. Likewise, TV stations prepared graphics from the summary, and nearly all also prominently posted the web address on their screens. The *Tacoma News Tribune* chose to dedicate two entire pages of their newspaper to printing the full original decision. And Westlaw picked up and published the full opinion.

As the days passed, editorial coverage continued to be plentiful and more often than not quite supportive, often describing the decision as a civics lesson or something comparable. There were also human-interest stories about judges and letters about the value of public debate along with articles and op-ed pieces posing such questions as "When a judge overturns a voter-approved initiative, does it mean the system of government is broken—or that it is working exactly as it should?"

Given the heightened level of public interest in the courts and constitutional issues, our court's leadership also thought this case presented a good opportunity to take one further step to help build public awareness. Referencing the ethical duty placed on the judiciary to educate the public, a provision found in most states' codes of judicial conduct, they urged me to meet and talk with members of the press.

Up to that time, in my decade on the bench I had never met with any member of print or electronic media to discuss or answer questions on any aspect of any case or decision from my court. I reluctantly consented to do interviews, but only upon the assurance that the interviewing media first agree that no questions would be asked about the substance of the ruling, and that I would focus instead on clarifying legal and judicial processes.

Only one television channel agreed to that limitation. They limited their questions to judicial process, including the inevitable question about the interaction of judges and citizenry in such a case. This was the exchange:

> Q: Because of your ruling, some people have said that their vote doesn't count. Do you feel like you were in a no-win situation?
>
> A: Not at all. I mean, this is a very reasonable question for people to ask: "What is one man doing? We had a million people vote in the following fashion . . .
>
> I think the best way to explain that is to say that if I am doing my job right, I'm not the voice of one man. When I do a case like this, I study the Constitution. I study a hundred years of decisions by our elected Supreme Court Justices. So, I think, properly viewed, my decision is not *my* decision. This is not the voice of a man speaking, but really if I have done my job right, it is the voice of the law developed over a hundred years.

Within a few weeks, letters and emails received by the court began shifting from mostly negative to mostly positive. Polls suggested that the tide of public opinion had begun to turn. We received word from the Washington State Supreme Court that thousands had downloaded my decision. And to my great pleasure, the state legislature passed a straightforward law doing away with the existing tax and implementing the $30 annual fee that I had ruled would be lawful and constitutional if standing alone.

But the good news didn't stop there.

Despite all the attention and speculation earlier in the year about likely adverse electoral consequences, and despite the fact that my ruling striking down tax referenda still stood, nobody declared to run against me.

Further, the Supreme Court affirmed my ruling 8–1 shortly before the end of the year.

And I heard one more time from the Midnight Rambler. In his last 2:00 a.m. message, which he left for me several months before the Supreme Court issued its opinion, he said, "I've been thinking about your ruling. I still think you were wrong. But I have decided that you were doing the best that you could do."

That may not seem like the greatest praise a judicial officer can receive, but I was delighted. Having a person who is firmly convinced that you made the wrong decision agree that you were acting in good faith, well, for a judge, it doesn't get much better than that.

10

Walking with My Ancestors: Tribal Justice for Salmon Running

Judge Allie Greenleaf Maldonado

Judge Allie Greenleaf Maldonado served as a litigator for the U.S. Department of Justice and an attorney for her Michigan tribe, the Little Traverse Bay Bands of Odawa Indians, and was appointed chief judge of her community in 2012.

As I held the white eagle feather speckled with subtle flecks of brown, I struggled with my options: to protect the community and send a message by giving the defendant the maximum sentence, or to offer a hand instead of a hammer. It was a difficult choice. She deserved to go to jail, but jail would guarantee that, when released, she would continue her life as a drug addict and dealer. Taking the feather out of its cedar box, I desperately wanted it to whisper the right decision into my ear. That is exactly what it did.

As chief judge for the Little Traverse Bay Bands of Odawa Indians I have limited criminal jurisdiction, and I rarely hear the serious drug cases that routinely plague big cities. My court is located in the extraordinarily beautiful town of Petoskey, Michigan. Petoskey lies within the boundaries of the Tribe's reservation in northern Michigan. Overall, it is a peaceful community. The spirits of my ancestors rest here somewhere between the beaches of Lake Michigan and the forests where the morels hide. People in this small community expect to feel safe. So, when one of our young women, whom I will call Salmon Running, allowed herself to be used by a downstate drug dealer to sell heroin and cocaine from the Tribe's hotel, it was a big deal.

The case first came to me when I was awakened at two in the morning by the tribal police. They were requesting a search warrant. Michigan State Police had pulled over and arrested Salmon Running, a tribal citizen, on an outstanding warrant for possession of a controlled substance. When she was searched, officers found illegal narcotics. In response to questions, she admitted that there were drugs in her tribal hotel room located on trust property. She claimed they were not her drugs but belonged to a friend. Because the state does not have criminal jurisdiction over tribal reservation land, they contacted the Tribal police. Hence the Tribal police were presenting me with an affidavit explaining the facts and requesting a search warrant to look for the drugs in Salmon Running's hotel room. Her self-incriminating statements gave me the probable cause to authorize the warrant. I then went back to bed troubled. I've watched my community suffer from alcoholism and addiction for years, and I've spent a great deal of my judicial career trying to address the underlying causes of addiction. I preside over a healing-to-wellness court that gives recovery tools and support to Native Americans who engage with the criminal justice system due to addiction.

Now this dealer had come into my community and infected more of my brothers and sisters and maybe even our children with the sickness of addiction. It felt as if for every person we saw succeed on the road to recovery, two more of our youth became sick with addiction. The tears of the families who have suffered in the wake of addiction in my community could fill Little Traverse Bay.

The police executed the search warrant and found heroin, cocaine, and marijuana in Salmon Running's room. With this evidence, the Tribal Prosecutor had to decide what charges to bring against her. The Tribal Prosecutor lives on the reservation. His wife is a tribal citizen, and he is the father to five of our young tribal women and grandfather to five of our children. He also has dedicated a tremendous amount of his time to helping to support community sobriety. His response to a drug dealer on the reservation wasn't surprising. He piled on drug charges as high as the law would allow: possession, use, sale, manufacture and/or distribution, conspiracy, and attempt. He even charged her with trespass. Under the Tribal law, if convicted, the total amount of jail time on all counts was four years, nine months. However, federal law caps the maximum time the Tribal Court can sentence an individual to at one year regardless of the tribal law.* So, if she was convicted, I could sentence her to only one year in jail. This one-year restriction is true for most tribal courts. Further complicating law enforcement on reservations, federal law allows tribal courts to exercise criminal jurisdiction only over Native Americans.** Consequently, because of these limitations, criminals often target reservations.

Vulnerable Native American women are often used to transport and distribute drugs for non-Indian drug dealers who choose Indian reservations because they know tribal courts cannot hold them accountable. When non-Indians commit crimes on reservations, tribes depend on the federal government to step in and prosecute. However, critics claim that the feds take only the most serious cases and usually only the ones they believe are slam-dunks. This leaves Indian country vulnerable to criminals who see an opportunity to exploit the tribes' lack of criminal jurisdiction.

In Salmon Running's case, the prosecutor wanted her to disclose the identity of her non-Indian supplier so that the feds could prosecute him. The prosecutor reasoned that the supplier, if not

---

* A limited exception under the Tribal Law and Order Act allows some courts to sentence up to three years. See The Tribal Law and Order Act of 2010, Pub.L. No. 111–211, 124 Stat. 2261 (Jul. 29, 2010) (codified as amended in various sections of 18 U.S.C., 21 U.S.C., 25 U.S.C., 28 U.S.C., and 42 U.S.C.

** The Violence Against Women Act offers tribes meeting set standards a very restricted exception for some domestic violence cases. The Violence Against Women Act was originally passed as Title IV of the Violent Crime Control and Law Enforcement Act of 1994, Pub. L. 103-322, 108 Stat. 1796. The 2013 revisions were passed as the Violence Against Women Reauthorization Act of 2013, Pub. L. No. 113-4, 127 Stat. 54.

prosecuted, would just replace Salmon Running with another native woman, and her case would do little to stop the flow of drugs onto our reservation. He offered Salmon Running a deal, but she wasn't going to talk. He then chose to make an example of her. Her personal history added reasons for him to do so. At just twenty-three she had a long criminal history. Salmon Running had been charged with possession of a concealed weapon, resisting arrest, and more than one drug-dealing offense, all in other jurisdictions. Her record suggested that she started as a user and then began selling to feed her habit. Furthermore, I would later learn that drugs had caused her to lose her parental rights to two children. Despite what would have been rock bottom and the first step to recovery for many people, she was digging deeper into a life of drugs and crime.

When she came in for her arraignment, her tough girl swagger didn't go unnoticed. She had an air about her that said, "Watch out, I'm the kind of woman that has brass knuckles in my pocket." The prosecutor was fired up and asked that she be held without bond. That is very unusual. Most people are entitled to bond unless they commit an extraordinarily serious crime and present an ongoing danger to the public or are a flight risk. The prosecutor passionately argued that Salmon Running's previous history of violation of her bond in another jurisdiction made her a flight risk. She responded that she had a sick grandmother whom she loved dearly for whom she provided care. She promised me she would appear for all future hearings. Her grandmother sat behind her looking frail, wearing an oxygen mask. Nonetheless, something in my gut told me that if I allowed her bond she would run. I denied her release on bond.

She requested that I appoint her an attorney. My tribal court always appoints attorneys for indigent people when they are facing jail time and so I honored her request. As soon as her attorney was appointed, he asked for another bond hearing. He skillfully argued that, under the Eighth Amendment of the U.S. Constitution and the Tribe's law, she had a right to a bond. Something in her eyes told me she would run, but I believe the court should err on the side of protecting people's rights. Therefore, I set her bond higher than

I believed she could post on her own, $50,000 cash, or a bond with 10 percent cash. (Simply put, a bond is purchased insurance that the defendant will appear in court. When a person violates their bond, the court can go after the insurance agency—the bondsman—for the total cash amount of the bond. This gives the bondsman an incentive to track down the person who has jumped bond and force their appearance in court.) I thought if Salmon Running had to depend on friends or family to post bond, she would be less likely to run because they would lose their money or collateral. It was not long before her grandma used her truck as collateral and hired a bondsman to post Salmon Running's bond. The bondsman accepted $2,500 in cash that her family raised and her grandma's truck, which he valued at $10,000, as collateral.

Over the next few weeks, the prosecutor and defense attorney continued with their preparation for trial. There was no plea deal. Requests for a jury trial, discovery, witness lists, and exhibit lists all went back and forth. I scheduled a pretrial status conference. Salmon Running didn't appear. Her attorney, embarrassed and tongue-tied, could not account for her whereabouts. I was furious. The prosecutor had this unbearable look of "I told you so" on his face. I knew this was going happen, but I did not follow my gut. Now she was in the wind. I wanted her back so I could hold her accountable for her actions. I was particularly disgusted by the way she had used her grandmother. People are creatures of habit, so I could guess where she had run. I figured she fled to Florida the way she did the last time she violated her release conditions.

Abiding by established legal requirements, I scheduled a subsequent "show cause" hearing to give her an opportunity to appear and explain her absence from the status conference. As I entered the courtroom for the hearing, draped in my black robe ornamented with traditional tribal beadwork, I was not surprised by the empty defendant's chair. As expected, she failed to appear. I found her guilty of contempt of court and revoked her bond. This caused the bondsman to be on the hook for $45,000. With such an incentive, he set out to find Salmon Running.

I issued a nationwide bench warrant for her arrest. Thanks to an internet database, if she came into contact with law enforcement anywhere in the country, they would arrest her. This would give the bondsman the opportunity to pick her up and bring her back to court.

It would take less than three months for us to get word of her location. Law enforcement in Florida arrested, charged, and found her guilty of possession of a controlled substance with intent to sell, possession of drug paraphernalia, possession of a concealed weapon, and resisting arrest. I thought, "How typical! She runs away from her problems only to reenact them somewhere else." I had little hope for her. She had all the makings of a lifelong criminal. She would have to serve her time in Florida before facing me again in Michigan. She cut a deal for one year and one day in prison in Florida. I placed a hold on her in jail, meaning that when her time was up she could not be released, but instead be held for the bondsman to pick her up.

As the year went by, the work of the court continued. As a new judge, only seated to the bench two years earlier, I inherited the Tribe's nationally lauded problem-solving court, the Waabshkii Miigwan ("White Feather") Healing-to-Wellness Court Program. My predecessor judge and her staff created an evidence-based, culturally appropriate treatment court that followed national drug court standards. I came to the bench with no background in recovery. However, Waabshkii Miigwan soon became my labor of love. Typical criminal and child welfare cases mostly focus on enforcement of the laws and hold people accountable for their actions regardless of the influence of addictions to narcotics or alcohol. Drug courts (also known as problem-solving courts or healing-to-wellness courts in Indian country) are different. Drug courts offer substance abusers in the criminal or family courts the opportunity to treat the addictions that prompted their court involvement. One might say it is intensive outpatient treatment with jail as a sanction for drug use relapse. Avoiding incarceration not only motivates sobriety but also generates substantial savings for taxpayers in terms of jail costs.

The National Association of Drug Court Professionals (NADCP) describes drug courts as follows:

> Drug Courts keep individuals in treatment long enough for it to work, while supervising them closely. For a minimum term of one year, participants are:
>
> - Provided with intensive treatment and other services they require to get and stay clean and sober;
> - Held accountable by the Drug Court judge for meeting their obligations to the court, society, themselves and their families;
> - Regularly and randomly tested for drug use;
> - Required to appear in court frequently so that the judge may review their progress; and
> - Rewarded for doing well or sanctioned when they do not live up to their obligations.[*]

I started learning everything I could about addiction and recovery. I took trainings and read books. However, that was not nearly enough for me to develop an expertise in recovery. Luckily, I had an amazing healing-to-wellness court team. The heart and soul of drug courts are the teams that make recommendations to the judge about how to manage the participants. For example, my team includes the Tribal Prosecutor, defense counsel, a probation officer, law enforcement, the court's cultural coordinator, a substance and mental health therapist, a Tribal elder, other court staff, and a mentor graduate of the program. Several of my team members have been in long-term recovery and understand the challenges facing addicts. Combined, my team has more than seventy-five years of experience in recovery. With that expertise, they encourage case participants to accept help that can change their lives. Thanks to such teamwork, I

---

[*] NADCP website at: http://www.nadcp.org/learn/drug-courts-work/what-are -drug-court.

became excited by the prospect of not only helping individuals suffering from addiction but facilitating the healing of Tribal families and making our community a healthier place.

Wednesday, healing-to-wellness days in my courtroom, soon became my favorite. Watching people transform their lives right in front of my eyes fed my soul. Although not every participant took advantage of the program, the ones who did gave my community and me hope. However, I had minimal expectations for Salmon Running. She was manipulative and had a terrible attitude. She even betrayed her family by jumping bond. So when she sent me a letter asking for mercy, I was not moved.

The handwritten letter on lined school paper arrived after she realized that when incarceration in Florida was finished she would be transferred to Tribal Court to face our charges against her. The letter was like many letters I received before it from people trying to avoid the consequences of their actions. She apologized to the court for running. She claimed that in prison she was a changed woman because she had dedicated her life to Jesus Christ. I have heard this one too many times to count. She also claimed that in jail she was completing some therapeutic courses to deal with trauma and anger from her childhood. It is not enough to go to therapy; you have to benefit from it for it to matter. She also told me that she would be receiving her GED before her release. I admit, that impressed me. That showed initiative and took work. However, when she talked about wanting to come home and take care of her sick grandmother, again, it reminded me of when she was arguing for bond before she ran. I remembered her betrayal of her family and her disrespect to the court. I doubted her sincerity. Her plea for leniency fell on deaf ears.

After the bondsman returned Salmon Running to Tribal Court, she entered my courtroom shackled in a blue jumpsuit. Something in her face and in her eyes looked different to me. Could something have clicked for her in jail after all? Could she finally be ready to change her life?

One thing had changed. The first tribal prosecutor had moved to a law firm; the new prosecutor offered Salmon Running a deal. If she would plead guilty, the prosecutor would drop some of the charges and recommend six months in jail and the completion of the Waabshkii Miigwan Healing-to-Wellness Program. This was a highly risky move for Salmon Running because I did not have to accept the prosecutor's recommendation. Despite her plea agreement, I could sentence her to jail for one year.

I feel very fortunate that I rarely struggle to come to the right decision. In most instances, the right decision is clear to me. This time was different. I was still incredibly angry with this young woman for endangering our community, disrespecting the court, and then betraying her family. She certainly deserved additional time in jail. However, jail did not feel right in my gut. I was not certain why, but I kept wondering if this young woman should get another chance. I decided that if the Healing-to-Wellness Court Team would accept her, I would follow the new prosecutor's recommendation. The team had to vote on the acceptance or denial of every participant. In my tenure on the bench, I had almost always accepted the recommendations of the team. I expected that this time would be no different.

The team unanimously rejected her request to participate in the program. I don't know why I was surprised. After all, the original prosecutor was still volunteering as a part of the team and was dead-set against her admission. He made the point that the program was for victims of substance abuse, not drug dealers. He persuasively argued that placing a known drug dealer in a program for people suffering from addiction was reckless.

It didn't cross my mind to overrule the team. Without the intense supervision of a Healing-to-Wellness Court, releasing her back into the community would put the community at risk. Yet every time I thought about putting her in jail I grew uneasy. I wasn't sure why.

She pled guilty to possession with intent to sell. When she came in for sentencing, I was not leaning towards any particular resolution. I listened with an open mind and open heart. Defense counsel begged me to consider a sentence of just six months with completion of Waabshkii Miigwan. He talked about the progress she had made in prison and argued that she was ready to change her life. He begged for leniency. Next, her grandma, a small, older woman, frail, with an oxygen mask trailing behind her, spoke about how much she loved her granddaughter. She shared her granddaughter's challenges growing up. She did not expect to live much longer and did not want to leave this world not knowing whether her granddaughter would be okay. After this, Salmon Running, with tears in her eyes, apologized to me. She acknowledged she had to be held accountable for the things she had done, but she wanted the opportunity to redeem herself. Most of all, she wanted to be there for her grandmother. This time was different. She really did want to take care of her grandmother. I looked in her eyes, but I didn't know if she was telling the truth. I wanted to believe her because I always want to believe everyone. However, I'm too experienced for that.

My mind and my heart began an epic battle. Her crimes against the community were serious. She brought drugs onto our reservation, sold them to our people, refused to turn over her supplier, and ran when she got caught. Furthermore, I can't count how many times I have heard people say they are sorry only after they're caught. She must be held accountable to the community for her choices. I needed to make an example out of her to deter others and keep the community safe. Furthermore, experience has taught me criminals and people wrapped in addiction lie. They lie to themselves and to everyone around them. She was not an out-of-control young person picked up for drunk and disorderly conduct who needed a second chance. She was a drug dealer. But the thought of even six months in jail didn't feel right in my gut. Did she deserve another chance? Maybe the story of her grandmother's illness was manipulating me and I was being weak. I just wasn't sure.

Walking with My Ancestors

I adjourned the proceedings until the next day. I knew I needed some time to think. When I got back to my office, I was drawn to the white eagle feather I keep in a cedar box on my desk. The eagle feather came to me not long after I took the gavel to preside over Waabshkii Miigwan. I draped the feather in a piece of felt and headed to the beach for a walk.

The feather reminds me of how the Waabshkii Miigwan Program came to be. One of our most respected Tribal elders, Rita Shepherd, inspired its creation. Born in 1939, Rita was an amazing Odawa woman. She was a wife and mother to four children. She understood the importance of education and encouraged her children to excel academically. After her children were grown, she took a job in a local law firm. When one of the attorneys at the firm became a local judge, she went to work for him as the probate court registrar. She learned a great deal about the legal system and wanted to use what she had learned to give back to her community. My Tribe has one seat on the appellate bench reserved for a Tribal elder. She became Little Traverse Bay Board's first elder appellate justice on May 17, 1998. She would serve several terms before retiring in 2008.

During her time on the bench she dedicated herself to addressing the problem of addiction in our community. While attending judicial training in Kake, a small village on an Alaskan island, she decided that she would take the opportunity to find an eagle feather.

Eagle feathers are sacred in my culture. Eagles are protected under federal law, and it is a felony for most people to possess eagle feathers. However, because of the unique spiritual connection between Native American people and the eagle, only tribal citizens may be in possession of eagle feathers. In my culture, the story is told like this:

The Creator was going to end all human life because people were not living the way the Creator intended. The eagle had hope that humanity could do better so he flew as high as he could and asked the Creator not to end human life. The Creator said, "I will give you three days to find one person living as I have asked of them. If you can find one person living in a good way, in the way in which I have taught, I will spare humanity."

On the first day, the eagle flew over hundreds of miles of land, water and mountains. He looked at every village. Despite flying from sunrise to sunset, he could not find one person living by the teachings of the Creator.

On the second day, the eagle flew even higher and faster. He passed valleys and streams and felt the weather change as the wind blew colder through his wings. He ignored hunger and exhaustion, but despite his best efforts he could not find one person living the way the Creator taught.

On the last day, the eagle pushed himself even harder. He flew through dense forests, over village after village. At the end of the third day, as the sun began to drop behind the crystal blue waters of Lake Michigan, the eagle found a person making an offering of tobacco to the Creator, to the earth and to the four directions. That person was an Anishinaabe (Native American). Exultant, the eagle flew as high as he could and told the Creator that he had found one person living the way he had taught and that person was an Anishinaabe. Today, the Anishinaabek use eagle feathers in the hopes of seeing what that eagle could see for humanity. The value of hope.

For Native Americans, it is one of life's greatest honors to be given an eagle feather as a gift. If a Native American finds an eagle feather, we believe that is a special gift directly from the Creator.

Rita had waited her whole life to find an eagle feather. It was spring in Kake, Alaska, and the island was teeming with wildlife. The eagles were moving from their nests to the water and river's edge. This was the perfect opportunity for Rita to fulfill her lifelong dream of finding an eagle feather. Rita shared her dream with the elder's guide for the trip. He assured her that she would be successful. He knew the eagles' favorite roosting spots and he would take her to them on the last day during their tour of the island.

Each day of her trip she took long walks in search of her eagle feather. She went to the beach below the cliffs where the eagles perched, but found nothing. She walked along the river where the salmon spawned and the eagles hunted. Again, found nothing. Other elders on the trip had found feathers. She didn't despair because their guide had promised to take them on a tour of the island, and she felt optimistic that would be her moment. However, the tour proved to be a disappointment. Although the tour itself was lovely, Rita did not find a feather. Sensing her sadness, the guide offered one last opportunity, the dump. The dump is not exactly the highlight of most tours, but eagles are scavengers, and on Kake they can often be found at the dump digging for a meal. The guide and several elders helped Rita look, but the day was ending, and it looked like her lifelong dream of finding an eagle feather would continue to elude her. Just as she was walking toward the bus, she looked down at her feet and saw a quill sticking out of the muck. She reached for it. Out from the rubbish came the sorriest and dirtiest feather she had ever seen. Her guide and the other elders tried to persuade her to throw it back on the ground. Her guide even kindly offered to gift her one of his many feathers. But it was an eagle feather and she had found it. Therefore, she believed it was the eagle feather the Creator meant for her to find. She was keeping it.

On the ride back to the hotel, the other elders on the bus gave Rita advice on how to care for the feather. Actually, they gave her a list of what not to do. As soon as she got back to her hotel room she promptly did everything she was advised against. She washed the feather with shampoo and water and fanned it to dry. That cleaned the feather. But it was how she held it in her hands and ran her fingers from one end to the next, over and over again, that brought the feather back to life. It was a beautiful white eagle tail feather.

As she cared for the feather, she thought about our people suffering from addiction. As the sorry, muck-covered feather slowly transformed back into the beautiful white feather that it had always been underneath the dirt, she came to a powerful realization. No matter what has been done to our people to dirty them or what they have done to themselves, they have the power to transform their lives. Tears welled in her eyes as she understood that if our people knew redemption was possible, they could forgive themselves. With care and support from their community and the Creator, they too could be clean again.

That experience inspired Rita and our Tribe to start the Waabshkii Miigwan, White Feather Healing-to-Wellness Court Program. Her story of the white eagle feather was not just about the search for the feather but about the transformation of the feather, which she viewed as symbolic of our lives. She said, "When something that is so dirty and mangled can become beautiful, clean, and white, then there is hope. Each one of us gets dirty, whether we get the dirt on ourselves or other people throw it on us. But with some gentle care, and with the help of the Creator, we can make ourselves clean and pure again."[*]

Northern Michigan is a breathtakingly beautiful place. The beaches are clean, the waters are blue, and the sunsets are an event. I am truly blessed to live on my ancestral lands. It is here that I have been at my best. My walk on the beach brought me to the edge where the water meets the sand. I sat down and buried my feet. Each wave that rolled in threatened to douse me. The white feather I held in my hand was not Rita's feather. She had given her feather to a young man in our tribe who was struggling but who she believed had great promise. She hoped it would serve him as an example of how he could transform his life. My feather had found its way to me not long after I began presiding over Rita's legacy, Waabshkii Miigwan. Rita was my mentor and friend. I often wonder if Rita's spirit had something to do with the feather finding me.

As I contemplated my decision regarding Salmon Running, I gazed at the feather, looking for answers just as Rita had done before

---

[*] For more of her story, better told by her and her grandson, please visit this web link: http://www.ltbbodawansn.gov/Tribal%20Court/DrugCourt /White%20Feather%20Story.html.

me. What was the right decision for the community? What did the community need me to do? Would the community be safer if I made an example of this young woman and sentenced her to the maximum imprisonment allowable under the law, or was there a different answer?

My Sentencing Decision

On the next day, I took a leap of faith and shocked the room by sentencing Salmon Running to no immediate jail time, not even the six months recommended by the new prosecutor. Instead, I sentenced her to one year of intensive probation, ordered her to complete a substance abuse assessment and follow all recommendations of the tribe's substance-abuse department. This was a huge opportunity for her to make a new start. Whether she deserved it or not, she was getting a second chance. I left 365 days of jail held in abeyance, meaning it could be used against her in the future. If she successfully completed probation, the jail sentence would be dropped. If I was wrong to give her a second chance and she continued to break the law I could still send her to jail for a year. At first, her defense attorney looked stunned. Then he smiled and turned to hug her. She was already embracing her grandmother. As I hit my gavel to adjourn the proceedings I still wasn't sure if I had made the right decision. Only time would tell. Giving a drug dealer a second chance wasn't easy. If she didn't change her life and instead went back to dealing, I would feel responsible for anyone she harmed. I hoped she wouldn't let our community or me down.

The terms of her probation lived up to their description as "intensive." She was to remain drug and alcohol free, not violate any other law, be subject to random drug and alcohol screenings, abide by a 12 a.m. curfew, not associate with any other person on probation or parole, get permission before leaving the county, have weekly contact with her probation officer, pay court costs and fines, and complete 150 hours of community service. Because our Tribal court probation office doesn't have as large a caseload as state court, our probation officers can keep a close eye on probationers. Each day every person on probation has a one-in-seven chance of being required to screen. Several times a week, a Tribal court probation officer is out checking to make sure the probationers are following curfew. If you're violating probation, you're probably going to get caught.

It wasn't long before Salmon Running was caught violating probation. Just over one month after giving her an opportunity to change her life, she tested positive for drugs. I was crushed. It looked like I was wrong to give her a second chance. I knew people in the community would expect me to respond by making her serve the 365 days held in abeyance. But I was now convinced that she was a drug addict who would only be able to stop using and transform her life with the intensive support that a Healing-to-Wellness Court can offer. Salmon Running also believed she needed help to stop using drugs. She wrote a letter to the Waabshkii Miigwan team asking them to reconsider admitting her to the program. Although her plea was passionate and articulate, the team rejected her for a second time.

Once again, I didn't know what to do. I was certain she needed the support of the Waabshkii Miigwan Program in order to stay sober. However, my team didn't believe that the risk of a drug dealer being in a program with recovering addicts was worth the potential benefit. Could I overrule the team? Should I?

I thought back to Rita's white feather story. Salmon Running was only twenty-three years old and potentially had a long life ahead of her. Her childhood was challenging. She fell into the wrong crowd at a young age. She became addicted to drugs, lost her parental rights to two children, and started selling drugs. Her life was like the white feather Rita pulled from the dump, a sorry mess. She needed help to make a new life for herself. I believed sentencing her to jail for a year without treating the addiction that led to her criminal behavior almost guaranteed that she would be back out on the streets using and selling after her release. I also thought sentencing her to jail without treatment would continue the cycle of substance abuse that plagued her family. I wanted to overrule the team and admit her to the Waabshkii Miigwan Program. But I worried about how that would affect my team. Would they feel disrespected? Would they lose respect for me? If I overruled the team and she failed the program, would I look like a weak, bleeding-heart jurist unfit for the bench? While trying to fall asleep, I fitfully negotiated battles between my thoughts as a sentencing judge from the ones that were not legally relevant.

Later that night, I dreamed about Rita. She was ahead of me on the beach leaving footprints on the sand. I was standing still, trying to decide if I would follow her. When I awoke I asked myself, what would Rita do? I knew what Rita would do, but was I bold enough to do it?

The next day I signed an order that overruled my team and admitted Salmon Running to the Waabshkii Miigwan Healing-to-Wellness Program. My team was not happy, but they're professionals. Once the decision was made, they accepted it and did everything they could to help her succeed.

Our program is extremely challenging and demands a great deal from participants. The Waabshkii Miigwan curriculum is a fifty-two-week program and six weeks of aftercare that utilizes Odawa values and teachings to encourage the adoption of the healthy and balanced lifestyle envisioned by our ancestors. The program's requirements balance spiritual, emotional, physical, and mental wellness activities. Spiritual health activities include self-help meetings, daily prayer, meditation, and twelve-step work in either AA or the White Bison Medicine Wheel Teachings. Other spiritual activities include participation in traditional Native American fires, sweat lodges, water ceremonies, and other tribal activities. The program requires abstinence from drugs and alcohol. Accordingly, participants are carefully monitored to make certain they are sober. They must call in daily to find out whether they have been randomly selected for a drug and alcohol screening. They wear an electronic device called a SCRAM (Secure Continuous Remote Alcohol Monitor) on their ankle twenty-four hours a day, seven days a week, that detects alcohol. They must live in an alcohol- and drug-free environment and stay away from establishments that exist primarily to sell alcohol. Unless excused for exceptional circumstances, they have to complete thirty hours a week of either work, school, or community service. Physical activity is encouraged. Finally, to address their emotional and mental health needs, all clients must attend weekly counseling.

Clients must fulfill all program requirements in order to advance to the next week's assignments. Failure to complete or follow program requirements can stop the client's progress and extend their time in the program. Repeatedly failing to complete or follow program requirements can result in expulsion from the program. When a client successfully accomplishes all program requirements, we celebrate with a graduation ceremony and feast. It's a demanding program, and not everybody is ready to change his or her life. But something happened that proved Salmon Running was finally ready to succeed.

As her grandmother was preparing to walk on, Salmon Running didn't want her nanna to die while her own life was in terrible disarray. She wanted to give her grandmother the gift of peace. With that as her guidepost, she dove into the program with an unparalleled level of commitment. Week after week she fulfilled each program requirement. She made all her meetings and began to enjoy them. She found a job, did well, and was quickly recognized as a valuable employee. This boosted her self-esteem. I doubt she ever had that kind of positive recognition before. A number of Native American people who slip into addiction are people who have little or no connection to the tribal community or culture. This was true for Salmon Running. Waabshkii Miigwan presented her first opportunity to learn about and connect with her culture. The court's cultural advisor provided her with traditional teachings that became the foundation of her recovery. The culture captivated her and helped her understand who she is and her place in the world as an Anishinaabe que (native woman).

Although we discourage participants in the program to become romantically involved during their first year of recovery, sometimes it happens. In this case, Salmon Running met a nice man who supported her sobriety. She became pregnant for the third time and gave birth towards the end of her time in the program. In Michigan, if the state feels it is necessary to challenge a person's fitness to parent, the burden of proof is on the state in most cases. However, in this case because the state had terminated Salmon Running's parental rights in the past, the burden of proof shifted to her to prove she was fit.

When the Department of Human Services first contacted her a few months before her due date, she panicked, but she didn't turn to alcohol or drugs. Instead, she turned to the team and asked for support. The former prosecutor who had once advocated for Salmon Running's incarceration was now a believer in her ability to transform her life. He became her best advocate. He reached out to the Department of Human Services on her behalf. He convinced the department that Salmon Running could prove not only that she'd been sober during her time in the program but also that she was working, had her own residence, and was 100 percent committed to a life in recovery. Without the program and the skillful advocacy of the former prosecutor, it is likely the state would have removed her newborn from her care at the hospital and she would have had to fight to prove she was a fit parent to get her child back. Instead, thanks to her strong record while in the program, Human Services left her alone.

We All "Walk On"

Not long before Salmon Running graduated, her grandmother walked on. She was the one tranquil person who, even in the darkest of days, never gave up on Salmon Running. She left this world knowing that her granddaughter had finally found her way and was walking the path of recovery. That gave both of them peace. Naturally, Salmon Running was grateful that, during her time in the program, she could be with her grandmother as a sober person who could truly take care of her. She became the person her grandmother always knew she could be—just in time.

Her graduation from the program was one of the happiest days of my career. With a new baby in her arms, surrounded by family, friends, her boyfriend, and the team, she spoke about her journey with tremendous gratitude. She thanked us for everything we had done, but most of all for taking a chance on her. I took my white feather into the graduation ceremony. It seemed only fitting, for it was the feather's spirit that had guided me back to the founding principles of why my elders and the Tribe created Waabshkii Miigwan.

After graduation, Salmon Running began focusing on cultivating her artistic skill. A few months after graduation, she gifted the court and the team with a painting she had made in our honor. It depicts a medicine wheel painted in the colors of the four directions on the landscape of a peaceful sunset. Hanging from the medicine wheel are four white feathers.

Since her graduation, she has become a role model for other young women in our community. Her greatest joy is being a mother, and she is grateful for her sobriety. Who knows what the future will bring, but she has been sober for several years and is still taking it one day at a time.

Her life explains why I chose Salmon Running as her pseudonym. I love the different layers of meaning the name symbolizes. The salmon run is sacred in my culture. It is celebrated because it represents the journey that adults must take in order to perpetuate life. The salmon endure this journey because instinct demands it for the next generation. I believe what we are doing in the Healing-to-Wellness Court is for the next seven generations. We are attempting to change not just individual lives but the life cycle of families that is passed on from one generation to the next. Lastly, I chose the name because of the irony involved with Salmon Running violating her release conditions. If I had not put her into the drug court program, she would have continued her toxic journey, passing on the cycle of addiction, dysfunction, and broken relationships to future generations.

Salmon Running's story has also changed me. On days when I am most challenged to see the possibility of change in tribal citizens, I think of her, and I know that if the person in front of me truly believes they can transform their life, I should take a risk and believe too.

I grew up in big cities full of noise and other negatives that come with city life. I love living in northern Michigan, not just for the epic sunsets that I love to watch from the break wall, but because I feel connected to the land. When I am here, I feel like I can hear my ancestors. They are telling me that we can't afford to throw away our community members who make mistakes. Giving people a second, third, or fourth chance won't always pay off. Yet we have to believe that if we treat each person with the same care, love, and respect with which my tribal elder Rita Shepard treated that white eagle feather, there is hope that, if they are ready and they too believe, they can heal.

11

Crazy or Cruel: The Trial of an Unexplained Filicide

JUDGE FREDERICK H. WEISBERG

 *Frederick H. Weisberg was appointed to the Superior Court of the District of Columbia in 1977 by President Jimmy Carter. He recently retired to take senior status after serving more than forty years as an active associate judge. He also recently stepped down after eighteen years as the chair of the District of Columbia Sentencing Commission. Before joining the bench he served on both the trial and appellate staff of the Public Defender Service in Washington, DC, eventually becoming chief of the Appellate Division.*

IT SHOULD HAVE BEEN A ROUTINE EVICTION. THE TENANT HAD NOT paid rent for many months. The landlord went to court and got a judgment for possession of his property by default. He arranged for an eviction crew and paid the required fee to the U.S. Marshal Service, which provides security for all evictions in the District of Columbia in case there is trouble. Sometimes evictions scheduled in January are canceled if the weather is too cold. The morning of January 9, 2008, was unseasonably warm.

The Deputy Marshal knocked twice on the door and received no response. The house, located in a rundown section of Washington, DC, looked unoccupied, and it seemed likely that the tenant had already moved out. Just as the Marshal was about to give the command to force the door, the tenant opened it and allowed them inside. As soon as the crew entered, it was obvious something was terribly wrong. The deputy immediately recognized the smell. It was the smell of death. The house had no furniture, and the water and electricity had been disconnected. The tenant, a thirty-three-year-old woman, had taken a seat on the stairs leading to the second floor. Twice they asked her to move so they could check upstairs for any possible source of danger. She remained seated, saying nothing, with a blank stare in her eyes. The Deputy gently moved her out of the way and preceded upstairs, the smell growing more malodorous with each step.

It was a three-bedroom townhouse. The first bedroom was empty. In the second bedroom, on the floor, were the decomposed bodies of what appeared to be three young children, mostly skeletal remains, with bugs crawling all over them. The bodies seemed to have been placed next to each other, lined up according to size. The third bedroom was sealed shut by a T-shirt and duct tape along the bottom of the door. It did not take much force to gain entry. Inside was the decomposed body of what appeared to be an older child, in roughly the same state of decay as the other three. The only object in the room was a steak knife on the floor near the body. Forensic technicians would later find no blood or DNA on the knife, even when viewed under a microscope.

The police officers and the Medical Examiner were dispatched to the scene. The homicide section of the U.S. Attorney's Office was notified. The tenant, who was soon to become the defendant, was taken into custody and brought down to the Metropolitan Police Department homicide office for interrogation. She gave a long rambling account punctuated by frequent references to her oldest daughter, whom she called Jezebel and who "had to be stopped." She claimed that the children had mysteriously died in their sleep within days of each other, in the order of their ages from youngest to oldest. The detectives did not believe her. When they asked directly whether she had killed her children or to explain how they had died, she refused to answer, invoking an unschooled version of her Miranda rights. Based on the strong circumstantial evidence, the police arrested her on four counts of first-degree murder.

The Medical Examiner described the bodies of the children as "mummified." He estimated initially that they had been dead approximately one to two months. Later, after consultation with other experts, including a forensic entomologist who studied the insects that had consumed the bodies of the children, the date of death was determined to be no less than three months before the eviction, and possibly as long as six months. It would be several more weeks before they could determine the probable cause and manner of death. Thus began the case of *United States v. Banita Jacks*.

Until they died, Ms. Jacks had four daughters: Aja Fogle, age five; N'Kiah Fogle, age six; Tatianna Jacks, age eleven; and Brittany Jacks, age sixteen. The shocking discovery of their remains generated the usual reactions of hand wringing and finger pointing. How could something like this have gone undetected? Where were the other family members? What about school officials and social workers, where were they? All good questions that would eventually be answered, though not to anyone's satisfaction. Low-level social workers would be scapegoated and fired. The politicians would vow never again. But virtually everyone who heard or read about the case had the same reaction. "What kind of mother could do this to her children? She must be completely crazy."

Whether Banita Jacks was crazy or cruel was the question that would bedevil the authorities and perplex this judge throughout the litigation of her criminal case. Ms. Jacks was presented in court on a single count of murder on January 10, 2008. One count was sufficient to start the process; other charges would surely be added at the grand jury. She was appointed counsel from the Public Defender Service, whose homicide lawyers were among the best criminal defense attorneys practicing in the District of Columbia courts. The judge who heard the case on January 10 ordered that she be held without bail pending trial. Told from the perspective of the trial judge, what follows necessarily fails to capture the communications between

Ms. Jacks and her lawyers, which must remain confidential. Even what is available on the public record, however, tells the story of one of the saddest, and one of the strangest, criminal trials in the history of the District of Columbia courts.

By all accounts, there was a time, around 2005 or 2006, when Banita Jacks was a fairly normal, if somewhat reclusive, single mother of four beautiful young girls. The children were bright and did well in school. The trouble seems to have begun around the time Brittany turned thirteen and became interested in boys or, perhaps more accurately, boys became interested in her. For reasons that remain largely a mystery, Ms. Jacks could not accept the awakening of hormones in her oldest daughter or the boys who took an interest in her. She began treating Brittany abusively, calling her a bitch and a whore in front of others, including the three younger girls. She no longer referred to her as Brittany and started calling her Jezebel, the name she used in her rambling statement to the police on the night of her arrest. To keep the boys away, she started locking Brittany in her room. The police found the door to the room sealed but unlocked, with the key on top of the door frame. At some point there was no longer any need to lock the door. Brittany was not sneaking out and no boys were sneaking in during the months leading up to January 9, 2008.

To make matters worse, Nathaniel Fogle, the father of the two youngest girls, died of cancer in 2007 after a long, debilitating illness. He had been a source of some stability for Ms. Jacks and her daughters. From her statement to the police on the day of her arrest, it was obvious that Ms. Jacks was preoccupied with his death, comparing Fogle to Jesus Christ, who had "gone to sit at the right hand of the Father." In her somewhat incoherent monologue, these religious tangents seemed unconnected to the death of her children, which she refused to talk about. But could they be a possible clue to motive—a belief that the family would be reunited in the hereafter?

What was known about the Jacks family was told to the grand jury by various friends and family members, none of whom appeared to have any idea of the depths to which Ms. Jacks had sunk in the months leading up to the death of her children. All of the witnesses expressed shock and dismay, but when one pieced the story together from different angles, there were signs that Ms. Jacks had reached a level of despair and depression that might make the thought of killing her children seem to her like a way out.

Most of the grand jury investigation involved expert witnesses trying to determine the cause and manner of death. This was not simple forensic pathology, to say the least. Given the state of decomposition of the bodies of all four children, the autopsies yielded very few clues. The authorities were fairly certain that the manner of all four deaths was homicide. After all, the defendant was the only living person in the home, she had been living in there for at least three months with the dead bodies of her children, there was a knife on the floor of the room in which the oldest child was found, that room had been sealed shut with a T shirt and duct tape, and the three younger children appeared to have been purposely lined up on the floor according to size, as if in a crypt. If these had been natural deaths—say, by accidental carbon monoxide poisoning from a gas leak—surely the defendant or someone else would have called the authorities to report it and to remove the bodies. But had they been beaten, starved to death, stabbed, deliberately poisoned? The answers to these cause-of-death questions would remain a mystery that would hang over the case all the way to the end.

Eventually, the grand jury indicted Banita Jacks on four counts of first-degree premeditated murder, four counts of first-degree felony murder based on child cruelty, and four counts of cruelty to children. Premeditated murder requires proof that the accused killed the victim after consciously forming the intent to kill. Felony murder is any killing—even an accidental killing—committed during the course of committing another felony. Each murder charge carried a mandatory sentence of not less than thirty years, although the law would permit only one conviction of murder per victim (regardless of the theory). The case was randomly assigned to me for arraignment on the indictment and all further proceedings.

The challenging legal issues in the case can be broken down into two categories: the defendant's mental state and the sufficiency of the evidence of guilt. Disputes about the defendant's mental condition dominated the pretrial proceedings in the case. Was she competent to stand trial? If she was competent, was she mentally ill at the time of the crimes? Did she intend to offer an insanity defense? If not, was she competent to make that decision, and could the judge force an insanity defense on the defendant against her will, particularly if the evidence of her legal insanity was compelling? If there were no insanity defense, could the prosecution prove beyond a reasonable doubt that she committed murder or cruelty to children with the requisite mental state, given the uncertainty surrounding the question of just how each child died? Throughout these preliminary proceedings I took comfort in the jury system. If the defendant presented an insanity defense, the complex question of criminal responsibility would be the jury's responsibility, not mine. And if there were no insanity defense, or if the jury rejected it, the jury, not the judge, would decide whether the evidence was sufficient to find the defendant guilty beyond a reasonable doubt. Or so I thought.

It did not take long for me to decide that Ms. Jacks was mentally competent to stand trial. The legal test is whether the defendant has a rational understanding of the nature of the proceedings and the charges against her and can cooperate with her lawyer with a reasonable degree of rational understanding. I initially ordered a mental evaluation for competency, which determined that she was competent, although the report was somewhat equivocal because there were certain subjects Ms. Jacks would not discuss. From the first time I saw her in court, it was apparent to me that Ms. Jacks was highly intelligent, though not well educated, and that she was actively engaged with her lawyers in the defense of her case. Although the lawyers complained on more than one occasion that their client was acting against their advice, they did not suggest that she lacked the capacity to understand what they were telling her or that she was unable to cooperate with them with a reasonable degree of rational understanding. In court, whenever it was necessary to address the defendant directly, rather than through counsel, her answers were invariably responsive and offered no hint that she had any difficulty understanding what she was being asked. In short, the defendant passed all the competency tests with flying colors, and I found her competent with little hesitation.

To be more accurate, she passed all the competency tests but one. On the question whether she was suffering from a mental illness, or was suffering from a mental illness in the fall of 2007, when her children died, Ms. Jacks was adamant that she was not mentally ill. In the law, the question of whether a criminal defendant is competent to stand trial and the question of whether, by reason of mental disease or defect, the defendant should be found not criminally responsible (i.e., not guilty by reason of insanity) are separate inquiries. Competency measures the defendant's mental state at the present time. Insanity relates to the defendant's mental state at the time of the crime. Indeed, the mischievous "doctrine" of temporary insanity (think Hostess Twinkies defense or, more recently, "Affluenza") is based on the notion that one can be quite disturbed at the time of the crime, but wholly sane, and in need of no treatment, by the time the case comes up for trial. The mischief is that if the defense succeeds, the defendant is not criminally responsible and cannot be punished; but at the same time the defendant is not, or is no longer, mentally ill and cannot be confined involuntarily to a hospital for treatment.

In Banita Jacks's case, the lines were more blurred. She could discuss the case rationally and cooperate with her lawyers, but when her lawyers recommended that she consider an insanity defense, she would have none of it. Everyone who heard about the case or knew anything about it assumed that she must have been suffering from an abnormal mental condition to have killed her children. But that assumption presupposed that Ms. Jacks killed her children. The question of her guilt was still very much unproven. She quite adamantly proclaimed her innocence. She also insisted that she was not crazy. If she did not kill her children and she was not crazy, how could she plead not guilty by reason of insanity? This was the perfectly rational question she put to me when I asked her whether it was true that, against her attorneys' advice, she was refusing to raise an insanity defense. I had no answer.

But this was not the end of the matter. Ms. Jacks and her lawyers were not in agreement. Although Ms. Jacks refused to allow her lawyers to enter an insanity plea, they intimated to me that they had retained at least one expert who was prepared to testify, to a reasonable degree of medical certainty, that at the time of the crime (what crime?) Ms. Jacks, as a result of mental illness, lacked the substantial capacity to appreciate the wrongfulness of her conduct (what conduct?) or to conform her conduct to the requirements of the law. In other words, in the opinion of the defense expert, the defendant met the standard for the insanity defense and, if she were to present such a defense, she could be found not criminally responsible for the death of her children, even if she caused their death.

The law in the District of Columbia is that a finding of competency to stand trial is not, by itself, sufficient to show that a defendant is capable of rejecting an insanity defense. The trial judge must make a further inquiry into whether the defendant has made an intelligent and voluntary decision not to plead insanity, at least where there is evidence that would support a finding of not guilty by reason of insanity. That evidence can come from the bizarre nature of the crime, mental evaluations of the defendant, the defense counsel's belief that an insanity defense would have merit and should be raised, and the defendant's reasons for not wanting to raise the defense, which may be indicative of both mental illness and an irrational refusal to plead insanity. Ultimately, however, if a competent defendant makes a rational and voluntary decision to reject a potential insanity defense, the judge must accept it. As the Supreme Court has held in other contexts, respect for the defendant's freedom as a person mandates that she be permitted to make fundamental decisions about the direction of her criminal case, even where her lawyer or the judge thinks the defendant's choices are not in her own interest. In the context of a defendant who voluntarily and intelligently decides not to present an insanity defense, a judge has no choice but to respect and accept that decision, no matter how strong the evidence of insanity is, and no matter how much the defendant's lawyer, or the judge, may disagree with the decision.

One other complicating factor deserves mention. If a defendant presents an insanity defense and the jury finds her not guilty by reason of insanity, she is automatically committed to a mental hospital, where she remains confined unless and until *the defendant* can prove that she is no longer mentally ill or no longer dangerous to herself or others as a result of mental illness. For a crime as serious as murder, it is not uncommon for an insanity-acquitted defendant to remain hospitalized for many years without being able to meet the statutory standard for release. However, the rules are different when the judge finds that the defendant is not making a rational or voluntary decision to forgo a viable insanity defense and imposes the defense on the defendant against her will (usually with the assistance of another lawyer appointed for that purpose). In such cases, if the jury finds the defendant not guilty by reason of insanity, the judge may not commit the defendant to a mental hospital based on the verdict. Instead, the defendant must be released unless *the government*, in a separate proceeding, proves that the insanity-acquittee should be civilly committed to a mental hospital on the ground that she is presently mentally ill and dangerous to herself or others. This is a burden the government may not be able to carry, even in cases where the evidence proves the defendant was mentally ill at the time of the crime.

In Banita Jacks's case, her lawyers urged me to appoint a different lawyer to present Ms. Jacks's insanity defense because she had instructed her lawyers not to present the defense and their duty to their client prohibited them from acting against her expressed wishes. I understood that I could not take that course under the law unless I could find that her decision not to present the insanity defense was irrational or involuntary; but in the back of my mind was the thought that if I were to make that finding, I was facing the very real prospect that Ms. Jacks could escape both punishment and hospitalization for what the evidence might ultimately prove to have been the murder of her four children. The cynic in me warned that the whole defense strategy might be a trap, set by a sane defendant and aided by her clever lawyers, whose goal was to obtain her freedom by any means necessary, within the limits of the law.

My next step in trying to reason through this procedural quagmire was to order another mental evaluation addressed to the question of whether a current mental illness was interfering with the defendant's decision not to plead insanity, which might provide a basis for finding that her decision was not rational or voluntary. I knew that up to that point Ms. Jacks had refused to discuss the idea of an insanity plea with her lawyers or with the doctors who had evaluated her for competency to stand trial. Here's how I put the matter to Ms. Jacks:

> Now Ms. Jacks, let me say a couple of things to you. You can—and I can't stop you—go into the evaluation on Tuesday and refuse to talk to the guy. And the only reason I'm mentioning that is because you have already told me that you have been unwilling to talk to your lawyers about it. If you do that [with the doctor], it won't accomplish anything, because if your goal is to convince me that you are making good decisions for your own reasons, then I need somebody to be able to tell me that she knows exactly what she is doing and she is making choices that she believes are correct for her.
>
> And the only way I can get that is for you to be willing to talk to the experts in the field to whom you can explain what your reasons are and what your thinking is and let them tell me "Judge, there's no reason to intervene. She knows what she is doing. She has talked to her lawyers. She understands their advice. She simply does not accept their advice. She is making her own decisions about that, and her decisions are competent."
>
> So I cannot tell you what to do or force you to do anything you do not want to do. But from what you have told me, it would be in your interest, I think, to at least explain yourself to the experts so that they can explain your reasoning to me.

It all made perfect sense to me, but it soon became apparent that my words had fallen on deaf ears. The evaluation—intended to answer one of the most complex questions in the law, a question located at the intersection of criminal law and forensic psychiatry— took approximately ten minutes. According to the psychiatrist's one-paragraph report, when the doctor asked Ms. Jacks if she understood why she was there, she refused to speak, and she remained mute for each of the succeeding questions until the doctor threw in the towel. As Ms. Jacks explained to me later, her behavior was not due to lack of comprehension or to the sudden onset of some form of catatonia. Quite the contrary. She knew precisely why she was there. She had made her position clear from the beginning: she was not crazy and did not wish to rely on an insanity defense, and she had nothing further to say on the subject—not to the doctor, not to her lawyers, and not to anyone else. I, on the other hand, was no closer to answering the question the law required me to answer than I was before ordering the evaluation.

It was now clear to me that I would have to decide whether Ms. Jacks was capable of making a voluntary and intelligent decision not to present an insanity defense without additional input from a mental health professional. By refusing to talk to the doctor about her reasons, she made it impossible for the doctor to offer any opinion about whether her reasons were rational or delusional. The only avenue left was to make my own inquiry of the defendant. But what if she refused to discuss her reasons with me? As it turned out, that was a bridge I did not have to cross.

At the next hearing in the case, I confirmed with defense counsel that nothing had changed in Ms. Jacks's resolve not to rely on an insanity defense. I told her I would need to ask her a number of questions so that I could be sure, as the law required me to be, that her decision was voluntary and intelligent, with a full understanding of the consequences. Ms. Jacks said she was not feeling well that day and she was not sure she could participate effectively in the process. I agreed to postpone the inquiry a few days until she felt better, but I was becoming increasingly concerned that the previously scheduled trial date was fast approaching, and there was a lot of work that remained to be done to prepare for a jury trial in a quadruple homicide case, whether or not there would be an insanity defense. Then Ms. Jacks made an unusual request, one that few criminal defendants in my experience would have had the intelligence or temerity to ask. She wanted to know if she could have the questions I would be asking her in advance. Her request caught me by surprise, but as I thought about it, the request was not unreasonable, and it would not make the proceeding any less reliable to give her that opportunity to prepare before having to explain herself to me. I told her I would write out the questions for her lawyers to take to her, but I also told her the written questions were just a starting point and that I might ask additional or different questions depending on her answers.

At the ensuing court hearing, I conducted the so-called Frendak inquiry, the legal mechanism for determining whether the defendant was capable of waiving an insanity defense or, if not, whether it would be my obligation to impose an insanity defense against her will.* Rather than paraphrase at this point, I will include the entire colloquy as it was transcribed, so the reader can decide whether my decision, bound by the law I swore an oath to uphold, was right or wrong.

---

* The inquiry takes its name from the case of *United States v. Paula Frendak*, in which the defendant shot and killed her co-worker and then fled to Abu Dhabi, where she was arrested with the murder weapon in her possession. She refused to present an insanity defense, and the jury found her guilty of premeditated first-degree murder. The trial judge, informed by the opinions of two psychiatrists who believed that Ms. Frendak was suffering from a major psychosis at the time of the murder, bypassed the defendant's lawyer and appointed another lawyer to present an insanity defense against the will of the defendant. This time the jury found the defendant not guilty by reason of insanity. She appealed both the murder conviction and the insanity acquittal. The prosecution joined her in arguing that the insanity acquittal should not stand. The appellate court reversed, holding that the trial judge erred by basing his decision to impose the insanity defense on the apparent strength of the evidence of insanity rather than on the quality of the defendant's decision not to present it. The murder conviction was affirmed.

THE COURT: All right. I'm going to begin then not with question number one, which I'll ask you in a minute, but I want to ask you whether you understand or what you understand about why I'm even asking you these questions.

THE DEFENDANT: From what I understand, it's for competency to waive the insanity plea.

THE COURT: Right. And when you say competency, do you mean—what do you mean?

THE DEFENDANT: Whether I'm able to waive it.

THE COURT: Right. Whether you understand it?

THE DEFENDANT: Whether I understand it.

THE COURT: Understand the consequences of waiving it?

THE DEFENDANT: Uhhuh.

THE COURT: And make a free and voluntary choice that that's what you want to do, right?

THE DEFENDANT: Yes.

THE COURT: Okay. That's exactly why I'm asking it. So I'm going to go according to the questions I had already prepared, but I may deviate depending on what your answers are, because that may suggest to me the need to explain other things. But let me start by asking how old you are.

THE DEFENDANT: I'm thirty-five.

THE COURT: And how far did you go in school?

THE DEFENDANT: Um, I'd like to explain that. How far did I go to—in school or how many years have I completed?

THE COURT: Either one. In your own words is fine.

THE DEFENDANT: All right. I completed six. I was held back for three years in the 7th grade. I attended reform school in the 8th and one semester in the 9th. So the last completed is 6th.

THE COURT: Where was the 9th grade where you did the one semester?

THE DEFENDANT: La Plata High School.

THE COURT: What caused you to stop at the 9th grade?

THE DEFENDANT: I was pregnant with my first child.

THE COURT: Did you ever take any—I'm not sure I need to go too deeply into this, but did you ever take any coursework after that toward a GED or any other education?

THE DEFENDANT: I took practice GED. Yes, I did.

THE COURT: All right. Have you had any difficulty discussing your case with your lawyers? Now, I'm not asking what you discussed. But have you had any difficulty discussing your case with your lawyers and understanding what they were saying to you?

THE DEFENDANT: No, I haven't.

THE COURT: In terms of written materials you had to read to prepare your case, did you have any difficulty reading those materials?

THE DEFENDANT: No, I did not.

THE COURT: And you do read then?

THE DEFENDANT: Yes, sir.

THE COURT: All right.

THE DEFENDANT: Read and write.

THE COURT: Okay. Before this case, which began sometime around January of 2008, had you ever been treated for a mental illness?

THE DEFENDANT: No, sir.

THE COURT: When you said reform school, was that just a behavioral thing?

THE DEFENDANT: It was for not attending school.

THE COURT: Truancy?

THE DEFENDANT: Yeah.

THE COURT: But it wasn't—

THE DEFENDANT: It wasn't for any problem learning—no. No.

THE COURT: Or any mental problems?

THE DEFENDANT: No.

THE COURT: Other than this last time you were there on my order, had you ever been to St. Elizabeths Hospital?

THE DEFENDANT: No, sir.

THE COURT: Any other mental hospital?

THE DEFENDANT: No, sir.

THE COURT: Other than the mental evaluations I ordered in this case, are you presently seeing a psychiatrist or any other doctor for a mental condition?

THE DEFENDANT: Not by choice. They have approached me at the jail though.

THE COURT: All right. Have they continued to tell you that they think you should take medication or is that not part of it?

THE DEFENDANT: That's not part of it because I choose not to speak to them.

THE COURT: Okay. Are you taking any medication for mental illness?

THE DEFENDANT: No, sir.

THE COURT: Other than the one time that the hospital gave it to you, maybe more than once, maybe a couple of times, have you ever taken medication for mental illness?

THE DEFENDANT: No, sir. Except twice at the St. Elizabeths Hospital, other than that, no.

THE COURT: When you were at St. Elizabeths, at least from what I understood about what was going on, they felt you should take medication. Is that right?

THE DEFENDANT: Until I began the process, yes.

THE COURT: Right. So at least some doctors there thought you would benefit from the medication. You opposed it. You exercised your rights, I guess, with [your lawyer's] help. And the outcome of that proceeding is that you would not be required to take the medication, is that right?

THE DEFENDANT: Yes, sir.

THE COURT: And you haven't taken any medication since then?

THE DEFENDANT: No, sir.

THE COURT: Are you thinking clearly today?

THE DEFENDANT: Yes, I am, sir.

THE COURT: All right. Can you tell me what the charges against you are in this case?

THE DEFENDANT: Four felony murder charges, cruelty to children, four premeditated murder, and four child cruelty felony charges.

THE COURT: Correct. Have you gone over with your lawyers what the possible sentences are should you be convicted of any of those crimes?

THE DEFENDANT: Yes, sir.

THE COURT: Well, you seem to hesitate. I assumed you—

THE DEFENDANT: Because it was kind of done in a hearing, not, you know, just with me and my lawyers. It was done during a hearing. It was said during a hearing.

THE COURT: By me? What kind of a hearing?

THE DEFENDANT: It was one of the status hearings.

THE COURT: I'm not sure I understand that answer. Have you talked to your lawyer about what your possible sentences would be if you were convicted of these crimes?

THE DEFENDANT: Yes. We've spoken about it.

THE COURT: What do you understand the sentence for first-degree murder to be?

THE DEFENDANT: Twenty-five to life.

THE COURT: It's actually thirty.

THE DEFENDANT: Yes.

THE COURT: Does my telling you that change your thinking about the case in any way?

THE DEFENDANT: No. No.

THE COURT: And it's not thirty to life—well, it is in a way. It's thirty years, but it could—actually, I take that back. It must be at least thirty. It can be up to sixty. And under certain circumstances, which may apply in your case, it can be life without any possibility of release. Is that what was explained to you?

THE DEFENDANT: Yes.

THE COURT: All right. So I'm going to go over it again. On a single count of first-degree murder—you have several—but on any one count, the sentence must be not less than thirty years. It can be up to sixty years. And under certain circumstances, which may apply in your case, it could be life without any possibility of release. And my question to you is, is that new information to you or did you already understand that?

THE DEFENDANT: I already understood it.

THE COURT: All right.

THE DEFENDANT: I just got the twenty-five and the thirty mixed up.

THE COURT: All right. Now, we got to this point because when your lawyers and I and doctors started to talk to you about the insanity defense, you basically refused to discuss it. It's more complicated than that, but I'll put it that way. You wouldn't talk to me about it. I got the impression you weren't talking to your lawyers about it, and you certainly weren't going to talk to the doctors about it. Did you have enough discussion with anybody, particularly your lawyers, so that you feel you understand what the insanity defense is?

THE DEFENDANT: Yes.

THE COURT: Can you tell me in your own words simply, not in an elaborate explanation, but tell me in your own words what you believe the defense is?

THE DEFENDANT: The defense is saying that at the time of the alleged crimes, that I was insane.

THE COURT: Right. And insane means unable to appreciate—because of a mental illness, unable to appreciate the wrongfulness of the conduct or to conform your conduct to the requirements of the law. And you would have the burden of proving an insanity defense by a preponderance of the evidence. Before you stopped talking about it, had you talked to your lawyers about that?

THE DEFENDANT: Yes, they have spoken to me.

THE COURT: All right. I'm not insisting on the answer to this next question, if [your lawyer] says I shouldn't have you answer, but I'd like to know the answer. Other than those doctors that I sent you to, most of whom you wouldn't talk to, have your lawyers sent you to talk to any doctors about an insanity defense in this case?

DEFENSE COUNSEL: Your Honor, we talked about this question and this is the one question she does not want to answer.

THE COURT: As I said, I don't think I'll require an answer to that question. I'll explain why I'm asking. Under the cases that require me to ask these questions in the first place, it seems important to the courts that have considered these issues if there's some report out there, that, in fact, says you would have a possible insanity defense based on a doctor's assessment of your condition at or about the time of the crimes in this case—I've never seen such a report. In fact, I've never seen any report that suggests to me in any way that you would have an insanity defense even if you wanted to raise one. And that's been part of my thinking in this case all along. There may be a report out there if your lawyers sent you to a doctor and a doctor formed that opinion. If there is such a report, I haven't seen it. So the purpose for my asking that question is to find out if there's something I'm missing. Because from everything I've seen, to be honest with you, I'm not sure I would have even conducted this inquiry. The only reason I did conduct it is because this whole question got raised when your lawyers said we've talked to her about an insanity defense. She won't discuss it with us. So that gave rise to the need for me to determine whether you were making your own decision about that with a full understanding of the consequences. All right. But, otherwise, I won't ask—I won't require you to answer that question. I can tell you this, though. If I conclude that you are competent to waive the insanity defense and I accept your waiver, and if you were convicted of the charges, any of the charges against you, if you were to then come forward with a report, at that stage that had been done as of this stage that said there's a very strong basis for an insanity defense in this case, I would consider that to have been waived because you knew about it and didn't . . . and you chose not to assert it. Do you understand what I'm saying?

THE DEFENDANT: I understand.

THE COURT: All right. Do you understand that because you refuse to cooperate with the doctors I sent you to for the evaluations that I ordered, those doctors were unable to tell me, one way or the other, if your decision not to raise an insanity defense was a competent decision? That is, one that was knowing and intelligent with a full understanding of the consequences and one that was not, itself, the product of some mental illness. Do you understand that?

THE DEFENDANT: Yes, I do.

THE COURT: Is it your present intention not to raise an insanity defense?

THE DEFENDANT: Yes.

THE COURT: Do you understand that even if you chose to raise the insanity defense, the defense would not arise unless and until the government proved beyond a reasonable doubt that you were guilty of one or more of the charges against you?

THE DEFENDANT: Yes.

THE COURT: Did you understand what I just said?

THE DEFENDANT: I understand that.

THE COURT: It's a complicated question. You sure you understand?

THE DEFENDANT: Yes, I do.

THE COURT: All right. Do you understand that even if you do raise the insanity defense, you could, at the same time, present any other defense you had to the charges against you?

THE DEFENDANT: Yes, I do understand.

THE COURT: All right. So that at trial, if you were raising the insanity defense, the government would first have to prove the charges against you, and you could present any other defense to those charges. And then if, but only if, the jury were to find you guilty of one or more of the charges against you would the insanity defense come into play. Do you understand that?

THE DEFENDANT: Yes, I do.

THE COURT: All right. Do you understand that if you do raise the insanity defense or if you were to make a decision to raise the insanity defense and if the jury decided that you were not guilty by reason of insanity at the time the crimes were committed, you would be sent to St. Elizabeths Hospital instead of to a prison?

THE DEFENDANT: Yes, I do understand.

THE COURT: Do you understand that you would then have a right to have a hearing within fifty days of that day to see whether you were at that time presently mentally ill and, if you were mentally ill, whether you were dangerous to yourself or others?

THE DEFENDANT: Yes, I do understand.

THE COURT: Do you understand that if a Court were to determine at that hearing that you were presently mentally ill and as a result of mental illness, dangerous to yourself or others, you would have a right to have a hearing on that issue every six months thereafter?

THE DEFENDANT: Yes, I do.

THE COURT: You might not ask for a hearing every six months but you would have a right to ask for it every six months. Do you understand that?

THE DEFENDANT: Yes, sir.

THE COURT: And do you understand, finally, that if at one of those hearings, the Court determined that you were either not mentally ill or no longer dangerous to yourself or others as a result of mental illness, you would be released from the hospital and you could not then be sent to prison because the jury will have determined that you were not guilty of the charges by reason of insanity if you had raised the insanity defense?

THE DEFENDANT: Yes, I do understand that.

THE COURT: Is there anything you want to ask me about the insanity defense or about your decision not to raise it?

THE DEFENDANT: No, sir.

THE COURT: All right. That's fine. Ms. Jacks, after everything we've talked about this morning, much of which I think you've already thought about before this morning, is it still your decision not to raise the insanity defense?

THE DEFENDANT: Yes, it is still my decision.

THE COURT: And can you tell me why, in your own words?

THE DEFENDANT: Basically, Your Honor, because I am not insane and these are alleged charges.

THE COURT: That's true. But I've already explained just a minute ago that even though the charges are alleged and the government has to prove them and you have every right to have a trial to defend against them, you could do that and still raise the insanity defense?

THE DEFENDANT: But I'm still not insane, your Honor.

THE COURT: All right.

THE DEFENDANT: That's like my major—

THE COURT: That's fair enough. I've already found that you were competent to stand trial. In fact, as I think I indicated last week, I personally have never had any doubt that you were competent to stand trial. I'm a layperson. I needed a doctor to tell me that. But it was always my perception that you understood the nature of the proceedings against you, the nature of the charges. And that except for the insanity defense, you were willing and able to cooperate with your lawyers with a reasonable degree of rational understanding and that has been confirmed and I have so found. I today find that you've been fully informed of the choices available to you with respect to the insanity defense, that you understand, in a rational and competent way, the consequences of failing to assert the defense, that you have freely chosen to waive the defense, and that you've made a voluntary, knowing, and intelligent decision to do so. Therefore, I'll accept the waiver and we'll proceed to trial on the merits of the charges.

The reader may disagree, but I found the defendant's responses to my questions rational, if not wise. Whatever her reasons were, she certainly understood the consequences of her choice; and her unwavering decision not to present an insanity defense was, from everything I could see, entirely voluntary. The issue was now settled. The trial would go forward on the charges of murder and related charges, and the jury would be instructed to decide whether the prosecution had proven the guilt of the defendant beyond a reasonable doubt, without considering a defense of not guilty by reason of insanity. All that remained was to prepare for the jury trial less than a month away. Selecting a fair and impartial jury would not be easy.

Just when I thought I had safely crossed one mine field, the defense dropped a bombshell. As we began to discuss the issues surrounding selection of a jury to hear this lengthy trial of a quadruple homicide with very graphic photographs and highly complex forensic evidence, not to mention extensive pretrial publicity that had undoubtedly colored the minds of most of the members of the community who would populate the pool from which we would pick the jury, the defendant's lawyer stood and said "Your honor, Ms. Jacks has indicated—once again against our advice—that she is considering waiving her right to a jury and having her case tried by the court."

I could feel a knot begin to form in the pit of my stomach as I tried to process the information calmly. Of course, in any felony case, the defendant has a constitutional right to a trial by jury. Like any right, it can be waived, as long as the court determines that the waiver represents "a voluntary relinquishment or abandonment of a known right or privilege." However, unlike some other rights, which belong exclusively to the defendant, the Supreme Court has held that the prosecutor also has a right to a jury trial. So even if the defendant wants to waive a jury, the prosecutor must also agree in order for the court to hear the case without a jury. As these thoughts were racing through my head in the wake of the defense counsel's surprise announcement, I found myself hoping that either the defendant would change her mind or the prosecutor would object and insist on a jury trial. The last thing I wanted was the solitary burden of deciding the guilt or innocence of this disturbed woman accused of murdering her four daughters with nothing more to go on than the circumstantial evidence the government had been able to piece together during its investigation.

One of the difficult things about being a judge is that the job affords little room for normal human emotions. If things are sad, one cannot cry. If things are funny, it is usually inappropriate to laugh. If things make you angry, anger must be expressed, if at all, in the most temperate of tones. So while these and other thoughts were rushing through my mind, the court reporter was writing everything down and everything said was on the record. I calmly pointed out to the parties that it would not make sense to spend hours working out the logistics of jury selection and certain other jury-related issues if this was going to be a non-jury trial. In addition, I explained that because this was such an important decision, I would not attempt to take a waiver from the defendant then and there, but would give her another week to discuss it with her lawyers and make a final decision. In the meantime, the prosecutors could use the time to figure out what the government's position would be in the event the defendant did decide to waive her right to a jury trial.

When we reconvened the next week, defense counsel advised me—and the defendant confirmed—that she had decided to waive a jury trial and try the case to the court. Before asking the defendant the series of questions necessary to determine whether her jury waiver was voluntary and intelligent, I asked the prosecutor to state the government's position. The response was "If the defendant wants to waive trial by jury, we're fine with trying this case non-jury." The only thing left was to ask the defendant a series of questions similar to those I had asked when she decided to give up an insanity defense, so I could satisfy myself, and the record would reflect, that she understood the right she was giving up and that she had made a voluntary and rational decision. What follows are my questions and her responses verbatim:

THE COURT: Ms. Jacks, I need to ask you a number of questions to make sure that you are giving up your right to a jury trial having thought about it and understanding fully the consequences of your decision. I know the last time I had to ask you a lot of questions about your decision not to raise an insanity defense, you got annoyed with me because you thought I was making things difficult for you. That is not my purpose. But I need to have a record that shows that you thought about this, that you discussed it with your lawyers, and that you made the decision that you feel is best for you, knowing the rights you are giving up and understanding all of the consequences. Let's start with the easy things. How are you feeling today? That's the easiest.

DEFENDANT: I feel fine.

THE COURT: Are you taking any medication at the jail?

DEFENDANT: No, I'm not.

THE COURT: Do you feel that you're thinking clearly today?

DEFENDANT: Yes.

THE COURT: Is there anything going on that is making it difficult to understand these proceedings?

DEFENDANT: No.

THE COURT: Do you understand that you have a constitutional right to have a trial by jury in your case that could not be taken away by me or by anyone else unless you chose to give it up voluntarily?

DEFENDANT: Yes, I do understand.

THE COURT: Did you talk to your lawyers about your jury trial rights?

DEFENDANT: Yes.

THE COURT: Was it explained to you and do you understand that if you exercise your right to a trial by jury, the prosecutor would have to convince all twelve jurors beyond a reasonable doubt that you were guilty of each charge before you could be found guilty?

DEFENDANT: Yes, they explained that.

THE COURT: And did they explain that if even one juror thought you were not guilty and all of the eleven others thought you were guilty, you could not be found guilty? And ordinarily in that case there would have to be another trial or trials until all twelve jurors either found you guilty or found you not guilty?

DEFENDANT: Yes, we discussed all of that.

THE COURT: Have you had any difficulty understanding what your lawyers explained to you about your right to a trial by jury?

DEFENDANT: No.

THE COURT: Can you tell me in your own words why—I don't want you to talk about anything you've discussed about your case with your lawyers—but I do want to know why you have decided you do not want a jury and prefer to have a trial by the court.

DEFENDANT: Can I decline to answer that because I would have to get into my case to answer that?

THE COURT: That is a reasonable response. Is it fair for me to assume from your answer that you've made an intelligent choice that you think it would be better for you to have a trial by the court without a jury than to have a trial with a jury? And by better for you I mean you feel it is more likely it would have a better outcome.

DEFENDANT: Yes, sir.

There were additional questions, but that was the gist of it; and in the end, I accepted the defendant's waiver of her right to a trial by jury. The government consented, and we were about to adjourn the proceedings until the trial, which would begin in two weeks, when the defense attorney made one last-ditch effort to escape the box his client had put him in.

DEFENSE COUNSEL: Well, I'm going to move to continue [i.e., postpone] the trial because I believe Ms. Jacks is not competent and not competent to waive the insanity defense. And I know the court has ruled and today you actually said again you believe her to be competent, you found her competent et cetera, but I think I have to make this motion and ask the court to start this whole inquiry again, at the risk of being at odds with my client, who doesn't want me to say that, and while I'm at it I'll put that on the record too.

THE COURT: Your motion for a continuance is denied. In my view, there is no basis to grant that motion. I've done everything I can do. I've observed her in court. I've had interactions with her in court. I've ordered an initial screening. I've ordered a full competency evaluation. The evaluation was unequivocal in my view in finding that she is competent to proceed. I conducted a lengthy and I thought very comprehensive Frendak inquiry about her decision to waive her insanity defense. Today I conducted another inquiry about her decision to waive her right to trial by jury. On each and every one of those occasions in court, I found her to be completely lucid, completely oriented to the circumstances she was in, entirely responsive to my inquiries—not always pleased with the fact that I was asking her those questions because, from her point of view, the answers seemed so obvious—but I explained to her why I had to ask and she understood. She went so far in the Frendak inquiry as to ask to review the questions in advance so she could be prepared, which I thought was an extremely intelligent thing for somebody to do. I just don't have any evidence of any kind from any source—and frankly never had any evidence from any source except for your own misgivings as counsel—that she is not competent to proceed. Now I realize that mental illness can be a very subtle process, and I don't claim to be an expert on the subject, but I just have no evidence in the record before me that Ms. Jacks is now, or in fact has ever been, incompetent. In my view, she has a factual and rational understanding of the nature of the proceedings and of the charges against her, and in my view she is able to cooperate with her lawyer with a reasonable degree of rational understanding. To be sure, she has her own way of looking at things, and it's been obvious at various stages of the case that she does not look at things the same way her lawyers do. And she has rejected some advice that her lawyers have given to her. We provide lawyers to give advice, but competent clients are free to reject that advice, whether they are making good decisions or bad decisions, prospectively or retrospectively. And I'm fully satisfied that Ms. Jacks is able to make those decisions and choices and that they are hers to make. So I do not see any reason to continue the trial or to conduct further competency proceedings.

The trial was scheduled to begin on July 13, 2009. Before we could start the actual trial, however, I had to decide a motion to suppress evidence. The defense had filed a motion to suppress Ms. Jacks's statement to the police on the day of her arrest on the ground that it was the product of an illegal arrest in violation of the defendant's Fourth Amendment rights, and that it was also inadmissible under the Due Process Clause of the Fifth Amendment and the Supreme Court's *Miranda* decision. So for part of two days I watched a videotape of Ms. Jacks's six-hour interrogation by the police. She had refused to answer most questions pertaining directly to the death of her children and admitted nothing; but the prosecutors wanted to introduce the tape to show the defendant's state of mind and to argue that her ability to answer some questions and to willfully refuse to answer others showed that she was in complete control of her faculties and conscious of her guilt.

After watching the tape and hearing arguments, I ruled that the tape was admissible. Ms. Jacks's defense attorney objected to my ruling and moved once again for the appointment of a separate lawyer to present an insanity defense, arguing that the tape provided additional evidence of mental illness that would support a verdict of not guilty by reason of insanity. I was not willing to revisit that question, which, in my opinion, I had put to rest, and I denied the request. It would not be the last time I would have to deal with that issue.

With the suppression motion out of the way, the prosecution's formal presentation of evidence began on the morning of July 15, 2009. The first three witnesses—a real estate property manager and two deputy U.S. marshals—traced the events leading up to the eviction and the discovery of the bodies of the children. Through the eyes of law enforcement, and with the benefit of hindsight, the marshals described actions by Ms. Jacks on January 9, 2008, that could be interpreted as indicative of her consciousness of guilt and an attempt to conceal what she knew to be a crime.

Next came the two grandmothers—the mother of Banita Jacks and the mother of Nathanial Fogle—to talk about their contact with the defendant and her children in 2006 and 2007. Ms. Jacks's mother had not seen her or the children after the fall of 2006, and did not know where they were living. Mr. Fogle's mother last saw Ms. Jacks and the girls early in 2007 about a month before her son died on February 19, 2007. Banita did not attend the funeral on February 28, nor did the two Fogle granddaughters. Ms. Fogle tried to maintain contact with Banita and the grandchildren in the next several months, but she could not break through the wall of silence.

The prosecution called several other friends and family members to fill in some of the gaps in the timeline, but the last time anyone reported seeing any of the children alive was in the summer of 2007. One friend testified that she visited in March of 2007 and saw Banita and the three younger girls, but not Brittany. There was no furniture in the house, and Banita said she had to throw it out because "ants got in it." The friend visited again in April of 2007 and saw Banita with the two youngest children, but not Brittany or Tatianna. She visited again in May of 2007 and believed she saw Banita with the three younger girls, but in June she was sure that she saw only Banita and the two youngest. Although she saw Banita once or twice after that, the last time she saw any of the children was in June of 2007.

Neighbors testified that they continued to see the mother from time to time into the late fall of 2007, but she looked more and more disheveled as the months went by, and no one reported seeing any of the children after June of 2007. Each witness described a good mother who was very attentive to her children, if a bit overprotective, until early in 2007, when things started to go downhill around the time Mr. Fogle died. A few friends of Brittany testified that Ms. Jacks's abuse of her oldest daughter began even earlier, in 2006.

Collectively, this evidence painted a picture of a family that became more and more insular and reclusive beginning in the spring of 2007 until the children entirely disappeared from view in the early summer. The evidence was corroborated by school officials and social workers who visited the home, or tried to visit, at various times during the year. After Brittany started to rack up absences from her high school, a social worker from the school made a home visit on April 27, 2007. She took a police officer with her. Ms. Jacks answered the door but refused to let them in. They did not see Brittany, though Ms. Jacks said she was there. Ms. Jacks was hostile but coherent. She said she did not like Brittany's school or its students, and she took her out of school to "home school" her. Through the open door the officer and the social worker could see and hear at least two other younger children. They did not appear to be injured or malnourished. When they asked why those children were not in school, Ms. Jacks told them "it is none of your business." They informed Ms. Jacks that they had a duty to report truancy and left. The visit lasted approximately five minutes.

In the following days, Brittany's school social worker made repeated calls to the agency responsible for investigating neglected children, to the police, and to the city's non-emergency hotline phone number to report the possible neglect of the younger children she had seen in the home. The only follow-up was a home visit by a youth division detective and two police officers on April 30, 2007. Ms. Jacks refused to let them in because they did not have a warrant, but she did bring the three youngest children to the door. Ms. Jacks said she did not like the public schools because they were teaching "sex education, homosexuality, and other topics that conflicted with her religious beliefs," and again she said she was "home schooling" her children, producing a textbook to substantiate her claim. They informed Ms. Jacks that she could not home school unless she "went through the process" and threatened that the children could be taken away from her. Ms. Jacks remained defiant, and the police eventually left. The next time that detective visited the Jacks home was January 9, 2008.

One of the police officers did stop by with a social worker a few days after the April 30 visit, and again by himself a few days after that, but no one answered the door on either occasion, and eventually he gave up. Between April 30, 2007, and January 9, 2008, there is no record of anyone from the children's school or anyone from the social service agency responsible for protecting the welfare of abused and neglected children ever visiting the Jacks residence or making any other contact with Banita Jacks or her children. After the story broke on January 9, 2008, the mayor of the District of Columbia, expressing outrage, fired several social workers.

Finally, there came a parade of medical examiners, forensic

pathologists, and other forensic scientists to try to explain how and when the children had died. No one would ever explain why. The long and short of it was that the experts did not know for sure what caused the death of any of the four children. They were virtually unanimous that all were homicides, but that was largely based on the nonscientific circumstantial evidence. The main problem standing in the way of definitive judgments as to cause was the state of almost total decomposition of the bodies of all four children. Clues to most homicides can be found by tracing the paths of bullets or stab wounds or bruising from blunt force through the skin and soft tissues of the victim. The bodies of Brittany, Tatianna, N'Kiah, and Aja were found with virtually no skin or soft tissue.

The medical examiner who did the autopsy on Brittany reported that the cause of her death was "undetermined." He did find what appeared to him to be three "slits" in her left torso that were consistent with stab wounds, but there was not enough tissue for him to be sure that they were stab wounds or that stab wounds were the cause of death. However, the chief forensic anthropologist at the Armed Forces Institute of Pathology—who is not a forensic pathologist but who specializes in autopsy of skeletal or very decomposed remains—testified that he consulted with the medical examiner who did Brittany's autopsy and looked at the autopsy photos, and he was certain that the three "slits" were stab wounds, although even he could not say for sure that stabbing was the cause of death. Suicide was unlikely, but it could not be definitively ruled out.

The forensic evidence regarding the three younger children was only slightly more illuminating. Again, all of the forensic pathologists who conducted the autopsies characterized the manner of death as homicide. The medical examiner who performed the autopsy on N'Kiah found two horizontal linear depressions on what was left of the child's neck that were consistent with ligature wounds (caused by bindings or ties), but there was too much decomposition for her to be sure they were ligature wounds or that strangulation by ligature was the cause of death. In her autopsy report she listed the cause of death as undetermined. The medical examiner who performed the autopsy on Aja found a "small dark grey area on the back of her neck with a weave pattern and a skin depression suggestive of a 'ligature furrow,'" but her testimony also was that the degree of decomposition was too great for her to conclude that Aja died from strangulation by ligature, and she too classified the cause of death as undetermined.

That same medical examiner observed the autopsy of Tatianna, whose body was even more decomposed than the others, in part because she had been laid to rest on her stomach, face down, with gravity having an effect. For this reason, while she also had a small depression on the back of her neck that could have been a "ligature furrow," it was less distinct than in the other two children, and again the cause of death was ruled undetermined.

Finally, the armed forces forensic anthropologist was almost certain that the marks on Aja and N'Kiah were ligature impressions and the mark on Tatianna was probably a ligature impression because it appeared to match the other two, but even he could not conclude that the cause of death in any of the three cases was strangulation by ligature because the degree of decomposition of all three bodies made it impossible to rule out other possible causes.

While there was little certainty about the cause of death, the experts generally agreed about the timing. Based primarily on the testimony of the forensic entomologist, who studied the life cycles of the insects that had feasted on the victims' dead bodies, corroborated by the findings of the army forensic anthropologist, it was determined that the children had been dead at least three months, and possibly as long as six months, when they were discovered. It was also determined that Brittany had died first, a month or more before her younger sisters, who died close in time to each other. I will spare the reader the grisly details of that testimony, but if credited, it meant that Ms. Jacks's statement to the police that all four children died in their sleep within days of each other, with Aja dying first and Brittany dying last, was almost certainly false.

All together the prosecution called twenty-three witnesses and introduced hundreds of exhibits. On July 24, 2009, the government rested. The defense called two brief witnesses that same day. The first was a textile and fiber expert from the Trace Evidence Unit of the police department. He testified that he had placed two autopsy specimens labeled "ligature remains" under a microscope and he was unable to detect any textile fibers in either specimen. The second witness was a defense investigator who testified that there were two skylights in the Jacks residence, thereby impeaching the testimony of several government witnesses who had described the house as having only one skylight. That was it. The defense rested.

I have a personal rule. Almost all of my colleagues disagree with me. When I am presiding in a non-jury trial, where I am acting as both the judge of the law and the finder of the facts, during the trial and during "deliberations" I will not discuss the facts with anyone, including judicial colleagues, intimate friends and family members, or even my law clerk. My reason is simple. In a jury trial we instruct the jury not to discuss the case with anyone, including each other, until all the evidence is in; and we instruct them that during deliberations they may discuss the case only among themselves when all twelve of them are present in the privacy of the jury room. I believe the same principles should apply when I am the sole fact finder, to ensure that the facts I find are based on the evidence as I assess it and are not based on the impressions or biases of anyone with whom I might have discussed the evidence. As I stated, most judges feel that my rule is excessively punctilious, but I nonetheless felt I should not make an exception for this tragic and difficult case. As a result, deciding the guilt or innocence of Banita Jacks was probably the loneliest assignment I have had in my forty years as a trial judge.

So after both sides rested and I heard the closing arguments of counsel, I announced to the parties that I would take the matter under advisement and deliberate on my verdict. Just as I was about to declare the recess for that purpose, Ms. Jacks's attorneys asked to approach the bench out of the hearing of the prosecutors. Although this request was somewhat irregular, I did not wish to be peremptory and I agreed at least to hear the subject matter of their request. When the lawyers came to the bench they attempted to hand me a legal pleading captioned a Motion For Reconsideration and Renewed

Motion For Appointment Of *Amicus Curiae* Counsel To Present
Insanity Defense.

I was hot. As soon as I saw the caption, I handed the document
back and refused to accept it. I sensed that this was another trap
by the defense, but even if it was not, I knew that I did not want
any verdict I reached to be tainted by a claim that I had considered evidence of insanity before I decided the guilt or innocence of
the defendant on the merits of the charges. I admonished defense
counsel that I had not even begun to consider whether the government had proven the charges against their client, and even if I were
willing to reconsider the insanity issue at some point in the future,
it was certainly premature to do so before reaching a verdict on
the charges. I insisted that they tell me whether their client had
authorized them to file that motion, because if not, they were acting unethically for all the reasons we had previously discussed so
many times. To my surprise, counsel stated "yes, she said we could
file it, but she asked that you not read it until after you reach your
verdict." That response confirmed to me once again the defendant's intelligence and competence to stand trial and said all that
needed to be said about the impropriety of attempting to present
such a motion at that critical juncture, not to mention trying to
present it without notice to the prosecution. I abruptly terminated
the bench conference and told the prosecutors generally what had
occurred, taking care not to reveal confidential attorney and client
communications.

I took all of my trial notes and boxes of exhibits into the jury
room to begin my deliberations. Using the jury room was both
symbolic and provided the privacy and quiet I needed to concen-
trate on the task at hand. There had been intense public interest and
media attention surrounding the trial, and I had no way of predict-
ing how long the deliberations would take. The Court's Director of
Media and Public Relations was bugging me to set a time certain
for announcing the verdict so she could alert the press in advance. I
declined, except to tentatively schedule a proceeding in court three
days later, with the understanding that I would cancel it if I was not

yet ready to decide. I went through the evidence over the next two days, working long into the evening on both days. I went over and over the forensic evidence relating to the possible stab wounds on Brittany's left torso and "ligature wounds" on the necks of the three younger girls. I found myself wondering why, if there was another side to these findings, didn't the defense call experts of their own to refute the prosecution's experts, but then I caught myself and consciously put the burden of proof back on the government where it belonged. When I was finally satisfied that I had considered the facts from every possible angle, including the very substantial circumstantial evidence of guilt, I felt ready to announce my verdict and gave notice that the court proceeding would go forward as scheduled.

At the appointed hour, I settled into my chair on the bench, staring out at a packed courtroom. After explaining that I had not discussed the facts of the case with anyone, either during the trial or during deliberations, here is how I began:

> Unlike other people who knew about this case, heard about the case, or read about the case, and who probably had a very normal human reaction to it when they heard about the events that unfolded on January 9, 2008, along the lines of "Well, she must have killed them, but what would drive a person to do that? Why would she do that?" I have not approached the case from that point of view, for obvious reasons. I have, as a finder of fact, started with the presumption that there are four unexplained deaths. I have done everything humanly possible to give Ms. Jacks the benefit of the presumption of innocence to which she is entitled, and I have required the government to prove its charges beyond a reasonable doubt. So the question for me as the factfinder is, and has always been: Was this a homicide? And if so, who did it and how? And can the government prove its charges against Ms. Jacks beyond a reasonable doubt?

I went on to describe my deliberations and my assessment of the evidence in some detail so as to make a record of my findings of fact. The Court rules require findings of fact in non-jury trials "upon request," but in this case I felt I owed it to the parties and to the public to explain my reasoning without waiting for a request. Announcing the verdict took more than an hour. In the end I found the defendant guilty of four counts of cruelty to children, four counts of first-degree felony murder based on cruelty to children, and three counts of first-degree premeditated murder of the three youngest girls. The ambiguous circumstances surrounding Brittany's death left me with a reasonable doubt as to precisely how she died (I even considered suicide), and I found Ms. Jacks not guilty of first-degree premeditated murder of Brittany. But as to felony murder, I had no doubt that Brittany was the victim of deliberate cruelty from her mother lasting many months, which led inexorably to her death. I ordered a presentence report and scheduled sentencing approximately two months later.

As I could have predicted, after the verdict the defense filed the motion they had tried to file before the verdict. The prosecution filed an opposition and I denied the motion. Although my decision to accept the defendant's waiver of an insanity defense had been difficult, I continued to feel that I had made the correct decision. Ultimately the Court of Appeals would decide that issue, and either the convictions would stand or the case would be sent back for an insanity trial. I had done my best, and I saw no need to revisit the issue once again.

I sentenced Ms. Jacks on December 18, 2009, to four consecutive mandatory thirty-year prison terms for the premeditated murders of the three youngest girls and the first-degree felony murder of Brittany. All other sentences were concurrent, resulting in an aggregate term of one hundred and twenty years in prison. Several weeks later I learned that Ms. Jacks had directed her lawyers not to file an appeal, making one last decision that a competent defendant is free to make.

Banita Jacks will live out her remaining days in prison for the murder of her four daughters. Sometimes I wonder if the result would have been different if she had presented an insanity defense or if I had imposed one on her over her objection. At the same time, I don't second-guess my decision. In our system we respect the right of a mentally competent person to decide her own fate, even when facing the most serious criminal charges and even when her decision is to forgo a possible avenue of escape. I do think about how she is doing in prison. I try to imagine what she thinks about as she tries somehow to come to grips with her crimes. I speculate about whether she has a will to live and whether her plan all along might have been to kill herself, so that she and her children could join Nathaniel Fogle in her conception of the afterlife. Mostly, though, I think about those four beautiful young girls and what they could have become, and I am haunted to this day by the gruesome photographs of their skeletal remains as they were discovered during what started out as a routine eviction on January 9, 2008.

12

Building Justice in Kosovo

JUDGE EDWARD S. WILSON

 *Judge Edward S. Wilson was appointed to the Minnesota District Court in 1987. He has served in the family, juvenile, civil, and criminal divisions and as the presiding judge of the criminal team. Before taking the bench, Judge Wilson worked for the Legal Aid Society of Minneapolis and Neighborhood Justice Center in Saint Paul. In 2002, Judge Wilson was nominated by* the U.S. Department of State to serve as an international judge with the United Nations mission in Kosovo.

AS A JUDGE, I SOMETIMES HAVE THE PRIVILEGE OF SPEAKING TO groups of students. At the end of these talks, I always invite the students to ask questions. Almost always, someone will ask "What was your hardest case?" The toughest cases do not necessarily present the most arcane legal issues, but are those that exhibit the tensions between competing values when one applies the rule of law. Transitional societies—particularly small, insular communities—can provide a perfect laboratory for revealing these tensions. When students ask that question, I now answer without hesitation that I've had cases that had more complex legal issues, with higher stakes for the litigants, but there is no question that my most challenging cases happened not in the United States, but in Eastern Europe, in the now-independent nation of Kosovo.[*]

Before 1989, Kosovo was part of the Federal Republic of Yugo-slavia. This is a region where memories, or more precisely, grudges run long and deep. For hundreds of years the overwhelming major-ity of Kosovo's residents were ethnic Albanians commonly known as Kosovars. Serbia, however, has long seen Kosovo as the cradle of its nation and part of its land. The Serbs still commemorate their defeat to the Turks on June 28, 1389, on The Field of Blackbirds, an area just outside Pristina, Kosovo. It was there, on the six hundredth anniversary of this historic defeat, that Slobodan Milosevic delivered a passionate nationalistic speech to a crowd of one million Serbs, reminding them of the courage that their Serb forebears exhibited in their heroic but fruitless battle to defend what was then their land, and exhorting them to exhibit that same courage.

In 1987 Slobodan Milosevic became president of Serbia on a nationalist platform, and in 1989 he pressed the Serbian parlia-ment to revise the constitution to regain control over Kosovo. The parliament acceded and annexed Kosovo. In response, the Kosovo Assembly, which was majority Kosovar, symbolically declared an independent Republic of Kosovo and began a nonviolent resistance movement. During this same period, a decidedly violent group, the Kosovo Liberation Army (KLA), was marshaling its forces, and began an armed conflict against Serbia. The conflict began on February 28, 1998, and continued until June 11, 1999. More than one million people were driven from their homes and an estimated 11,000 Kosovo Albanians and 2,000 Serbs were killed.

The conflict did not proceed according to the accepted norms of warfare; Serbian forces and militia engaged in mass killings and

---

[*] Kosovo was a semi-autonomous United Nations (UN) protectorate when the writer served there from 2002 to 2003, but it formally declared its independence on February 17, 2008. As of November 2017, 112 of 193 UN member states, in-cluding the United States, have recognized Kosovo as a sovereign state.

"ethnic cleansing" of Kosovars, and massive human rights violations that ultimately led to international intervention. NATO engaged in a bombing campaign against Serbian military targets to pressure the Serbian government to stop its operations in Kosovo. The campaign was successful, but left a power vacuum in Kosovo.

In the aftermath of the war, the United Nations established a governing structure known as the United Nations Mission in Kosovo (UNMIK) to administer the province of Kosovo on an interim basis, pending a final determination of its status. When UNMIK originally began its mission, there was no provision for a court system other than that which already existed. It soon became apparent, however, that it was necessary to impose a revamped court structure over this stew of simmering ethnic hatred. In addition to the day-to-day criminal offenses that are common in any society, many charges arose from the war including war crimes and weapons-trafficking, as well as organized criminal activity that presented unique judicial challenges. Even more basic, as Kosovo moved from the transitional stage to a more stable government, it had to cultivate a justice system worthy of the name. It had to develop a justice system that operated under the constraints of the rule of law. Under the new system, everyone, regardless of their station in life or position in government, had to be held accountable to laws that were clear, just, and, crucially, fairly administered by competent, unbiased officials. The idea of "fairness" assumes that people who have roughly similar cases will be treated in roughly the same manner. A justice system will not be respected if its constituents do not believe it is fundamentally fair.

There were few Serb lawyers and judges in Kosovo before the conflict, and fewer afterwards. Most Serbs left Kosovo for Serbia during the conflict, and those few attorneys and judges who remained generally refused to cooperate with the post-conflict Kosovo justice system, as they believed it to be illegitimate and biased against Serbs. The Kosovars had been, as a practical matter, barred from participating in the justice system, such as it was, during the presidency of Slobodan Milosevic. When, in 1989, Milosevic abruptly ended Kosovo's status as an autonomous province of Serbia, as part of his scheme he removed Kosovars from the judiciary. The end result, as is often the case in transitional societies, was that UNMIK was faced with the intractable problem of constructing a justice system from whole cloth that would fairly address a daunting volume of high-intensity cases involving war crimes, ethnic violence, and organized crime. These cases had to be adjudicated by an inadequate number of judges and prosecutors who were predominately Kosovars. As they had been previously "shut out" of the justice system by the Milosevic regime, few of them had sufficient training or experience to handle such cases. Even more important, the long-standing enmity between the Kosovars and the Serbs—with all the social pressure as well as physical intimidation that entailed—posed a perceptual as well as a factual barrier to the possibility of Kosovars providing fair trials to all parties.

Nevertheless, out of necessity, and to circumvent the charge that it was in essence a neocolonial operation, UNMIK began the court system by allowing the Kosovars to prosecute and judge all the cases that came into the system. It quickly became obvious that this was an untenable situation. The Kosovar judges exhibited an obvious bias against the Serbs who appeared before them; that is, they tended to detain Serbs in cases for which they would release Kosovars, and would mete out harsh sentences for the most minimal offenses committed by Serbs. Conversely, the Kosovar prosecutors were less likely to charge Kosovars for alleged war crimes than they were to charge Serbs for similar offenses. This behavior may have been attributed to threats, fear of retaliation from other Kosovars, bribery—Kosovar judges were paid only about 600 Euros per month (approximately U.S. $732)—or some combination of factors. After the first cases in which Serbs were parties, it was clear that the Kosovars could not be relied upon to give them a fair trial. In addition, local judges had little security provided for them and they were vulnerable to pressure from organized crime by either threats or bribery. To put it bluntly, the rule of law did not exist.

UNMIK initially tried to counter this problem by developing an innovative solution of placing international judges and international prosecutors to work with the national (i.e., local) judges. This was groundbreaking because all previous international judges and prosecutors had served on international tribunals that were separate and distinct from the national court system. UNMIK took a baby step in this process by assigning one international judge and one international prosecutor to the Mitrovica District Court, one of the five district courts of Kosovo. This move was inadequate on its face, as it covered only one court. Further, as the courts were composed of multi-judge panels—either three or five members, depending upon the type of case—the international judge could and often would be outvoted by the Kosovar judges. (The five-member panels were composed of two professional [legally trained] judges and three lay judges. The lay judges were people who lived in the community, were selected by the local president of the court, and were not legally trained.) This often resulted in unjust convictions for Serb defendants and undercharging or improper acquittals of Kosovar defendants.

UNMIK had to devise a means of ensuring that justice—which must, perforce, embrace the appearance of justice—could be fairly rendered in this transitional society. It did this with UN Regulation 2000/64 (Reg. 64). This regulation included several features to guarantee that cases would be fairly charged and would receive a fair hearing. Under Reg. 64, UNMIK could recommend that international judges and/or prosecutors be assigned to a case "if it determines that this is necessary to ensure the independence and impartiality of the judiciary or the proper administration of justice." The United Nations Special Representative could then designate for any given case an international prosecutor, an international investigating judge, and/or a panel of only three judges, *including at least two international judges*, one of whom would be the presiding judge.[*]

With Reg. 64 in place, UNMIK could now provide assurances, at least facially, that each stage of a case, be it charging, investigation,

---

[*] Reg. 64, Sec.2 (emphasis added).

trial, or appeal, would be fairly administered. In effect, the rule of law was about to begin in Kosovo for the first time.

Sometime in April 2002, all Minnesota state court judges received an email advising them that UNMIK was seeking international judges to serve in Kosovo for six-month terms with possible extensions. This was an opportunity to see the world, do justice, and work in the exciting field of international law. I applied immediately and was chosen as one of the first group of American judges to serve as international judges in Kosovo.

We arrived in Kosovo in November 2002, and immediately after we were sworn in as judges, a UN Justice Department official stressed to us that our charge was not merely to preside over cases but to act as mentors to the local lawyers and judges. I initially felt that it would be presumptuous of me, unversed as I was in the Kosovo/Yugoslavian criminal code and procedural rules, to try to guide its players through the justice system. I was to learn that mentoring has less to do with familiarity with legal texts and more with adherence to a process.

We were quickly assigned a variety of cases including war crimes, weapons smuggling, homicide, and organized crime. I landed in Prizren, Kosovo's second largest city, said to be the jewel of Kosovo because of its abundance of Ottoman era architecture. Among the most visually striking sites is the Old Stone Bridge, crossing the Bistrica River, which meanders through the center of town. There are numerous historic mosques and Orthodox churches in the city and the surrounding area, and Prizren is in close proximity to the scenic Shar Mountains. Lest this sound too much like a travelogue, it must be said that while Prizren is a jewel, it is by no means a flawless gem. Like all of Kosovo, Prizren suffered from constant power outages, intermittent water shutdowns, and inadequate street water drainage. This left the streets muddy most of the year, and choked with an all-covering dust in the summer. The lights always seemed to go out at the most inconvenient times—such as when one was in the middle of making dinner. When the lights went out, there was nothing to do but leave the house and walk around aimlessly with everyone else in the city until they came back on—usually within forty-five minutes.

Three international judges were assigned to Prizren: a German, a Hungarian, and me, an African American originally from Chicago's Southside, but a longtime Minnesota resident. During our tenure in Prizren, while all three of us sat on most of the cases that arose in our district, we alternated in presiding over cases. Dierk Helmken, the German judge, presided over our first case, which involved one Sali Veseli, a Kosovar charged with the murder and conspiracy to murder Commander Drini. This was the commander's *nom de guerre*, his real name was Ekrem Rexha. Commander Drini was also a Kosovar and a leader of the KLA during the conflict with Serbia. Veseli, who was a former KLA member, and later a major general in the Kosovo Protection Corps, a "civil defense" spin-off of the KLA, was alleged to have conspired with others to kill Commander Drini in an apparent postwar political power struggle.

This case was a prime example of the need for international judges to preside over local trials, even when they did not involve ethnic violence, war crimes, or drug or weapons smuggling. The evidence against Veseli for participation in a conspiracy to commit murder was persuasive—several witnesses gave statements to the effect that Veseli had ordered the murder of Commander Drini and bragged about it later. But it was clear that Veseli's standing in the local community was so strong that the Kosovar judges and their potential citizen-judges would probably not convict him because of either bribery, fear of retribution, admiration for his war deeds, or some combination of these factors.

We held the trial starting in January 2013 in the Prizren courthouse, a white cinderblock three-story, nondescript building a few blocks from the town center. The courtroom itself was wholly unsuited for judicial hearings of any length, not to mention a major trial. The room was long and narrow—about 130 feet by 25 feet—and the lighting came from a few flickering, naked, humming fluorescent bulbs. The seating consisted of long wooden benches with no back support. The heating ranged from oppressive to minimal. And the ventilation? There was none.

While the acoustics, physical layout, and lack of climate control made the setting uncomfortable, the security, or lack thereof, made the court unsafe. There was no separate entryway for detainees, and there was no secure holding area when they were not in the courtroom. As a result, detainees would routinely pass through hallways in close proximity to judges, attorneys, victims, and witnesses during the course of a trial. This would prove to be problematic in my final trial.

The trial days were long and punctuated only by brief breaks for lunch and dinner. Given the number of witnesses that had to be called in a brief period of time, it was necessary that we maintain this unrelenting pace. The trial continued off and on for several weeks. As it wore on, though, it became increasingly evident that there would be no witness, and no smoking gun that could link Veseli directly to the killing, as opposed to the conspiracy to murder Drini. In the end, after countless hours of testimony, our panel of international judges acquitted Veseli of murder, but convicted him of conspiracy to commit murder and sentenced him to ten years in prison. One year later, the Kosovo Supreme Court, also composed of international judges, overturned our verdict. Sali Veseli was again tried in 2005–2006 before yet another international panel. He was finally brought to justice when, on August 4, 2006, after eleven months of trial, nearly four years after the start of his first trial, and six and a half years after the act, he was convicted of the murder of Commander Drini and was sentenced to fifteen years. While such quirks in trial procedure may appear bizarre by western standards, this is what sometimes happens in a transitional society with a nascent justice system.

I presided over the second trial in which I participated. It was also a murder case but was played out on an international scale. The defendant, Arben Ramadani, a Kosovo resident, was charged with committing a murder . . . in Turkey. This presented some major logistical and procedural problems.

As Kosovo was not then a sovereign nation, it had no treaties that would allow Ramadani to be extradited to Turkey. In order for him to be brought to justice, it was necessary to implement an innovative, albeit cumbersome process. Under the Kosovo Code of Criminal Procedure in force at the time, the Kosovo courts had jurisdiction over any case in which a defendant allegedly committed a criminal offense outside of the territory of Kosovo but currently resided in Kosovo.* A procedure known as a "Special Investigative Opportunity" allowed testimony to be heard by me in Turkey and to be fully admissible in the main trial as long as I was one of the judges on the main trial panel, and the witnesses were "unavailable due to . . . lack of presence in Kosovo." In a nutshell, a substantial portion of the parties involved in the trial—but not all—had to travel to Mugla, Turkey, to hear testimony. Our contingent included Ramadani's defense attorney, the prosecutor, a human rights monitor, and me. The witnesses in Turkey included the victim's sisters and Ramadani's local associates. Ramadani, who was in custody in Kosovo, did not accompany us. Neither did the other two judges. The judicial authorities in Turkey were more than gracious in allowing us to use their court facilities and ensuring that the witnesses were brought to court when required.

The factual background of Ramadani's case was almost tragicomic. Ramadani was a small-time hustler who moved between Turkey and Kosovo, depending on how much pressure he was under from the law. He figured he had made a big score when he met Mehmet Erdem,** who lived with his two older sisters in a small village near Mugla, an ancient Turkish city near the Mediterranean. To say that Erdem and his two older sisters lived meagerly would be a gross understatement; they lived in a tiny home with no electricity or modern conveniences, and dressed shabbily. But Erdem and his

---

* (Kosovo Procedural Code 2003, Art. 32, Para. 1).
** "Erdem" is a pseudonym.

sisters lived frugally in order to put money aside for the future. By selling yogurt and other homemade food over the years and from his odd jobs, Erdem and his sisters had amassed savings equivalent to about U.S. $20,000.

Somehow, Ramadani caught wind of this and determined that he would relieve Erdem of his earnings. He devised a childishly crude but brutally effective scheme to do so. He befriended Erdem and learned that he might be interested in buying some land—either as an investment opportunity or as somewhere to build a home for his sisters and himself. Ramadani and a confederate drove Erdem to a deserted area on the pretense of showing him some property. When they reached the designated location, Ramadani told him to look out of the window to his right to see the property and promptly shot him in his head. He then dumped the body, after taking the money that Erdem had brought to pay for the land, and left. Erdem's body was discovered weeks later, largely devoured by animals. Ramadani repaired to Kosovo, thinking he was safe from justice.

The Turkish law enforcement authorities were more than up to the task of investigating this case and quickly determined that Ramadani was the key suspect. They notified UNMIK, who in turn advised the Kosovo police to arrest Ramadani. He was arrested and, after an investigative hearing, brought to trial before our panel.

Erdem's sisters gave moving and persuasive testimony about how they and Erdem had scrimped over the years to build a small nest egg, and how Ramadani had told Erdem about a land investment opportunity. We also heard from one of Ramadani's associates who drove the car in which they rode to the crime scene and testified that Ramadani shot Mehmet.

We returned to Kosovo for the main trial, where all parties, including Ramadani and the other two judges on the panel, were present. The main trial was actually quite swift. I read into the main trial record a transcript of the testimony that we heard in Turkey, and we then heard testimony from Ramadani. The attorneys gave perfunctory final arguments and we retired to deliberate.

We held a brief discussion of the evidence and then voted. We all agreed that Ramadani was guilty of Erdem's murder beyond a reasonable doubt. But it was the sentencing discussions that took me aback. Although it was not specifically denominated as such under the Criminal Code, there was no doubt in my mind (nor was there in the other judges' minds, for that matter) that this offense was a clear case of Murder in the First Degree. Ramadani planned weeks in advance to befriend and gain Erdem's trust so that he could take his money and devised a scheme to take him to an isolated area where he could carry out his plan. When they reached the area, he shot him in the head, took his money, and literally threw his body to the wolves.

In every state in the United States this would be punishable by life imprisonment, if not the death penalty. In the state of Minnesota, a person convicted of Murder 1 would be sentenced to life imprisonment which carries a thirty-year minimum term of imprisonment. I realized that the European justice system generally gave more lenient sentences than those in the United States, so, in a spirit of compromise, I suggested that he be sentenced to a fifteen-year term. Each of my colleagues felt that this was overly harsh, and suggested a term of five years. After some haggling back and forth, we agreed to sentence him to a term of seven years. I felt this was grossly inadequate, given the degree of planning involved, the cruel manner in which he disposed of the body, and the collateral harm done to the victim's sisters, who lost their only brother and the money on which they depended to help them in their old age. But this was the manner in which sentences were determined in Kosovo—by a process of judges talking together and reaching a rough compromise which hopefully approximated justice.

The final case, and the most challenging, involved a Kosovar named Bujar Basha, who was the head of a local organized crime family. Basha, his family, and his associates were infamous in the Prizren region for their brazen armed robberies, home invasions, and burglaries and thefts from merchants. They had a penchant for preying upon jewelers and jewelry makers, as they were likely to have gold, precious stones, and large sums of cash in their workplaces and homes. While the issues were not particularly complicated, did not involve the murder of a high-profile political figure, and did not require international travel, the notorious nature of the family required someone who was not part of the Kosovo culture and not as vulnerable to threats and intimidation. This was precisely the type of case that required an international judge. But, as I would soon learn, the mere presence of an international judge on a panel did not guarantee that the case would be tried free from any improper influences.

As noted previously, the international judges in Kosovo served on panels of three or five. In those cases involving war crimes or with region-wide political implications, such as the murder of Commander Drini, the international judges always made up a majority of the panel, to ensure that the panel would not be swayed by local pressure. Even though the Basha family was a notorious criminal organization that had wreaked havoc on the Prizren community for years, the UNMIK administration determined that this case did not require a majority panel of international judges, presumably because the case did not fit into the categories of cases in which there was a reasonable fear that local judges might base their decisions on factors not related to the case itself. As a consequence, the case of *The People v. Bujar Basha, et al.*, was composed of a panel of three lay judges, one local attorney, and me.

The three lay judges had been chosen by the local chief judge. They were all elderly men from Prizren, and, other than that, I never learned much about them. What was their work background, their family life? Had they or any members of their family or friends ever had any run-ins with Basha or members of his crew? These are questions that would be routinely asked of jurors in the common law system. If they had had any previous negative interactions with the accused, or even if they or a close family member had been a victim of a crime similar to those for which the accused were being tried, they would, in all likelihood, be thanked and excused from service on this trial. But I was assured, and had no reason to disbelieve, that they were all respected members of the community. All were gray-haired and stern and probably much younger than they appeared. The attorney panelist was much younger than the lay judges. He lived on the outskirts of Prizren. He always seemed to have transportation problems, which sometimes required that I or some court assistant pick him up and bring him to court. The lay judges, attorneys, and defendants all spoke Albanian, so we required an interpreter at every stage of the proceedings, including our deliberations.

The prosecutor was a middle-aged, rather pudgy man with an officious air. In the early stages of the trial, I observed that he made a show of sauntering into the courtroom at the same time as the judges entered, as though he were one of us. Initially, I found this vaguely amusing and let it pass, but I quickly adjusted that position and advised him to enter before us. It may have been the Kosovo model of decorum, but it did not seem right that the prosecutor and the judicial panel should be perceived as a cohesive unit. He was annoyed at this directive but grudgingly complied.

The opening stages of the trial proceeded predictably for a case of this nature. The court panel, as is the custom in the civil law system, started first and asked most of the questions. We examined several witnesses who told stories of how they were victims of robbery, burglary, or theft. Their testimony about the losses they suffered was at once both poignant and horrifying. One goldsmith was accosted just outside his home as he was returning from work and beaten and robbed. Another family had the rudest of awakenings when four masked gunmen armed with pistols and rifles broke into their home and demanded their gold and money, or see their children killed. Another jeweler came to his shop one morning to discover that someone had broken in through the roof the night before and cleaned out his entire inventory. Yet another jeweler was driving home and his car was blocked on the road by other cars. Masked gunmen then robbed him.

The defense attorneys followed us. The attorneys did not, frankly, seem to have much interest in providing a vigorous defense for their clients. There were four defense attorneys, and they had a pattern of leaving the courtroom on the spur of the moment, ostensibly to attend to other matters. When they did so, they would explain that their co-counsel would act in their absence. I determined that this behavior was not sufficient to meet their clients' needs and directed them to stop this practice. When they were present, they seemed either distracted or bored. Their questions were, to be kind, pro forma at best.

The prosecutor's performance—and that is what it was—was hardly better. He made a show of excitedly gesticulating when he questioned witnesses, and of exhibiting righteous indignation at the defense attorneys' courtroom antics, but did little to prove the case against the defendants.

The biggest challenge to completing the trial came from an event that happened outside the courtroom. As mentioned, the "courthouse" where we heard trials was not designed with an eye for security. This would be troublesome, to say the least, in any country. But it raises special problems in a relatively insular area such as Prizren, Kosovo. During one of our breaks, the defendant, Bujar Basha, passed by one of our lay judges in the hall while being led away from the courtroom and yelled at him in Albanian in an angry, agitated tone. While I couldn't understand what he said, I knew that he either threatened or cursed him. As it turned out, he did both. The lay judge said that Basha had insulted his mother and threatened to kill his son if Basha were convicted. He was understandably shaken by these remarks and took the threats seriously, as he, like the other judges, was well-known in Prizren. He immediately declared that he would no longer serve as a judge on this panel. This was a vexing problem, as we were well into the trial and had heard several witnesses. I and the other judges asked him to reconsider his decision in view of the implications of having him leave in the middle of the trial, but he was not swayed. I asked the president of the court to talk with him. He did, but to no avail.

In the United States, this turn of events would have required me to hold the defendant in contempt and to declare a mistrial. While I admonished Basha for his threats, the Code of Procedure did not provide for a contempt sanction. Of course, that was not the most pressing issue. How could we continue the trial when one of the original judges refused to serve?

Fortunately, to my surprise and gratitude, the Code of Procedure had a solution. In cases where one of the judges becomes incapacitated or is otherwise unable to serve, the Code provides that another judge can step into the case, after he has read or had read to him the testimony the witnesses gave before he entered the case. The president of the court hastily appointed another judge. This procedure caused a delay of two days, but after the new judge was brought up to speed, we were able to continue with the trial apace.

The trial continued for several more days without further incident. The remaining witnesses testified along the same lines as had the others. They said they were subjected to frightening robberies or home invasions at the hands of ruthless gunmen, or their stores were burglarized. While there was no doubt that these people had been the victims of horrendous crimes, a nagging thought kept growing in my mind: Except for one case, in which Basha and his parents admitted responsibility, where was the solid evidence that linked these defendants to the offenses? Almost all of the offenses happened at night and were executed by masked gunmen. As a result, none of the witnesses could positively identify their attackers. Because all of the jewelers in the area fashioned or sold similar styles of jewelry without personal identifying marks, none of them could swear that any of the jewelry that was placed in evidence belonged to them. The most that they could say was that it appeared similar to the jewelry that they sold. None of the defendants implicated any of their cohorts. None of the defendants made any incriminating statements. There was no fingerprint evidence obtained from the homes or stores to compare with the defendants' prints. There was no identification of any vehicle that was used in any of the crimes. To be frank, the overwhelming majority of the charges in this case had no evidence to support them. On the positive side, I joked to myself, at least the deliberations will be brief.

After we heard all of the evidence, we filed into our "deliberation room," which was actually the chambers of Judge Haynalka Karpati, my Hungarian colleague, who was out of the office that day. I reviewed the counts in the indictment and suggested that we take a vote on each count for each defendant.

One of the lay judges spoke up immediately. "They are all guilty," he said. "They should all be found guilty of all the charges." I looked at the other lay judges and they nodded gravely in agreement. I was shocked. How could they reach this decision? Had they heard the same evidence (or lack thereof) that I had heard over the past two weeks?

But perhaps I should not have been surprised. These judges, who were functionally more akin to jurors, did not endure the rigorous *voir dire*, or questioning process, to determine their fitness to serve as would jurors in the United States. Had they been so examined, and answered with a grain of truth, their predispositions would have been apparent to the greenest attorney, who would have used a peremptory challenge to remove them from the panel before they could be sworn in as jurors. More likely, if they exhibited such a degree of bias that the judge believed that they could not fairly hear and decide the case, the judge would have excused them "for cause" from the trial. But this was Kosovo, and such measures were not in the Code of Procedure.

I painstakingly went over the facts we had heard and reminded them that we had to adhere to a high standard of proof before we could convict anyone of any crime, not to mention offenses that carried consequences as severe as these. "But they are bad people!" they insisted. "They have been bad as long as they have been here!" We went back and forth in this way for some time, and I realized that the attorney/judge had been listening quietly during this entire debate. Finally, when I had run out of arguments, he weighed in. "There is not enough evidence," he said. That was all it took. After that we were able to quickly determine the verdicts for all of the defendants. Except for the cases involving Basha, his parents, and two other family members where the evidence of guilt was clear, we determined that the remaining defendants were not guilty of all charges.

This did not complete our work or, I should say, my work. Under the civil system of justice, the presiding judge must produce an extensive set of findings that explain and justify the decision that the panel reached. I prepared the verdicts with findings in two days and we were ready to present them to the public.

It was an unseasonably hot day when I read our verdict. Not surprisingly, the courtroom was packed beyond capacity, because of the notoriety of the defendants and the sheer quantity of their alleged misdoings in Prizren. Given these conditions, the one air conditioning unit was completely inadequate. I began by acknowledging that the Prizren community had suffered for several months from a crime spree that appeared to be perpetrated by a single criminal organization. At the same time, I said, that while the people who committed these crimes should be brought to justice, it would be wrong to do so without proper evidence that proved their guilt. I explained that, with one exception, such evidence was not presented in this case. We found Bujar Basha guilty of two robberies and sentenced him to a compounded sentence of twelve years of imprisonment. We found four of his family members guilty of complicity in one of the robberies for which Basha was convicted and sentenced three of them to three years and one of them to four years.

The crowded room was eerily silent as I read the verdicts and findings, which were immediately translated into Albanian by an interpreter. Afterwards, the people filed out quietly, and Basha and his family were led away to begin their sentences.

As I neared the end of my tenure in Kosovo, I reminisced about what our group of international judges had accomplished. Did we work diligently and do our best to render fair and impartial justice? The answer is clearly yes. Did we make a lasting impact on the legal culture of Kosovo? I believe we did. While we were charged with the task of mentoring, we learned more than we taught. I was reminded that individual trials, no matter how significant they may appear at the moment, fade from memory with time. But properly administered justice, like wisdom, will linger.

A few months after the Basha trial, I ran into the lay judge who had vociferously argued that all of the defendants should be found guilty of all charges because they were "bad people." He reached out and shook my hand warmly, and spoke earnestly for some time. Of course, I could not understand a word that he said, but I would like to believe that in essence it was "thank you."

13

Elián

JUDGE JENNIFER D. BAILEY

 *Jennifer D. Bailey has been a circuit court judge in Miami-Dade, Florida, for twenty-five years. She is the administrative judge for the twenty-five-judge Circuit Civil Division and handles a docket of Complex Business Litigation cases. She previously ministered justice to Miami's families in the Family Court for nearly a decade. Judge Bailey served as dean of the Florida College of Advanced Judicial Studies and has taught as faculty for the Florida New Judge's College, the Florida College of Advanced Judicial Studies and for the Florida Conference of Circuit Court Judges. She currently lectures nationally on civil justice innovation.*

TO UNDERSTAND THIS CASE, YOU HAVE TO UNDERSTAND MIAMI. Miami sprawls on beaches at the southeastern edge of the Florida peninsula, cradled between the Everglades and the Atlantic Gulf Stream. The first globalists, migrants from the northeast and the Bahamas, settled southern Florida in the 1800s with a vision of growing exotic fruit in eternal sunshine. Shortly thereafter, entrepreneurs like Henry Flagler realized that sunshine was South Florida's critical commodity. They built railroads and tourist destinations. World War II brought military training centers to Miami Beach. After the war, thousands of veterans returned. It was a city defined by sand, sun, and the dreams of those seeking opportunity. By the middle of the twentieth century, air conditioning had tamed the heat, humidity, and mosquitos. The city, with its decidedly southern cadence, drew swarms of new inhabitants and tourists to its perfect weather.

Events to our south in the late 1950s were about to produce upheaval. Fidel Castro led a revolt against the reigning regime in Cuba. What started as a promise of democracy turned to repressive communism. Those who spoke against Castro were beaten, jailed, or killed. Families lost everything; businesses were nationalized and properties seized. The Cuban elite fled, predominantly settling in Miami to await Castro's collapse. Doctors, lawyers, and engineers flooded Miami and took any job they could find. It was not unusual to have a college professor from University of Havana driving a cab or an engineer busing restaurant tables.

The Cuban community in Miami was an exile community, forced from their beloved country. They hated the charismatic leader who had taken their homeland from them. America's CIA, fearing a communist regime on the U.S. doorstep, sponsored an armed invasion by Cuban exiles in 1961. The attack, commonly known as the Bay of Pigs, failed. Many Cubans blamed lack of promised U.S. military support for the failure. More than one hundred men died in the invasion, and more than one thousand men were captured. Castro executed hundreds, and others were jailed for years. These men were the fathers, grandfathers, sons, and uncles of families living in Miami. The mismanaged invasion was an embarrassment for the United States, which ultimately negotiated the return of many of the prisoners who survived. Huge segments of the Cuban community in Miami never forgot nor forgave the U.S. government that betrayed them.

Meanwhile, much of "old Miami" was uneasy with the changes to the city caused by the influx of Cubans. The immigrants worked hard, took any job they could get, and made the most of every opportunity, despite daily discrimination. The tempo of the city seemingly changed overnight. The Cuban community cherished its language, cultural traditions, and customs. Despite Cuban distrust of the U.S. government, Congress passed the Cuban Adjustment Act in 1966, to exempt Cuban migrants from immigration quotas or providing required reasons for entry. The federal law also permitted Cubans access to an expedited path to permanent residency.

Cubans continued to migrate, frequently fleeing the island on hand-built rafts. Many drowned in the rough Florida Straits that separate Cuba from Florida. Cubans on the island continued to face political executions, beatings, and imprisonment. Every reported death, on land or sea, grieved relatives or friends in Miami. The Mariel boatlift brought 125,000 Cubans to Miami's shores between April 15 and October 31, 1980. The resulting social upheaval in Miami placed significant demands on the immigration, medical, police, and court systems and the housing and job markets. Ethnic tensions simmered across the city.

By the year 2000, Miami was socially polarized across ethnic lines. Hispanics represented 57 percent of Miami-Dade County's tri-ethnic community. Cuban immigrants dominated local politics and were a force to be considered in all elections—from presidential to local judicial races. Hatred for Castro dominated political debates. Some in the white and African American communities perceived disenfranchisement by virtue of the growing political, economic, and cultural influence of Cubans. Others across the community celebrated Miami's growing ethnic diversity and international character stemming from its new status. Business opportunities improved the economic status of many. Planted geographically halfway between the capitol of Castro's Cuba and the all-American vacationland Orlando, Miami's roots extend in both directions. I joined this melting pot in 1983 after graduating from law school in Georgia. I was lucky to partake in the unique opportunities the community offered. If you worked hard, success could be yours in Miami. Ten years after beginning my legal practice in Miami, this wildly eclectic community elected me as a state court trial judge, a position I continue to hold today.

It is against this backdrop that the Elián González state court case came my way in the winter of 2000.

The Boy from Cardenas

Elián González was born in Cárdenas, Cuba. His mother, Elizabet Broton, and his father, Juan Miguel González, divorced when he was young but had a friendly co-parenting relationship. Elizabet had custody, but the child stayed at his father's house when attending school. On Tuesday, November 22, 1999, Elizabet, five-year-old Elián, and twelve other adults crowded into a fifteen-foot boat to cross the ocean to the United States and freedom. The mother apparently did not discuss her illegal departure from Cuba with anyone in advance and left no record of the reasons she left Cuba. Juan Miguel and his remaining family learned of the departure after the boat launched. The father then phoned the González relatives in Florida to be on the lookout for and to take care of them.

Off the Florida shore, the boat capsized in five-foot swells. Elián was tied to an inner tube. He never saw his mother again. With the exception of two other survivors, who washed up on Key Biscayne, everyone else was lost at sea. He miraculously survived two days alone in the Atlantic Ocean. Elián was spotted off the coast of Fort Lauderdale by fishermen on Thanksgiving morning, November 25, 1999. The U.S. Coast Guard met the rescuers and brought the dehydrated and hypothermic child to a Florida hospital where, as "an unaccompanied minor," he passed into the custody of the U.S. Immigration and Naturalization Service (INS). Lázaro González, the Miami brother of Elián's paternal grandfather, came to the hospital. INS determined that Lázaro González was Elián's great-uncle and paroled the boy to him pending further investigation.

At the moment of the temporary parole, INS had no idea where the child's parents were, whether there were other survivors, or what relatives other than Lázaro were in the United States. INS immediately commenced its inquiries while worldwide media celebrated the child's safety—nowhere more deliriously than in Miami's Little Havana neighborhood. Unsure who might be out there to claim the boy, an INS spokesman stated that any custody question would be referred to state court.

This winsome, dark-haired boy with a beautiful smile captured the world's attention. Crowds gathered outside the modest little Havana home of Lázaro and Angela González. It was soon to become a permanent media encampment. Every time the child stepped out of the house, camera shutters clicked away. He achieved instant single-name celebrity status: "Elián."

INS determined the mother had died and the father remained in Cuba. Upon learning of Elizabet's death and Elián's survival, Juan Miguel immediately asked Cuban authorities to assist in returning Elián to him. Consequently, INS officials made arrangements to interview Mr. González in Cuba. Bilingual American diplomats conducted multiple interviews, in settings to assure that the father could speak freely—including having him write answers to written questions to avoid listening devices. Juan Miguel brought Elián's birth certificate, proving paternity. He provided ample evidence that the boy lived with him during the school year and attended school in Juan Miguel's district, that the paternal grandmother watched Elián while the parents worked, and that Juan Miguel was an involved and caring parent for Elián. He produced medical records, school records, and photographs evidencing uninterrupted parenting. He also told them that he did not want to pursue political asylum for Elián in the United States. The Cuban government also demanded the return of the child.

By mid-December, INS determined that the father was a fit and appropriate parent and, under U.S. and international norms, entitled to parent his child upon the mother's death. Federal authorities announced their intent to return Elián to his father in Cuba by January 14, 2000.

The Miami relatives opposed returning Elián to Cuba, despite his father's wishes. The family argued that Elián's mother had died to bring him to freedom and her wishes should be honored. On December 13, Lázaro González filed a petition for political asylum with INS on Elián's behalf. On December 15, the five-year-old, who could not read or write, filed his own petition for political asylum. By the first week of January 2000, INS rejected the petitions, determining that Lazaro had no right to file on Elián's behalf and that Elián was too young to file on his own. INS also determined that Elián's father had the right as the sole surviving parent to determine what should happen with Elián.

Many in the Cuban community rallied to Lazaro's vow to seek freedom for Elián in the United States. Every day crowds gathered outside the Miami family's modest home. Elián's appearances in the yard were accompanied by puppies, politicians, and celebrities, documented by paparazzi. The entire world watched as the Miami family, the father, and the governments of both countries increasingly squared off while the little boy played in Lázaro González's front yard.

By January 7, the family assembled a task force of publicists, political operatives, and lawyers to keep Elián in Miami. The Cuban exile community's political clout was fully deployed. Simultaneously, the Castro government held national marches of thousands demanding the return of the child to his father. In the face of all this, some in Congress discussed filing a special bill to grant Elián residency or U.S. citizenship. Elián (now six) was subpoenaed to testify before the House of Representatives Government Reform Committee chaired by Congressman Dan Burton. Whether Elián would go to Cuba or stay in Miami was now playing out on a national political stage.

See You in Court

By 1999, I had served in Miami's family court for more than six years. Much like the general public, my fellow judges and I speculated about Elián's future: Should he go home to his father, or stay in Miami with relatives? As community positions hardened and debate intensified, we began to contemplate the possibility that sooner or later a lawsuit could be filed. We thought about the relationship of federal court and immigration issues to any potential state court case. Under well-established law, immigration issues were the responsibility of federal courts, and family disputes were the state court's responsibility. How would these diverging jurisdictions reconcile? We also speculated on the political consequences for any elected judge caught in the middle of the growing national and local frenzy over the adorable boy.

Given the political support that state government officials were offering to keep Elián in Miami, it seemed likely that the state of Florida would declare him a ward of the state subject to Florida's laws and file a dependency petition in juvenile court. Our court has a separate specialized division for juvenile cases brought by the state regarding children who do not have parents or who are at risk for abuse or neglect. There was no living parent in Florida to consent or make arrangements for Elián. In addition, our court has a separate family division for matters such as divorce and child support, where I was assigned.

The jurisdictional limitations that governed family division cases made it unlikely that Elián's case would be brought before a family court judge, where I sat. These jurisdictional laws require that the child must have lived in Florida for at least six months before the case was filed. The law was designed to avoid conflicting custody orders from different states, and to prevent parents from traveling to a new state just to secure or avoid a custody decision. The only exception was emergency jurisdiction, in which the judge had to find a threat of imminent harm to the child.

The only legal right that the Miami family had to Elián's custody was based on the INS parole—which could be terminated by INS at any time. Nevertheless, on January 7, the family filed a petition for custody signed on their behalf by seven prominent Miami lawyers. Surprisingly, they filed in family court under a Florida statute designed to facilitate short-term voluntary placement of children with extended family members. This law is typically used by living parents for military deployments, parents entering into residential rehabilitation, and similar major life events. The statute contemplates parental consent and restoration of parental custody within a specific time. Florida law, as in most states, presumes that the child belongs with his parent. If a parent objects to the award of temporary custody of the minor child to other relatives, the court is required to take evidence and find by clear and convincing proof that the objecting parent is unfit due to a likelihood of abuse, abandonment, or neglect of the child if placed with the objecting parent. Only if this risk is proven can a child be placed with a nonparent relative by the family court and even then only temporarily.

Relying on this statute, Lázaro González sued Juan Miguel González. The great-uncle sought custody until such time as there was a final disposition of the application for political asylum on behalf of Elián. He also sought an order preventing Elián from being removed from the jurisdiction. Elián clearly had not lived in Florida prior to being brought ashore by the Coast Guard. Thus, traditional Florida family court jurisdiction was not available. Instead Lázaro invoked emergency jurisdiction, claiming that Elián was at risk of abuse or neglect if he were to be returned to Cuba. He invoked the Court's inherent emergency authority to protect children within the state from danger and abuse. The petition claimed that Elizabet's consent to Lázaro's custody could be inferred from her high-risk efforts to reach Florida and alleged that the father would be committing abuse by seeking Elián's return to communist Cuba because of the repressive character of the Cuban state. The petition also claimed that Juan Miguel could not freely express his wishes with regard to

Elián because the Castro government had "seized the plight of Elián as a mechanism to promote the communist agenda and degradation of the United States." The petition alleged that the court could not consider any objection by Juan Miguel until he was removed from his coercive environment and could speak openly about his wishes. There were no allegations that Elián had ever actually been abused or neglected when he lived in Cuba.

Lázaro's filing prompted court watchers to wonder: Why hadn't the State of Florida filed in juvenile court? The Governor and state politicians publicly supported the Miami family's fight against returning the child. Juvenile court was the logical place for an unaccompanied minor with no parents in the state. Filing there would have brought state juvenile lawyers and a complete set of independent evaluative resources into the case, including supervised services such as grief counseling for a child who had watched his mother drown. Federal law provided the answer: the State of Florida could not file a dependency action involving an unaccompanied minor alien without the U.S. attorney general's consent. Since it was increasingly clear the attorney general would not give that consent, Lazaro's attorneys initiated a contorted path through our family system.

The case was assigned to one of my colleagues. On January 10, she granted Lázaro, Elián's great uncle, emergency temporary custody, to preserve the status quo, prevent the child's removal from Miami, and provide time to assert Elián's right to seek asylum under U.S. immigration law. She based court jurisdiction on the inherent right of the state to protect children within its borders in an emergency. She ordered the family's lawyers to serve notice to Juan Miguel in Cuba, and set a future hearing date in March. In an effort to comply with legal notice requirements, the Miami family published notice of the court case in a Miami newspaper—one that the father would surely not see. They also sent a certified letter to the address for Juan Miguel in Cuba.

Many family law experts viewed the state family court's exercise of jurisdiction with skepticism as the child had never resided in Florida prior to being brought ashore by the Coast Guard, and immigration is exclusively a matter for federal government control. Elián was a resident of Cuba and had only been in Florida a matter of weeks. From the sidelines, I watched the growing tension and intolerance for differing viewpoints. Many in the Cuban community felt that their decades-long agony and genuine fear of reprisal and repression against the child was being dismissed by those who thought he should be returned to his father. They protested loudly that Juan Miguel could not in any way express his wishes honestly while he was under the control of Castro and that, if he did want his child returned, he was unfit and selfish. Others felt that the child belonged with his father, whom INS had determined was acting independently of the Cuban government. Some believed the Miami family's attitude was disrespectful of the role of the father and the many relatives left in Cuba. Co-workers and family members fought over what should happen and stopped speaking to each other. Workplaces forbade employees from discussing Elián's future.

The state court case went dormant after the custody order was issued, and the legal battle shifted back to the asylum issue before immigration authorities. On January 11, Lázaro González filed another asylum petition with the INS. Attorney General Janet Reno advised the family by letter that the state court order "has no force or effect as far as INS's administration of the immigration law is concerned." On January 13, INS again rejected the asylum application. INS would not open an immigration case. It determined that the father was entitled to legal custody under Cuban law as the surviving parent, and therefore had the sole authority to speak for Elián in immigration matters. The agency found no evidence that Elián would be at risk of harm in Cuba or that he and his father had conflicting interests. INS remained resolute in its determination that the proper remedy was the reunification of Elián with his father and attempted to work with the Miami family to create a graceful reunification process, involving psychologists and counselors. It offered to bring Juan Miguel to the United States for his son, or to have the

Miami relatives personally escort Elián to Cuba. Attempts at mediation through the Catholic Church repeatedly failed. Elián's grandmothers flew to Miami to see him, which turned into a media fiasco. No matter what, Lázaro González steadfastly refused to return the child to his father. The street in front of the Miami house had crowds in the thousands every day, complete with port-a-potties. The media rented nearby neighbors' patios and driveways to establish "Camp Elián." But still, thankfully, it was not my case. Not my worry to solve.

My gratitude was short-lived. Shortly after the state court judge ruled, the media discovered that the judge who granted custody to Lázaro González had been represented, in her judicial election campaign, by the publicist serving as family spokesman for the Miami family. With a risk that the public would perceive judicial bias, she removed herself from the case. Her action was followed by other judges who had used the same publicist for their election campaigns. As I had no relationship with the publicist, the case ended up assigned to me on February 28, 2000. This increasingly surreal case was now my responsibility.

On March 1, the family filed a case in the U.S. District Court for the Southern District of Florida, suing INS and the U.S. Justice Department for failing to process the asylum petition Lázaro made on Elián's behalf. Lázaro asserted authority to file for Elián based on the INS parole and the state court custody order. He argued that the failure to process the asylum petition violated Elián's constitutional rights. Lázaro was doing exactly what the state court order gave him authority to do: pursuing the child's rights under the immigration laws. It was now up to the federal court to decide who was right, INS and the attorney general or the Miami family. Did Elián have a right to a political asylum process, or was INS correct in determining that only the father could speak for Elián and that the father had the right to decline to seek political asylum for the child and have Elián returned to him to live in Cuba? INS and the Justice Department urged the federal judge to dismiss the case.

The Legal Questions

In March, all activity was occurring in the federal matter. This afforded me time to research and deliberate the tough questions in the remaining state court case. How should a state court judge proceed when assigned a troubled case like this, involving the federal immigration agency, the U.S. Justice Department, a federal court, and her state court, especially after another state court judge had already issued orders? The first filings had come solely from the Miami family. The father was in Cuba. The United States had no direct relationships with Cuba. If, as the family contended, Juan Miguel was under the direct control of Castro, how could the court ever determine whether he received proper legal notice about the case? I knew the father's position because the family attached INS letters reflecting the government's decision to honor the father's wish to return Elián to Cuba. Nothing had been filed by the father or on his behalf in the state court action. The state case was truly one-sided. I had to retain my focus and remember that my obligation was to the law and to one small boy—not to the competing politics of the clamoring voices, despite my status as an elected judge who would need their votes in the future.

During March, I ordered the family to file all the federal case documents into the state court case and indicated I would wait for the outcome of the federal case. In the meanwhile, I examined international treaties regarding children and protocols regarding the status of refugees. I explored every legal avenue I could imagine about child custody, even child custody in war zones. I read cases on immigration, unaccompanied minors, and political asylum.

The critical point of these inquiries was to meet my obligation to uphold the law. Judges should not twist the facts or bend the law to achieve a popular result. The right to parent one's child, free of interference, is a core principle of American freedom. The only relevant exception involved risk of abuse or neglect of the child. Could the father's choice to live in communist Cuba, where he had always lived and where the child had lived apparently happy and healthy, equate to abuse and neglect? I worried that such a finding had implications for American freedoms—one that could be exploited here by warring parents in future custody cases. In addition, I routinely presided over cases where one parent had kidnapped a child to another country. What did a ruling in this case imply for future efforts to secure the return of American children? I prepared a series of draft orders for different actions, so that I would be ready if they were needed. I hid my discarded drafts after I learned reporters were going through the garbage from my office in an effort to "scoop" what I might do.

Political pressure was growing. Commentators, not understanding the law, kept suggesting that the case should be decided in Florida family court so that the "best interests of the child" could be determined. They failed to understand that Florida's temporary custody law did not use the "best interests" test when a parent objected to a third party's custody petition. The "best interests" test applied to custody disputes between parents. The statute Lazaro sued under required a much higher standard of "lack of fitness" if a nonparent is seeking temporary custody over a parent.

The Miami family was asking me to conclude the father was unfit essentially because he was living in communist Cuba. They contended that Juan Miguel, by demanding return to Cuba, was condemning the child to substandard housing, deprivation of food, and deprivation of basic human needs and placing his physical and emotional health at risk. Yet there was no allegation that Elián had suffered any of these deprivations during his years in Cuba. The petition dramatically pleaded that "Little Elián, at age 6, has already experienced the differences of existence in Cuba's totalitarian and oppressive regime and the life and liberty (not to mention the material differences) of life in the United States . . . genuine fear of returning to a world that can only be described as a living hell." An affidavit in support of the family's petition asserted that Elián would be the "victim of an imposed, manipulative, atheist educational system, the only goal being the indoctrination of Cuban children and where Fidel Castro is worshipped as a god." The tone of their papers made clear that this would not be a hearing with measured focus on the child. The family lawyers intended to put Castro and Cuba on trial. There would be no evidence available about the particulars of Elián's life in Cuba as no U.S. court could compel witnesses to come from Cuba to testify. This seemed to be a dispute about nations, best suited for the diplomats and the federal government, not for a state court judge.

The Dispute Unfolds on Camera

Unrelenting media coverage remained surreal. While Lázaro González's financial affidavit in the court file reflected an extremely modest income with limited means to support Elián, material support for the Miami family flowed in from the community. Elián was afforded a private VIP trip to Disney World with an entourage of thirty relatives, publicists, and reporters. At Lázaro's home and beyond, his every move was treated as a photo op. Packs of journalists followed him to the private school that had given him a full scholarship.

Elián was the subject of constant and heated debate in every corner of Miami. People from all walks of life were emotionally invested in outcomes that could never be reconciled. This case had released years of hatred, anger, and loathing for Castro and the evil he had perpetrated on families who could never go home, who had been isolated for years from loved relatives—grandparents, sisters, brothers—who had remained on the island. People were getting into fistfights over what should happen to Elián, and the crowds at the house were growing more and more restive. Two hundred miles to the south, from Cuba, his father gave a television interview suggesting that the family in Miami was acting under pressure from the powerful exile community. The father was outraged that his son had been turned over to Lázaro without any proof of relationship, just by showing up at the hospital in November. In contrast, Juan Miguel pointed out how he had to prove paternity, produce a birth certificate, and answer questions about his relationship with his son. He told television reporters that the Miami relatives were using Elián for material benefit without concern for his emotional well-being.

I watched television, with the rest of the world, as adoring crowds thronged outside the Little Havana home. As a family court judge, my priority was following applicable laws and preserving the well-being of Elián. I worried that people no longer saw a little boy who had lost his mother in a harrowing sea journey. Instead Elián had become a geopolitical vessel into which people had poured their hopes, frustrations, and anger. Personal experience shaped many views of the respective importance of fatherhood, family, and freedom. The increasingly defiant tone in public discourse caused me to worry about what this case meant for the rule of law. Elián had become a symbol for both sides: he would either serve as the personification of a defiant exile community if he remained, or serve as the emblem of Castro's Cuba if he returned.

Focus Shift to State Court

On March 21, 2000, the federal judge ruled against Elián's great uncle Lázaro González, finding that INS and the Justice Department had the authority to give Elián's father the exclusive right to pursue political asylum on his son's behalf. The judge declined to enter an injunction preventing INS from repatriating the child to Cuba. On March 27, INS revoked Elián's parole status and ruled he was subject to return to Cuba. In response, crowd leaders at Lázaro's house promised a human chain to prevent the federal government from taking Elián. Legal and political maneuvers went into overdrive as the family appealed the federal order to the United States Court of Appeals for the 11th Circuit. Elián's father was permitted to travel to Washington, DC, and stay at the Cuban diplomatic compound in Maryland. The Miami family lawyers met over and over again with INS, but Lázaro would not agree to any plan to return the child to his father.

Having lost in federal court, the lawyers for the Miami relatives returned to state court, filing a series of urgent requests. They wanted to fly to Maryland to take Juan Miguel's deposition at Cuba's diplomatic compound. They also wanted a trial in ten days, despite Florida law requiring at least thirty days' notice prior to a trial date. And, while it was questionable whether the father received the required legal notice of all components of the state court claims, the Miami relatives sought a default judgment against him.

My intensive research convinced me this was a straightforward case of applying Florida's temporary custody statute and evaluating the family court's jurisdiction under Florida law in comparison to federal immigration law. My conscience directed me to treat this case as it deserved under the law, ignoring the swirling debate. What made this case daunting was the constant and pervasive expressions of community passion about its outcome. I was determined that the state court proceedings would not contribute to or inflame the turmoil. I would do my best to assure dignity and respect for this small child. It was evident that patience was running out after the family ignored INS's repeated requests for Elián's return.

I needed to hear directly from the parties, but there was still only one side appearing in the case. Holding a one-sided court hearing would only increase the outsized drama. On April 9, when it became obvious that mediation efforts were going nowhere, I selected from the orders I had prepared and issued an "Order to Brief." It directed the petitioner, Lázaro González, to address several technical but fundamental legal issues, namely, whether Florida law authorized me to address the issues raised by the parties, whether federal immigration law takes priority over the application of any relevant state law, the lingering questions about legal notice to Juan Miguel González, and the legal authority for his temporary custody claim under Florida law. In addition, I requested that the U.S. Justice Department file a traditional "Friend of the Court" brief, although they were not a party to this case, as a means to obtain the federal government's view in the case.

Although the father was not participating in the state court case, I hoped what I received from the briefs would guide me in terms of what should happen next.

Political Pressure Increases

The Miami family's filings were not subtle. Their filings included the prospect of direct political pressure on me. In their demand for a default judgment against the father and a trial within ten days, they included a letter from the speaker of the House of Representatives to President Clinton demanding that Attorney General Reno allow the case to be decided in state court so that "the Florida family court should decide what is in the best interests of Elián." The letter was signed by Congressional leaders Dick Armey, Tom DeLay, Dennis Hastert, and J.C. Watts. Also attached was a letter from Mr. DeLay, the House majority whip, stating that for special citizenship bills to proceed, "It is of significance for there to be a final judgment by Florida's family court concerning the permanent custody of Elián González. . . . We believe it relevant and most helpful for Florida's family court to move forward with an evidentiary hearing which will permit all sides to be heard before the court with the legal authority to handle child custody disputes." Politicians were overlooking the fact that this highly publicized case had ramifications for the rights that American parents take for granted. This reality began to get traction when the media reported that efforts in Congress to secure special citizenship legislation for Elián were quietly abandoned after some conservative family advocacy groups pointed out that such a move would undermine parental authority.

The Miami relatives' briefs also included letters from Florida Governor Jeb Bush and Florida Attorney General Bob Butterworth and a resolution of the Florida Cabinet, noting that tensions were rising over the inflammatory and heavy-handed approach by INS and the Department of Justice. They demanded the INS and Justice rescind their demand that Lázaro González turn over Elián if he were to lose his appeal of the federal order. They urged the federal government to consent to "full and impartial evidentiary hearing . . . in which Elián's fate will be decided not on procedural issues but rather on whether his best interests are served by returning to Cuba or remaining in the United States." The filings also included similar demands signed by forty Florida state senators. Presidential candidates Al Gore and George W. Bush both asserted that the case should be decided in Florida's family court under a best-interests standard. The family's court filings did not include factual information about Elián's life. No one was stopping long enough to look at what the actual legal standard was that a judge must apply.

The letters from political leaders reflected a continuing misunderstanding of what was before me. They kept demanding a "best-interests" hearing—which was not the legal test I had sworn to uphold. The Florida statute on extended family placement allowed only a grant of temporary custody for limited duration, not permanent custody. The only way Lázaro could "win" even temporary custody of Elián required proof by clear and convincing evidence that the father was unfit. Only after unfitness was established could the court consider "best interests."

The Florida relatives also misunderstood important legal requirements. They wanted a hearing in my courtroom without the father present because he had not responded to the case. Florida law in these temporary custody cases requires the court to observe fundamental procedural safeguards including "most critically, notice and an opportunity to be heard." The Miami family was proposing to take Juan Miguel's son away on the strength of a notice letter they mailed to Cuba. Well-established due process principles require verified (usually under oath) notice of a complaint be given to all parties. Absence of this crucial evidence was not cured merely because the Cuban government subsequently brought Elián's father to a diplomatically protected compound in Maryland. Hence, I was not going to conduct a hearing when there were real questions about whether the defendant had adequate notice and an opportunity to present evidence.

There were other legal problems with the U.S. family's case. First, the statute under which they were suing had an extremely high burden of proof in cases where there was no parental consent and claims of paternal unfitness. Second, their papers kept taking illogical and inconsistent positions. They argued that the father was Castro's virtual prisoner and therefore his wishes couldn't be considered, and also asserted they gave him proper legal notice by mailing a letter to Cuba. They were seeking temporary custody in state court to pursue federal immigration remedies when the federal court already ruled they had no such remedies. The original temporary custody order they obtained from the first state judge required Elián's father to present himself in Miami and bring his witnesses. But there were no means by which he, a Cuban citizen, could subpoena other Cubans or even present himself in Miami.

There was yet another problem. The statute under which Lazaro sued in family court provided a very limited list of relatives who could seek temporary custody. The statute authorized only brother, sister, grandparent, aunt, uncle, or cousin as qualified custodians. Lázaro, as great-uncle, was not on the list. Hence, he did not have legal authority to seek custody under this statute. While I knew that some would view this as a technicality, it was the law. The legislature had adopted it and the Governor approved it. It was my job to apply it, regardless of the anger or political risk it would incur on either side. The result under that law was going to either disappoint those in favor of the father or those in favor of the family. If I ignored the law, then Elián would be treated differently from other children simply because he had a vocal and politically powerful community advocating custody to his great-uncle. In a democracy, the law must prevail.

The fever-like condition of the community was best demonstrated when the mayor of Miami-Dade County warned that local police would not support any effort by INS to return Elián to his father and that the mayor would hold the federal government responsible for resulting civil unrest. Tens of thousands of supporters held vigils outside Lázaro's house. Those who opposed Elián's return to communist Cuba emphasized how Elizabet had died to bring Elián to America. In their eyes, anyone who supported the father lacked respect for freedom and democracy and ignored the agonies that Castro had imposed on the Cuban people—risks Elián would surely face. Those on the father's side were appalled at the protestors' lack of respect for the father, the federal government, and the rule of law. There was a daily diet of fistfights, street fires, and constant police presence.

Time to Decide

Given all that was happening, the trial risked becoming a one-sided, multi-day media free-for-all. The idea was troubling, not only for trial management reasons but also for its impact on foreign relations. I had had more than one case in which a child had been abducted by one parent to another country, and I entered orders to get those children back that depended on the cooperation of a foreign government. Case law for decades established strong precedent that the federal government, not states, controlled immigration issues. If I unilaterally determined that Florida did not approve of the living conditions in Cuba, what were the international ramifications? Would other countries that disapproved of the American lifestyle use this as an excuse to refuse to return American children?

I also worried that the existing custody order and continued prosecution of the case had the goal of creating a state court basis to resist the federal court, INS, and the Justice Department orders. The timing certainly implied such a conclusion. The Miami relatives had not come back to state court until they lost in federal court. It seemed all the more problematic when one looked at the original petition in state court. The purpose was to ensure Elián's immigration rights were fully explored. Lázaro had been given authority to go to federal court to pursue those rights, and the federal judge had ruled that INS and the Justice Department had followed the law by determining that only the father had the right to decide whether or not to pursue asylum for Elián. The reasons for the original custody order, to resolve the immigration question, had been fulfilled, although not to the satisfaction of the Miami relatives.

It was clear that community resistance was spiraling towards defiance. The leader of one protest group outside Lázaro's house declared that his group was ready to die for Elián's freedom. The Miami police department barricaded the street. Crowds outside the home braced for any attempt to remove Elián. Lázaro announced that, "they will have to take this child from me by force." Lázaro's daughter was quoted as saying, "they are going to have to come get him," despite the fact that the U.S. Attorney General, by the commissioner of the Immigration and Naturalization Service and by a United States district court judge, told the family the decision to reunite Elián and Juan González would stand. The U.S. family refused to accept this result. They argued to the 11th Circuit Court of Appeals in Atlanta that the federal trial court judge erred in throwing out their case because the original state court temporary custody order created Lázaro's right to go to federal court. I did not want the state court order to serve as an excuse to defy the federal government or provide a means to justify defiance of the law.

Throughout, I worried about the child. Most of us cannot imagine the press camped outside our houses as adults. It had to be exhausting for Elián. As a parent myself, I knew this was no life for a six-year-old child. People were chanting outside the house into the evening. In fact, filings in the case indicated that Lázaro's daughter had to be hospitalized for exhaustion during the proceedings. The Elián story was on TV every night and the subject of jokes for late-night comedians including skits on *Saturday Night Live*. I am glad the case predated ubiquitous use of social media.

I deeply respected the agony of those who wished to keep Elián here. I could never know how they felt. The Cuban exiles and their families had suffered directly at Castro's hands. Their family members had been murdered and jailed by Castro's government. There were genuine reasons for their passion and fears. While this case provoked fights over ideology, at bottom it was about *who* could legally decide where Elián spent his childhood, not *where* he would live.

The Final Ruling

Two days later, on April 11, 2000, I received the requested briefs from Lázaro González and the U.S. government. The same day, Attorney General Reno appeared on television. Federal patience had been exhausted. She set a firm deadline of April 14 at 2 p.m. for the Miami relatives to deliver Elián to a local airport so that he could be reunited with his father. Conflict seemed inevitable. My timetable had been set for me. I studied the briefs. My work over March had paid off. There were no surprises; no cases or arguments that I had not carefully considered through earlier research.

I decided that holding an unnecessary, one-sided hearing in the matter would only aggravate the already tense situation. There were no unresolved evidentiary questions. These were legal questions that I decided on the briefs: The child was a resident of Cuba and was an unaccompanied minor alien. The reasons for the grant of temporary custody, to determine Elián's right to pursue political asylum, had been accomplished by virtue of the order of the federal court. The proof of notice to the father was questionable, but he effectively knew about the case. Elián remained in the country by grace of the federal government, and it was up to the federal government to determine who should speak for him in connection with immigration matters. In essence, the local family was contending that Cuba was unfit—clearly a federal diplomatic and immigration matter.

Further, the law was well established that a state court custody order could not prevent federal immigration authorities from returning Elián to his father. Even if I had entered an order, unjustified by the law, to keep him here, it was clear that such an order would not supersede the federal government's immigration authority. And under Florida law, great-uncle Lázaro González did not qualify for temporary custody under the extended family definition. The law required me to end the state court case. I wanted to rule quickly so as to eliminate justification for any more delays or resistance. I also hoped to cool temperatures down before Miami boiled over.

I wrote a twenty-two-page order terminating the original temporary custody order and dismissing the state court case. This prevented the Miami family from refusing to comply with the federal orders based on anything that had happened in state court. I tried to express my grief and sympathy for all those who felt so strongly about the case and acknowledged the very real concerns on all sides. I was convinced that the law of Florida required this result. As I wrote the order, I grieved for Elián, for everyone who loved this child, and for Miami. Conflict at this level should not have had to happen. I knew the lawyers involved in this case for the family, I knew the Attorney General and the U.S. Attorney in Miami. They were all honorable people with a deep dedication to the rule of law. Sadly, they became entangled in a nightmare of external forces and intractable client positions.

My purpose in writing to explain my ruling and doing so quickly was to avoid this little boy being the subject of any physical confrontation. In the end, no matter my efforts, that is exactly what happened. Lázaro González refused to turn Elián over to authorities. In the morning on April 22, a federal government SWAT team, fully armed and armor-protected, raided the house at five in the morning. The journalist who snapped the photo of a terrified Elián being seized at gunpoint out of the arms of the fisherman who had found him, won the Pulitzer Prize that year. I was heartsick.

Elián was soon reunited with his father. Juan Miguel remained in the United States at the Cuban compound in Maryland until the federal appeals court affirmed the federal trial court ruling that dismissed the federal claims. The family's appeal of my ruling to a higher Florida court was dismissed as moot.

Trauma from these events reverberated for years—on both a community and a personal level. A few judicial colleagues refused to speak to me ever again. Friends called me to express their disappointment or to congratulate me on what they perceived as a job "well done." Others praised me for resisting the political forces. In truth, I did not deserve praise for resisting. I simply ignored the politics, which is what judges are supposed to do.

Now years later, Elián is an adult in Cuba. I have seen him interviewed on television. He has a close relationship with his father and family, appears to be happy and healthy, and is pursuing a career in engineering. This is a case that always stays with me. I know I followed the law and kept my oath. Doing so insured a little boy would grow up with his father as a family. My decision also cost that little boy the American freedom that his Miami relatives sought for him. It was the correct result under the law. Whether it was "right" in the end depends, for each of us, on what we value most.

Acknowledgments

THIS BOOK HAS BEEN IN THE MAKING FOR MORE THAN THREE YEARS. Starting with casual conversations at the courthouse and, in one instance, on a tennis court, we editors shared stories about the cases we could not forget long after they were over in court. As we took turns telling stories of our most difficult and perplexing cases, the thought occurred to us that they might be of interest to a wider audience. We realized that the stories captured the essence of a trial judge's vocation and showed how the commitment to do justice—and equal justice—is often challenging and sometimes even painful.

As the idea for the book began to take shape, we also realized our real-life case stories might present teaching vehicles for future lawyers and judges. We decided to put pen to paper, knowing that our three stories were a small sample of the similar stories that could be told by trial judges in every part of the country. So while writing up our own "tough cases," we went looking for the others we knew were out there.

Engaging our fellow judicial authors was not the product of a Google search or perusal of our lists of contacts. Success in finding gifted authors and instructive cases took time and the help of many persons. Some authors of this book came to our attention through our individual professional circles and others serendipitously. No matter which way it all came together, we now acknowledge and salute the following persons who have made this collection of judicial stories possible.

We start by giving thanks to our fellow authors: Michelle M. Ahnn, Robert H. Alsdorf, Jennifer D. Bailey, Gail Chang Bohr, Mark Davidson, Lizbeth González, George W. Greer, Allie Greenleaf Maldonado, Reggie B. Walton, and Edward S. Wilson. Besides giving us the gift of their case stories, they each opened our eyes to the almost unimaginable varieties of legal challenges that arise in trial courts everywhere.

We salute also the following persons who gave us their wisdom, encouragement, and suggestions for improvements: state chief justices Tani Cantil-Sakauye and Nathan Hecht; judges Jeb Boasberg, Frank Burgess, Kevin Burke, Danya Dayson, Jennifer Di Toro, Ramsey Johnson, and Steve Leben; and professors Paul Butler, David Cole, Angela Davis, Michael Diamond, Andrew Ferguson, James Forman, Mike Seidman, and Abbe Smith.

We recognize the wonderful team of editors, collaborators, and production experts at The New Press. These consummate professionals tutored us in the ways of book publishing, smoothed out wrinkles in our texts, and inspired us with their confidence in our vision for this book. Thank you Emily Albarillo, Jed Bickman, Sarah Passino, for her help on George W. Greer's chapter, Sharon Swados, and Diane Wachtell.

On a personal level, we editors give thanks to these family members and friends who bolstered our spirits and resolve to reach the finish line: Sharon Burka, Ethan Canan, Lukas Canan, Lee Coykendall, Liz Coykendall, Mary Davey, Marshall Dayan, Michael Diamond, Gerry Kittner, Tim Kochis, Kerry Malawista, Colman McCarthy, Marisa Mize, Kathy Noel, Jeffrey O'Toole, Jenny Q, John Q, JoAnne Richardson, John Scheibel, Barbara Stevenson, Heidi Lee Turner, Greta Van Susteren, Caitlin Weisberg, Jessica Westerman, and Penelope Wong.

About the Editors

Russell F. Canan is currently a judge on the Superior Court of the District of Columbia and an adjunct professor at the George Washington University School of Law. He lives in Washington, DC.

Gregory E. Mize is a currently a judge on the Superior Court of the District of Columbia and is a judicial fellow at the National Center for State Courts and an adjunct professor at the Georgetown University Law Center. He lives in Washington, DC.

Frederick H. Weisberg is currently a judge on the Superior Court of the District of Columbia and teaches annually in the Trial Advocacy Workshop at Harvard Law School. He lives in Washington, DC.

Publishing in the Public Interest

Thank you for reading this book published by The New Press. The New Press is a nonprofit, public interest publisher. New Press books and authors play a crucial role in sparking conversations about the key political and social issues of our day.

We hope you enjoyed this book and that you will stay in touch with The New Press. Here are a few ways to stay up to date with our books, events, and the issues we cover:

- Sign up at www.thenewpress.com/subscribe to receive updates on New Press authors and issues and to be notified about local events
- Like us on Facebook: www.facebook.com/newpressbooks
- Follow us on Twitter: www.twitter.com/thenewpress

Please consider buying New Press books for yourself; for friends and family; or to donate to schools, libraries, community centers, prison libraries, and other organizations involved with the issues our authors write about.

The New Press is a 501(c)(3) nonprofit organization. You can also support our work with a tax-deductible gift by visiting www.thenewpress.com/donate.